C-2576   CAREER EXAMINATION SERIES

This is your
PASSBOOK for...

Pharmacy Aide

Test Preparation Study Guide
Questions & Answers

NATIONAL LEARNING CORPORATION®

COPYRIGHT NOTICE

This book is SOLELY intended for, is sold ONLY to, and its use is RESTRICTED to individual, bona fide applicants or candidates who qualify by virtue of having seriously filed applications for appropriate license, certificate, professional and/or promotional advancement, higher school matriculation, scholarship, or other legitimate requirements of education and/or governmental authorities.

This book is NOT intended for use, class instruction, tutoring, training, duplication, copying, reprinting, excerption, or adaptation, etc., by:

1) Other publishers
2) Proprietors and/or Instructors of "Coaching" and/or Preparatory Courses
3) Personnel and/or Training Divisions of commercial, industrial, and governmental organizations
4) Schools, colleges, or universities and/or their departments and staffs, including teachers and other personnel
5) Testing Agencies or Bureaus
6) Study groups which seek by the purchase of a single volume to copy and/or duplicate and/or adapt this material for use by the group as a whole without having purchased individual volumes for each of the members of the group
7) Et al.

Such persons would be in violation of appropriate Federal and State statutes.

PROVISION OF LICENSING AGREEMENTS – Recognized educational, commercial, industrial, and governmental institutions and organizations, and others legitimately engaged in educational pursuits, including training, testing, and measurement activities, may address request for a licensing agreement to the copyright owners, who will determine whether, and under what conditions, including fees and charges, the materials in this book may be used them. In other words, a licensing facility exists for the legitimate use of the material in this book on other than an individual basis. However, it is asseverated and affirmed here that the material in this book CANNOT be used without the receipt of the express permission of such a licensing agreement from the Publishers. Inquiries re licensing should be addressed to the company, attention rights and permissions department.

All rights reserved, including the right of reproduction in whole or in part, in any form or by any means, electronic or mechanical, including photocopying, recording, or by any information storage and retrieval system, without permission in writing from the Publisher.

Copyright © 2025 by
National Learning Corporation

212 Michael Drive, Syosset, NY 11791
(516) 921-8888 • www.passbooks.com
E-mail: info@passbooks.com

PASSBOOK® SERIES

THE *PASSBOOK® SERIES* has been created to prepare applicants and candidates for the ultimate academic battlefield – the examination room.

At some time in our lives, each and every one of us may be required to take an examination – for validation, matriculation, admission, qualification, registration, certification, or licensure.

Based on the assumption that every applicant or candidate has met the basic formal educational standards, has taken the required number of courses, and read the necessary texts, the *PASSBOOK® SERIES* furnishes the one special preparation which may assure passing with confidence, instead of failing with insecurity. Examination questions – together with answers – are furnished as the basic vehicle for study so that the mysteries of the examination and its compounding difficulties may be eliminated or diminished by a sure method.

This book is meant to help you pass your examination provided that you qualify and are serious in your objective.

The entire field is reviewed through the huge store of content information which is succinctly presented through a provocative and challenging approach – the question-and-answer method.

A climate of success is established by furnishing the correct answers at the end of each test.

You soon learn to recognize types of questions, forms of questions, and patterns of questioning. You may even begin to anticipate expected outcomes.

You perceive that many questions are repeated or adapted so that you can gain acute insights, which may enable you to score many sure points.

You learn how to confront new questions, or types of questions, and to attack them confidently and work out the correct answers.

You note objectives and emphases, and recognize pitfalls and dangers, so that you may make positive educational adjustments.

Moreover, you are kept fully informed in relation to new concepts, methods, practices, and directions in the field.

You discover that you are actually taking the examination all the time: you are preparing for the examination by "taking" an examination, not by reading extraneous and/or supererogatory textbooks.

In short, this PASSBOOK®, used directedly, should be an important factor in helping you to pass your test.

PHARMACY AIDE

DUTIES
Working under the direct and immediate supervision of a pharmacist, a Pharmacy Aide assists in preparing medications for the pharmacist to dispense, and performs administrative tasks such as maintaining files, preparing reports and logs, and managing product recalls; serves as a receptionist/office manager; maintains an inventory of pharmaceutical supplies; assists in preparing pharmaceutical orders, receiving pharmaceutical supplies, and entering data in appropriate records; assists in prepackaging prescriptions, the repackaging and delivery of drugs and maintaining a clean, safe, and professional environment within the pharmacy.

SUBJECT OF EXAMINATION
The written test is designed to test for knowledge, skills, and/or abilities in such areas as:
1. Clerical operations with letters and numbers;
2. Name and number checking; and
3. Office record keeping.

HOW TO TAKE A TEST

I. YOU MUST PASS AN EXAMINATION

A. *WHAT EVERY CANDIDATE SHOULD KNOW*

Examination applicants often ask us for help in preparing for the written test. What can I study in advance? What kinds of questions will be asked? How will the test be given? How will the papers be graded?

As an applicant for a civil service examination, you may be wondering about some of these things. Our purpose here is to suggest effective methods of advance study and to describe civil service examinations.

Your chances for success on this examination can be increased if you know how to prepare. Those "pre-examination jitters" can be reduced if you know what to expect. You can even experience an adventure in good citizenship if you know why civil service exams are given.

B. *WHY ARE CIVIL SERVICE EXAMINATIONS GIVEN?*

Civil service examinations are important to you in two ways. As a citizen, you want public jobs filled by employees who know how to do their work. As a job seeker, you want a fair chance to compete for that job on an equal footing with other candidates. The best-known means of accomplishing this two-fold goal is the competitive examination.

Exams are widely publicized throughout the nation. They may be administered for jobs in federal, state, city, municipal, town or village governments or agencies.

Any citizen may apply, with some limitations, such as the age or residence of applicants. Your experience and education may be reviewed to see whether you meet the requirements for the particular examination. When these requirements exist, they are reasonable and applied consistently to all applicants. Thus, a competitive examination may cause you some uneasiness now, but it is your privilege and safeguard.

C. *HOW ARE CIVIL SERVICE EXAMS DEVELOPED?*

Examinations are carefully written by trained technicians who are specialists in the field known as "psychological measurement," in consultation with recognized authorities in the field of work that the test will cover. These experts recommend the subject matter areas or skills to be tested; only those knowledges or skills important to your success on the job are included. The most reliable books and source materials available are used as references. Together, the experts and technicians judge the difficulty level of the questions.

Test technicians know how to phrase questions so that the problem is clearly stated. Their ethics do not permit "trick" or "catch" questions. Questions may have been tried out on sample groups, or subjected to statistical analysis, to determine their usefulness.

Written tests are often used in combination with performance tests, ratings of training and experience, and oral interviews. All of these measures combine to form the best-known means of finding the right person for the right job.

II. HOW TO PASS THE WRITTEN TEST

A. NATURE OF THE EXAMINATION

To prepare intelligently for civil service examinations, you should know how they differ from school examinations you have taken. In school you were assigned certain definite pages to read or subjects to cover. The examination questions were quite detailed and usually emphasized memory. Civil service exams, on the other hand, try to discover your present ability to perform the duties of a position, plus your potentiality to learn these duties. In other words, a civil service exam attempts to predict how successful you will be. Questions cover such a broad area that they cannot be as minute and detailed as school exam questions.

In the public service similar kinds of work, or positions, are grouped together in one "class." This process is known as *position-classification*. All the positions in a class are paid according to the salary range for that class. One class title covers all of these positions, and they are all tested by the same examination.

B. FOUR BASIC STEPS

1) Study the announcement

How, then, can you know what subjects to study? Our best answer is: "Learn as much as possible about the class of positions for which you've applied." The exam will test the knowledge, skills and abilities needed to do the work.

Your most valuable source of information about the position you want is the official exam announcement. This announcement lists the training and experience qualifications. Check these standards and apply only if you come reasonably close to meeting them.

The brief description of the position in the examination announcement offers some clues to the subjects which will be tested. Think about the job itself. Review the duties in your mind. Can you perform them, or are there some in which you are rusty? Fill in the blank spots in your preparation.

Many jurisdictions preview the written test in the exam announcement by including a section called "Knowledge and Abilities Required," "Scope of the Examination," or some similar heading. Here you will find out specifically what fields will be tested.

2) Review your own background

Once you learn in general what the position is all about, and what you need to know to do the work, ask yourself which subjects you already know fairly well and which need improvement. You may wonder whether to concentrate on improving your strong areas or on building some background in your fields of weakness. When the announcement has specified "some knowledge" or "considerable knowledge," or has used adjectives like "beginning principles of…" or "advanced … methods," you can get a clue as to the number and difficulty of questions to be asked in any given field. More questions, and hence broader coverage, would be included for those subjects which are more important in the work. Now weigh your strengths and weaknesses against the job requirements and prepare accordingly.

3) Determine the level of the position

Another way to tell how intensively you should prepare is to understand the level of the job for which you are applying. Is it the entering level? In other words, is this the position in which beginners in a field of work are hired? Or is it an intermediate or advanced level? Sometimes this is indicated by such words as "Junior" or "Senior" in the class title. Other jurisdictions use Roman numerals to designate the level – Clerk I, Clerk II, for example. The word "Supervisor" sometimes appears in the title. If the level is not indicated by the title, check the description of duties. Will you be working under very close supervision, or will you have responsibility for independent decisions in this work?

4) Choose appropriate study materials

Now that you know the subjects to be examined and the relative amount of each subject to be covered, you can choose suitable study materials. For beginning level jobs, or even advanced ones, if you have a pronounced weakness in some aspect of your training, read a modern, standard textbook in that field. Be sure it is up to date and has general coverage. Such books are normally available at your library, and the librarian will be glad to help you locate one. For entry-level positions, questions of appropriate difficulty are chosen – neither highly advanced questions, nor those too simple. Such questions require careful thought but not advanced training.

If the position for which you are applying is technical or advanced, you will read more advanced, specialized material. If you are already familiar with the basic principles of your field, elementary textbooks would waste your time. Concentrate on advanced textbooks and technical periodicals. Think through the concepts and review difficult problems in your field.

These are all general sources. You can get more ideas on your own initiative, following these leads. For example, training manuals and publications of the government agency which employs workers in your field can be useful, particularly for technical and professional positions. A letter or visit to the government department involved may result in more specific study suggestions, and certainly will provide you with a more definite idea of the exact nature of the position you are seeking.

III. KINDS OF TESTS

Tests are used for purposes other than measuring knowledge and ability to perform specified duties. For some positions, it is equally important to test ability to make adjustments to new situations or to profit from training. In others, basic mental abilities not dependent on information are essential. Questions which test these things may not appear as pertinent to the duties of the position as those which test for knowledge and information. Yet they are often highly important parts of a fair examination. For very general questions, it is almost impossible to help you direct your study efforts. What we can do is to point out some of the more common of these general abilities needed in public service positions and describe some typical questions.

1) General information

Broad, general information has been found useful for predicting job success in some kinds of work. This is tested in a variety of ways, from vocabulary lists to questions about current events. Basic background in some field of work, such as sociology or economics, may be sampled in a group of questions. Often these are principles which have become familiar to most persons through exposure rather than through formal training. It is difficult to advise you how to study for these questions; being alert to the world around you is our best suggestion.

2) Verbal ability

An example of an ability needed in many positions is verbal or language ability. Verbal ability is, in brief, the ability to use and understand words. Vocabulary and grammar tests are typical measures of this ability. Reading comprehension or paragraph interpretation questions are common in many kinds of civil service tests. You are given a paragraph of written material and asked to find its central meaning.

3) Numerical ability

Number skills can be tested by the familiar arithmetic problem, by checking paired lists of numbers to see which are alike and which are different, or by interpreting charts and graphs. In the latter test, a graph may be printed in the test booklet which you are asked to use as the basis for answering questions.

4) Observation

A popular test for law-enforcement positions is the observation test. A picture is shown to you for several minutes, then taken away. Questions about the picture test your ability to observe both details and larger elements.

5) Following directions

In many positions in the public service, the employee must be able to carry out written instructions dependably and accurately. You may be given a chart with several columns, each column listing a variety of information. The questions require you to carry out directions involving the information given in the chart.

6) Skills and aptitudes

Performance tests effectively measure some manual skills and aptitudes. When the skill is one in which you are trained, such as typing or shorthand, you can practice. These tests are often very much like those given in business school or high school courses. For many of the other skills and aptitudes, however, no short-time preparation can be made. Skills and abilities natural to you or that you have developed throughout your lifetime are being tested.

Many of the general questions just described provide all the data needed to answer the questions and ask you to use your reasoning ability to find the answers. Your best preparation for these tests, as well as for tests of facts and ideas, is to be at your physical and mental best. You, no doubt, have your own methods of getting into an exam-taking mood and keeping "in shape." The next section lists some ideas on this subject.

IV. KINDS OF QUESTIONS

Only rarely is the "essay" question, which you answer in narrative form, used in civil service tests. Civil service tests are usually of the short-answer type. Full instructions for answering these questions will be given to you at the examination. But in case this is your first experience with short-answer questions and separate answer sheets, here is what you need to know:

1) Multiple-choice Questions

Most popular of the short-answer questions is the "multiple choice" or "best answer" question. It can be used, for example, to test for factual knowledge, ability to solve problems or judgment in meeting situations found at work.

A multiple-choice question is normally one of three types—
- It can begin with an incomplete statement followed by several possible endings. You are to find the one ending which *best* completes the statement, although some of the others may not be entirely wrong.
- It can also be a complete statement in the form of a question which is answered by choosing one of the statements listed.

- It can be in the form of a problem – again you select the best answer.

Here is an example of a multiple-choice question with a discussion which should give you some clues as to the method for choosing the right answer:

When an employee has a complaint about his assignment, the action which will *best* help him overcome his difficulty is to
  A. discuss his difficulty with his coworkers
  B. take the problem to the head of the organization
  C. take the problem to the person who gave him the assignment
  D. say nothing to anyone about his complaint

In answering this question, you should study each of the choices to find which is best. Consider choice "A" – Certainly an employee may discuss his complaint with fellow employees, but no change or improvement can result, and the complaint remains unresolved. Choice "B" is a poor choice since the head of the organization probably does not know what assignment you have been given, and taking your problem to him is known as "going over the head" of the supervisor. The supervisor, or person who made the assignment, is the person who can clarify it or correct any injustice. Choice "C" is, therefore, correct. To say nothing, as in choice "D," is unwise. Supervisors have and interest in knowing the problems employees are facing, and the employee is seeking a solution to his problem.

2) True/False Questions

The "true/false" or "right/wrong" form of question is sometimes used. Here a complete statement is given. Your job is to decide whether the statement is right or wrong.

SAMPLE: A roaming cell-phone call to a nearby city costs less than a non-roaming call to a distant city.

This statement is wrong, or false, since roaming calls are more expensive.

This is not a complete list of all possible question forms, although most of the others are variations of these common types. You will always get complete directions for answering questions. Be sure you understand *how* to mark your answers – ask questions until you do.

V. RECORDING YOUR ANSWERS

Computer terminals are used more and more today for many different kinds of exams.

For an examination with very few applicants, you may be told to record your answers in the test booklet itself. Separate answer sheets are much more common. If this separate answer sheet is to be scored by machine – and this is often the case – it is highly important that you mark your answers correctly in order to get credit.

An electronic scoring machine is often used in civil service offices because of the speed with which papers can be scored. Machine-scored answer sheets must be marked with a pencil, which will be given to you. This pencil has a high graphite content which responds to the electronic scoring machine. As a matter of fact, stray dots may register as answers, so do not let your pencil rest on the answer sheet while you are pondering the correct answer. Also, if your pencil lead breaks or is otherwise defective, ask for another.

Since the answer sheet will be dropped in a slot in the scoring machine, be careful not to bend the corners or get the paper crumpled.

The answer sheet normally has five vertical columns of numbers, with 30 numbers to a column. These numbers correspond to the question numbers in your test booklet. After each number, going across the page are four or five pairs of dotted lines. These short dotted lines have small letters or numbers above them. The first two pairs may also have a "T" or "F" above the letters. This indicates that the first two pairs only are to be used if the questions are of the true-false type. If the questions are multiple choice, disregard the "T" and "F" and pay attention only to the small letters or numbers.

Answer your questions in the manner of the sample that follows:

32. The largest city in the United States is
    A. Washington, D.C.
    B. New York City
    C. Chicago
    D. Detroit
    E. San Francisco

1) Choose the answer you think is best. (New York City is the largest, so "B" is correct.)
2) Find the row of dotted lines numbered the same as the question you are answering. (Find row number 32)
3) Find the pair of dotted lines corresponding to the answer. (Find the pair of lines under the mark "B.")
4) Make a solid black mark between the dotted lines.

VI. BEFORE THE TEST

Common sense will help you find procedures to follow to get ready for an examination. Too many of us, however, overlook these sensible measures. Indeed, nervousness and fatigue have been found to be the most serious reasons why applicants fail to do their best on civil service tests. Here is a list of reminders:

- Begin your preparation early – Don't wait until the last minute to go scurrying around for books and materials or to find out what the position is all about.
- Prepare continuously – An hour a night for a week is better than an all-night cram session. This has been definitely established. What is more, a night a week for a month will return better dividends than crowding your study into a shorter period of time.
- Locate the place of the exam – You have been sent a notice telling you when and where to report for the examination. If the location is in a different town or otherwise unfamiliar to you, it would be well to inquire the best route and learn something about the building.
- Relax the night before the test – Allow your mind to rest. Do not study at all that night. Plan some mild recreation or diversion; then go to bed early and get a good night's sleep.
- Get up early enough to make a leisurely trip to the place for the test – This way unforeseen events, traffic snarls, unfamiliar buildings, etc. will not upset you.
- Dress comfortably – A written test is not a fashion show. You will be known by number and not by name, so wear something comfortable.

- Leave excess paraphernalia at home – Shopping bags and odd bundles will get in your way. You need bring only the items mentioned in the official notice you received; usually everything you need is provided. Do not bring reference books to the exam. They will only confuse those last minutes and be taken away from you when in the test room.
- Arrive somewhat ahead of time – If because of transportation schedules you must get there very early, bring a newspaper or magazine to take your mind off yourself while waiting.
- Locate the examination room – When you have found the proper room, you will be directed to the seat or part of the room where you will sit. Sometimes you are given a sheet of instructions to read while you are waiting. Do not fill out any forms until you are told to do so; just read them and be prepared.
- Relax and prepare to listen to the instructions
- If you have any physical problem that may keep you from doing your best, be sure to tell the test administrator. If you are sick or in poor health, you really cannot do your best on the exam. You can come back and take the test some other time.

VII. AT THE TEST

The day of the test is here and you have the test booklet in your hand. The temptation to get going is very strong. Caution! There is more to success than knowing the right answers. You must know how to identify your papers and understand variations in the type of short-answer question used in this particular examination. Follow these suggestions for maximum results from your efforts:

1) Cooperate with the monitor

The test administrator has a duty to create a situation in which you can be as much at ease as possible. He will give instructions, tell you when to begin, check to see that you are marking your answer sheet correctly, and so on. He is not there to guard you, although he will see that your competitors do not take unfair advantage. He wants to help you do your best.

2) Listen to all instructions

Don't jump the gun! Wait until you understand all directions. In most civil service tests you get more time than you need to answer the questions. So don't be in a hurry. Read each word of instructions until you clearly understand the meaning. Study the examples, listen to all announcements and follow directions. Ask questions if you do not understand what to do.

3) Identify your papers

Civil service exams are usually identified by number only. You will be assigned a number; you must not put your name on your test papers. Be sure to copy your number correctly. Since more than one exam may be given, copy your exact examination title.

4) Plan your time

Unless you are told that a test is a "speed" or "rate of work" test, speed itself is usually not important. Time enough to answer all the questions will be provided, but this does not mean that you have all day. An overall time limit has been set. Divide the total time (in minutes) by the number of questions to determine the approximate time you have for each question.

5) Do not linger over difficult questions

If you come across a difficult question, mark it with a paper clip (useful to have along) and come back to it when you have been through the booklet. One caution if you do this – be sure to skip a number on your answer sheet as well. Check often to be sure that you have not lost your place and that you are marking in the row numbered the same as the question you are answering.

6) Read the questions

Be sure you know what the question asks! Many capable people are unsuccessful because they failed to *read* the questions correctly.

7) Answer all questions

Unless you have been instructed that a penalty will be deducted for incorrect answers, it is better to guess than to omit a question.

8) Speed tests

It is often better NOT to guess on speed tests. It has been found that on timed tests people are tempted to spend the last few seconds before time is called in marking answers at random – without even reading them – in the hope of picking up a few extra points. To discourage this practice, the instructions may warn you that your score will be "corrected" for guessing. That is, a penalty will be applied. The incorrect answers will be deducted from the correct ones, or some other penalty formula will be used.

9) Review your answers

If you finish before time is called, go back to the questions you guessed or omitted to give them further thought. Review other answers if you have time.

10) Return your test materials

If you are ready to leave before others have finished or time is called, take ALL your materials to the monitor and leave quietly. Never take any test material with you. The monitor can discover whose papers are not complete, and taking a test booklet may be grounds for disqualification.

VIII. EXAMINATION TECHNIQUES

1) Read the general instructions carefully. These are usually printed on the first page of the exam booklet. As a rule, these instructions refer to the timing of the examination; the fact that you should not start work until the signal and must stop work at a signal, etc. If there are any *special* instructions, such as a choice of questions to be answered, make sure that you note this instruction carefully.

2) When you are ready to start work on the examination, that is as soon as the signal has been given, read the instructions to each question booklet, underline any key words or phrases, such as *least, best, outline, describe* and the like. In this way you will tend to answer as requested rather than discover on reviewing your paper that you *listed without describing*, that you selected the *worst* choice rather than the *best* choice, etc.

3) If the examination is of the objective or multiple-choice type – that is, each question will also give a series of possible answers: A, B, C or D, and you are called upon to select the best answer and write the letter next to that answer on your answer paper – it is advisable to start answering each question in turn. There may be anywhere from 50 to 100 such questions in the three or four hours allotted and you can see how much time would be taken if you read through all the questions before beginning to answer any. Furthermore, if you come across a question or group of questions which you know would be difficult to answer, it would undoubtedly affect your handling of all the other questions.

4) If the examination is of the essay type and contains but a few questions, it is a moot point as to whether you should read all the questions before starting to answer any one. Of course, if you are given a choice – say five out of seven and the like – then it is essential to read all the questions so you can eliminate the two that are most difficult. If, however, you are asked to answer all the questions, there may be danger in trying to answer the easiest one first because you may find that you will spend too much time on it. The best technique is to answer the first question, then proceed to the second, etc.

5) Time your answers. Before the exam begins, write down the time it started, then add the time allowed for the examination and write down the time it must be completed, then divide the time available somewhat as follows:
    - If 3-1/2 hours are allowed, that would be 210 minutes. If you have 80 objective-type questions, that would be an average of 2-1/2 minutes per question. Allow yourself no more than 2 minutes per question, or a total of 160 minutes, which will permit about 50 minutes to review.
    - If for the time allotment of 210 minutes there are 7 essay questions to answer, that would average about 30 minutes a question. Give yourself only 25 minutes per question so that you have about 35 minutes to review.

6) The most important instruction is to *read each question* and make sure you know what is wanted. The second most important instruction is to *time yourself properly* so that you answer every question. The third most important instruction is to *answer every question*. Guess if you have to but include something for each question. Remember that you will receive no credit for a blank and will probably receive some credit if you write something in answer to an essay question. If you guess a letter – say "B" for a multiple-choice question – you may have guessed right. If you leave a blank as an answer to a multiple-choice question, the examiners may respect your feelings but it will not add a point to your score. Some exams may penalize you for wrong answers, so in such cases *only*, you may not want to guess unless you have some basis for your answer.

7) Suggestions
    a. Objective-type questions
        1. Examine the question booklet for proper sequence of pages and questions
        2. Read all instructions carefully
        3. Skip any question which seems too difficult; return to it after all other questions have been answered
        4. Apportion your time properly; do not spend too much time on any single question or group of questions

5. Note and underline key words – *all, most, fewest, least, best, worst, same, opposite,* etc.
   6. Pay particular attention to negatives
   7. Note unusual option, e.g., unduly long, short, complex, different or similar in content to the body of the question
   8. Observe the use of "hedging" words – *probably, may, most likely,* etc.
   9. Make sure that your answer is put next to the same number as the question
   10. Do not second-guess unless you have good reason to believe the second answer is definitely more correct
   11. Cross out original answer if you decide another answer is more accurate; do not erase until you are ready to hand your paper in
   12. Answer all questions; guess unless instructed otherwise
   13. Leave time for review

   b. Essay questions
   1. Read each question carefully
   2. Determine exactly what is wanted. Underline key words or phrases.
   3. Decide on outline or paragraph answer
   4. Include many different points and elements unless asked to develop any one or two points or elements
   5. Show impartiality by giving pros and cons unless directed to select one side only
   6. Make and write down any assumptions you find necessary to answer the questions
   7. Watch your English, grammar, punctuation and choice of words
   8. Time your answers; don't crowd material

8) Answering the essay question

Most essay questions can be answered by framing the specific response around several key words or ideas. Here are a few such key words or ideas:

M's: manpower, materials, methods, money, management
P's: purpose, program, policy, plan, procedure, practice, problems, pitfalls, personnel, public relations

   a. Six basic steps in handling problems:
   1. Preliminary plan and background development
   2. Collect information, data and facts
   3. Analyze and interpret information, data and facts
   4. Analyze and develop solutions as well as make recommendations
   5. Prepare report and sell recommendations
   6. Install recommendations and follow up effectiveness

   b. Pitfalls to avoid
   1. *Taking things for granted* – A statement of the situation does not necessarily imply that each of the elements is necessarily true; for example, a complaint may be invalid and biased so that all that can be taken for granted is that a complaint has been registered

2. *Considering only one side of a situation* – Wherever possible, indicate several alternatives and then point out the reasons you selected the best one
3. *Failing to indicate follow up* – Whenever your answer indicates action on your part, make certain that you will take proper follow-up action to see how successful your recommendations, procedures or actions turn out to be
4. *Taking too long in answering any single question* – Remember to time your answers properly

IX. AFTER THE TEST

Scoring procedures differ in detail among civil service jurisdictions although the general principles are the same. Whether the papers are hand-scored or graded by machine we have described, they are nearly always graded by number. That is, the person who marks the paper knows only the number – never the name – of the applicant. Not until all the papers have been graded will they be matched with names. If other tests, such as training and experience or oral interview ratings have been given, scores will be combined. Different parts of the examination usually have different weights. For example, the written test might count 60 percent of the final grade, and a rating of training and experience 40 percent. In many jurisdictions, veterans will have a certain number of points added to their grades.

After the final grade has been determined, the names are placed in grade order and an eligible list is established. There are various methods for resolving ties between those who get the same final grade – probably the most common is to place first the name of the person whose application was received first. Job offers are made from the eligible list in the order the names appear on it. You will be notified of your grade and your rank as soon as all these computations have been made. This will be done as rapidly as possible.

People who are found to meet the requirements in the announcement are called "eligibles." Their names are put on a list of eligible candidates. An eligible's chances of getting a job depend on how high he stands on this list and how fast agencies are filling jobs from the list.

When a job is to be filled from a list of eligibles, the agency asks for the names of people on the list of eligibles for that job. When the civil service commission receives this request, it sends to the agency the names of the three people highest on this list. Or, if the job to be filled has specialized requirements, the office sends the agency the names of the top three persons who meet these requirements from the general list.

The appointing officer makes a choice from among the three people whose names were sent to him. If the selected person accepts the appointment, the names of the others are put back on the list to be considered for future openings.

That is the rule in hiring from all kinds of eligible lists, whether they are for typist, carpenter, chemist, or something else. For every vacancy, the appointing officer has his choice of any one of the top three eligibles on the list. This explains why the person whose name is on top of the list sometimes does not get an appointment when some of the persons lower on the list do. If the appointing officer chooses the second or third eligible, the No. 1 eligible does not get a job at once, but stays on the list until he is appointed or the list is terminated.

X. HOW TO PASS THE INTERVIEW TEST

The examination for which you applied requires an oral interview test. You have already taken the written test and you are now being called for the interview test – the final part of the formal examination.

You may think that it is not possible to prepare for an interview test and that there are no procedures to follow during an interview. Our purpose is to point out some things you can do in advance that will help you and some good rules to follow and pitfalls to avoid while you are being interviewed.

What is an interview supposed to test?

The written examination is designed to test the technical knowledge and competence of the candidate; the oral is designed to evaluate intangible qualities, not readily measured otherwise, and to establish a list showing the relative fitness of each candidate – as measured against his competitors – for the position sought. Scoring is not on the basis of "right" and "wrong," but on a sliding scale of values ranging from "not passable" to "outstanding." As a matter of fact, it is possible to achieve a relatively low score without a single "incorrect" answer because of evident weakness in the qualities being measured.

Occasionally, an examination may consist entirely of an oral test – either an individual or a group oral. In such cases, information is sought concerning the technical knowledges and abilities of the candidate, since there has been no written examination for this purpose. More commonly, however, an oral test is used to supplement a written examination.

Who conducts interviews?

The composition of oral boards varies among different jurisdictions. In nearly all, a representative of the personnel department serves as chairman. One of the members of the board may be a representative of the department in which the candidate would work. In some cases, "outside experts" are used, and, frequently, a businessman or some other representative of the general public is asked to serve. Labor and management or other special groups may be represented. The aim is to secure the services of experts in the appropriate field.

However the board is composed, it is a good idea (and not at all improper or unethical) to ascertain in advance of the interview who the members are and what groups they represent. When you are introduced to them, you will have some idea of their backgrounds and interests, and at least you will not stutter and stammer over their names.

What should be done before the interview?

While knowledge about the board members is useful and takes some of the surprise element out of the interview, there is other preparation which is more substantive. It *is* possible to prepare for an oral interview – in several ways:

1) Keep a copy of your application and review it carefully before the interview

This may be the only document before the oral board, and the starting point of the interview. Know what education and experience you have listed there, and the sequence and dates of all of it. Sometimes the board will ask you to review the highlights of your experience for them; you should not have to hem and haw doing it.

2) Study the class specification and the examination announcement

Usually, the oral board has one or both of these to guide them. The qualities, characteristics or knowledges required by the position sought are stated in these documents. They offer valuable clues as to the nature of the oral interview. For example, if the job involves supervisory responsibilities, the announcement will usually indicate that knowledge of modern supervisory methods and the qualifications of the candidate as a supervisor will be tested. If so, you can expect such questions, frequently in the form of a hypothetical situation which you are expected to solve. NEVER go into an oral without knowledge of the duties and responsibilities of the job you seek.

3) Think through each qualification required

Try to visualize the kind of questions you would ask if you were a board member. How well could you answer them? Try especially to appraise your own knowledge and background in each area, *measured against the job sought*, and identify any areas in which you are weak. Be critical and realistic – do not flatter yourself.

4) Do some general reading in areas in which you feel you may be weak

For example, if the job involves supervision and your past experience has NOT, some general reading in supervisory methods and practices, particularly in the field of human relations, might be useful. Do NOT study agency procedures or detailed manuals. The oral board will be testing your understanding and capacity, not your memory.

5) Get a good night's sleep and watch your general health and mental attitude

You will want a clear head at the interview. Take care of a cold or any other minor ailment, and of course, no hangovers.

What should be done on the day of the interview?

Now comes the day of the interview itself. Give yourself plenty of time to get there. Plan to arrive somewhat ahead of the scheduled time, particularly if your appointment is in the fore part of the day. If a previous candidate fails to appear, the board might be ready for you a bit early. By early afternoon an oral board is almost invariably behind schedule if there are many candidates, and you may have to wait. Take along a book or magazine to read, or your application to review, but leave any extraneous material in the waiting room when you go in for your interview. In any event, relax and compose yourself.

The matter of dress is important. The board is forming impressions about you – from your experience, your manners, your attitude, and your appearance. Give your personal appearance careful attention. Dress your best, but not your flashiest. Choose conservative, appropriate clothing, and be sure it is immaculate. This is a business interview, and your appearance should indicate that you regard it as such. Besides, being well groomed and properly dressed will help boost your confidence.

Sooner or later, someone will call your name and escort you into the interview room. *This is it*. From here on you are on your own. It is too late for any more preparation. But remember, you asked for this opportunity to prove your fitness, and you are here because your request was granted.

What happens when you go in?

The usual sequence of events will be as follows: The clerk (who is often the board stenographer) will introduce you to the chairman of the oral board, who will introduce you to the other members of the board. Acknowledge the introductions before you sit down. Do not be surprised if you find a microphone facing you or a stenotypist sitting by. Oral interviews are usually recorded in the event of an appeal or other review.

Usually the chairman of the board will open the interview by reviewing the highlights of your education and work experience from your application – primarily for the benefit of the other members of the board, as well as to get the material into the record. Do not interrupt or comment unless there is an error or significant misinterpretation; if that is the case, do not hesitate. But do not quibble about insignificant matters. Also, he will usually ask you some question about your education, experience or your present job – partly to get you to start talking and to establish the interviewing "rapport." He may start the actual questioning, or turn it over to one of the other members. Frequently, each member undertakes the questioning on a particular area, one in which he is perhaps most competent, so you can expect each member to participate in the examination. Because time is limited, you may also expect some rather abrupt switches in the direction the questioning takes, so do not be upset by it. Normally, a board member will not pursue a single line of questioning unless he discovers a particular strength or weakness.

After each member has participated, the chairman will usually ask whether any member has any further questions, then will ask you if you have anything you wish to add. Unless you are expecting this question, it may floor you. Worse, it may start you off on an extended, extemporaneous speech. The board is not usually seeking more information. The question is principally to offer you a last opportunity to present further qualifications or to indicate that you have nothing to add. So, if you feel that a significant qualification or characteristic has been overlooked, it is proper to point it out in a sentence or so. Do not compliment the board on the thoroughness of their examination – they have been sketchy, and you know it. If you wish, merely say, "No thank you, I have nothing further to add." This is a point where you can "talk yourself out" of a good impression or fail to present an important bit of information. Remember, *you close the interview yourself*.

The chairman will then say, "That is all, Mr. _____, thank you." Do not be startled; the interview is over, and quicker than you think. Thank him, gather your belongings and take your leave. Save your sigh of relief for the other side of the door.

How to put your best foot forward

Throughout this entire process, you may feel that the board individually and collectively is trying to pierce your defenses, seek out your hidden weaknesses and embarrass and confuse you. Actually, this is not true. They are obliged to make an appraisal of your qualifications for the job you are seeking, and they want to see you in your best light. Remember, they must interview all candidates and a non-cooperative candidate may become a failure in spite of their best efforts to bring out his qualifications. Here are 15 suggestions that will help you:

1) Be natural – Keep your attitude confident, not cocky

If you are not confident that you can do the job, do not expect the board to be. Do not apologize for your weaknesses, try to bring out your strong points. The board is interested in a positive, not negative, presentation. Cockiness will antagonize any board member and make him wonder if you are covering up a weakness by a false show of strength.

2) Get comfortable, but don't lounge or sprawl

Sit erectly but not stiffly. A careless posture may lead the board to conclude that you are careless in other things, or at least that you are not impressed by the importance of the occasion. Either conclusion is natural, even if incorrect. Do not fuss with your clothing, a pencil or an ashtray. Your hands may occasionally be useful to emphasize a point; do not let them become a point of distraction.

3) Do not wisecrack or make small talk

This is a serious situation, and your attitude should show that you consider it as such. Further, the time of the board is limited – they do not want to waste it, and neither should you.

4) Do not exaggerate your experience or abilities

In the first place, from information in the application or other interviews and sources, the board may know more about you than you think. Secondly, you probably will not get away with it. An experienced board is rather adept at spotting such a situation, so do not take the chance.

5) If you know a board member, do not make a point of it, yet do not hide it

Certainly you are not fooling him, and probably not the other members of the board. Do not try to take advantage of your acquaintanceship – it will probably do you little good.

6) Do not dominate the interview

Let the board do that. They will give you the clues – do not assume that you have to do all the talking. Realize that the board has a number of questions to ask you, and do not try to take up all the interview time by showing off your extensive knowledge of the answer to the first one.

7) Be attentive

You only have 20 minutes or so, and you should keep your attention at its sharpest throughout. When a member is addressing a problem or question to you, give him your undivided attention. Address your reply principally to him, but do not exclude the other board members.

8) Do not interrupt

A board member may be stating a problem for you to analyze. He will ask you a question when the time comes. Let him state the problem, and wait for the question.

9) Make sure you understand the question

Do not try to answer until you are sure what the question is. If it is not clear, restate it in your own words or ask the board member to clarify it for you. However, do not haggle about minor elements.

10) Reply promptly but not hastily

A common entry on oral board rating sheets is "candidate responded readily," or "candidate hesitated in replies." Respond as promptly and quickly as you can, but do not jump to a hasty, ill-considered answer.

11) Do not be peremptory in your answers

A brief answer is proper – but do not fire your answer back. That is a losing game from your point of view. The board member can probably ask questions much faster than you can answer them.

12) Do not try to create the answer you think the board member wants

He is interested in what kind of mind you have and how it works – not in playing games. Furthermore, he can usually spot this practice and will actually grade you down on it.

13) Do not switch sides in your reply merely to agree with a board member

Frequently, a member will take a contrary position merely to draw you out and to see if you are willing and able to defend your point of view. Do not start a debate, yet do not surrender a good position. If a position is worth taking, it is worth defending.

14) Do not be afraid to admit an error in judgment if you are shown to be wrong

The board knows that you are forced to reply without any opportunity for careful consideration. Your answer may be demonstrably wrong. If so, admit it and get on with the interview.

15) Do not dwell at length on your present job

The opening question may relate to your present assignment. Answer the question but do not go into an extended discussion. You are being examined for a *new* job, not your present one. As a matter of fact, try to phrase ALL your answers in terms of the job for which you are being examined.

Basis of Rating

Probably you will forget most of these "do's" and "don'ts" when you walk into the oral interview room. Even remembering them all will not ensure you a passing grade. Perhaps you did not have the qualifications in the first place. But remembering them will help you to put your best foot forward, without treading on the toes of the board members.

Rumor and popular opinion to the contrary notwithstanding, an oral board wants you to make the best appearance possible. They know you are under pressure – but they also want to see how you respond to it as a guide to what your reaction would be under the pressures of the job you seek. They will be influenced by the degree of poise you display, the personal traits you show and the manner in which you respond.

ABOUT THIS BOOK

This book contains tests divided into Examination Sections. Go through each test, answering every question in the margin. We have also attached a sample answer sheet at the back of the book that can be removed and used. At the end of each test look at the answer key and check your answers. On the ones you got wrong, look at the right answer choice and learn. Do not fill in the answers first. Do not memorize the questions and answers, but understand the answer and principles involved. On your test, the questions will likely be different from the samples. Questions are changed and new ones added. If you understand these past questions you should have success with any changes that arise. Tests may consist of several types of questions. We have additional books on each subject should more study be advisable or necessary for you. Finally, the more you study, the better prepared you will be. This book is intended to be the last thing you study before you walk into the examination room. Prior study of relevant texts is also recommended. NLC publishes some of these in our Fundamental Series. Knowledge and good sense are important factors in passing your exam. Good luck also helps. So now study this Passbook, absorb the material contained within and take that knowledge into the examination. Then do your best to pass that exam.

EXAMINATION SECTION

EXAMINATION SECTION
TEST 1

DIRECTIONS: Each question or incomplete statement is followed by several suggested answers or completions. Select the one that BEST answers the question or completes the statement. *PRINT THE LETTER OF THE CORRECT ANSWER IN THE SPACE AT THE RIGHT.*

Questions 1-10.

DIRECTIONS: Questions 1 through 10 are to be answered on the basis of the following information.

Assume you are in charge of ordering the following supplies for Unit X:

DESCRIPTION	REORDER ONLY WHEN AMOUNT FALLS TO:	AMOUNT OF EACH REORDER
Copier paper (500 pkgs/ream)	15 reams	20 reams
Copier fluid (5 bottles/carton)	2 cartons	15 cartons
Copier toner (4 bottles/pack)	1 pack	10 packs
Writing pads (12 pads/pack)	4 packs	10 packs
Typing paper (500 pkgs/ream)	3 reams	15 reams
Correction fluid (12 bottles/carton)	1 carton	5 cartons

You should assume that no supplies are reordered more than once in any one week, and that no reordering was done the first week. Reorders occur only when stated, when the facts indicate supplies have fallen below the level required, or when the facts show logically that reordering must have occurred in order for the given totals to make sense. All reorders are filled the same day they are requested.

Other important facts:

Twenty bottles of copier fluid were used in the first week.

The amount of copier fluid at the beginning of the fourth week was double the amount of copier fluid in the unit at the beginning of the first week.

Eight bottles of copier toner were used in the first week.

Forty writing pads were used in week one, and fifty writing pads were used in week two.

The unit had twice as many cartons of correction fluid at the beginning of the first week as it had at the beginning of the third week.

In the first week, twenty-seven reams of copier paper were used.

A total of six reams of copier paper were used in the second and third weeks.

There were twelve reams of typing paper in the unit at the beginning of the third week.

Now that you have the facts, here is a table to help you in answering the questions that follow. Please note that some information has already been provided. All figures in the table are in terms of reams, packs, or cartons.

	Copier paper	Copier fluid	Copier toner	Writing pads	Typing paper	Correction fluid
Beginning of week 1	42			11		
Beginning of week 2		3	2		5	
Beginning of week 3						2
Beginning of week 4						

1. How many reams of copier paper were left in the unit at the beginning of the fourth week?

    A. 9 B. 16 C. 29 D. 41

2. How many cartons of copier fluid were in the unit at the beginning of the first week?

    A. 7 B. 5 C. 23 D. 18

3. How many cartons of copier fluid were used in the unit in the second and third weeks if copier fluid was only reordered once during this time?

    A. 4
    B. 28
    C. 11
    D. Cannot be determined from the information given

4. How many packs of copier toner did the unit have at the beginning of the first week?

    A. 12 B. 4 C. 6 D. 1

1.____

2.____

3.____

4.____

5. If the unit used a total of sixteen bottles of copier toner in the second and third weeks, how many bottles did the unit have at the beginning of the fourth week? Assume that the copier fluid was only reordered once during this time. 5.____

    A. 8 B. 6 C. 24 D. 32

6. Writing pads were reordered the first time in week 6.____

    A. one B. two C. three D. four

7. The number of packs of writing pads at the beginning of the fifth week was half the amount of the number of packs of writing pads left at the beginning of the third week. How many writing pads were left at the beginning of the fifth week? 7.____

    A. 6.75 B. 7 C. 81 D. 84

8. How many reams of typing paper were used by the unit in the second week? 8.____

    A. 8 B. 7 C. 12 D. 15

9. How many bottles of correction fluid did the unit use in the first and second weeks if none were reordered during this time? 9.____

    A. 2 B. 6 C. 12 D. 24

10. In the third week, fourteen bottles of correction fluid were used. This means that correction fluid was reordered 10.____

    A. the second week
    B. the third week
    C. the fourth week
    D. there was no need to reorder

KEY (CORRECT ANSWERS)

1. C   6. B
2. A   7. C
3. A   8. A
4. B   9. D
5. D   10. B

EXAMINATION SECTION
TEST 1

DIRECTIONS: Each question or incomplete statement is followed by several suggested answers or completions. Select the one that BEST answers the question or completes the statement. *PRINT THE LETTER OF THE CORRECT ANSWER IN THE SPACE AT THE RIGHT.*

1. When picking items from a shelf at least 10 feet high, the one of the following that is BEST to use is a　　　　　　　　　　　　　　　　　　　　　　　　　　　　　　　　　1.____

    A. cart　　　　　B. table　　　　　C. stool　　　　　D. ladder

2. Cardboard boxes, wrapping paper, and cord are all very useful items in　　　　2.____

    A. packaging　　　B. typing　　　　C. cleaning　　　D. filing

Questions 3-6.

DIRECTIONS: Questions 3 through 6 are to be answered by picking the answer which is in the correct numerical order, from the lowest number to the highest number, in each question.

3. A. 44533, 44518, 44516, 44547
    B. 44516, 44518, 44533, 44547
    C. 44547, 44533, 44518, 44516
    D. 44518, 44516, 44547, 44533

4. A. 95587, 95593, 95601, 95620
    B. 95601, 95620, 95587, 95593
    C. 95593, 95587, 95601, 95620
    D. 95620, 95601, 95593, 95587

5. A. 232212, 232208, 232232, 232223
    B. 232208, 232223, 232212, 232232
    C. 232208, 232212, 232223, 232232
    D. 232223, 232232, 232208, 232212

6. A. 113419, 113521, 113462, 113588
    B. 113588, 113462, 113521, 113419
    C. 113521, 113588, 113419, 113462
    D. 113419, 113462, 113521, 113588

Questions 7-10.

DIRECTIONS: Questions 7 through 10 are to be answered on the basis of the information given below.

The most commonly used filing system and the one that is easiest to learn is alphabetical filing. This involves putting records in an A to Z order, according to the letters of the alphabet. The name of a person is filed by using the following order: first, the surname or last name; second, the first name; third, the middle name or middle initial. For example, *Henry C. Young* is filed under Y and thereafter under *Young, Henry C.* The name of a company is filed in the same way. For example, *Long Cabinet Co.* is filed under L, while *John T. Long Cabinet Co.* is filed under L and thereafter under *Long, John T. Cabinet Co.*

7. The one of the following which lists the names of persons in the CORRECT alphabetical order is

    A. Mary Carrie, Helen Carrol, James Carson, John Carter
    B. James Carson, Mary Carrie, John Carter, Helen Carrol
    C. Helen Carrol, James Carson, John Carter, Mary Carrie
    D. John Carter, Helen Carrol, Mary Carrie, James Carson

8. The one of the following which lists the names of persons in the CORRECT alphabetical order is

    A. Jones, John C.; Jones, John A.; Jones, John P.; Jones, John K.
    B. Jones, John P.; Jones, John K.; Jones, John C.; Jones, John A.
    C. Jones, John A.; Jones, John C.; Jones, John K.; Jones, John P.
    D. Jones, John K.; Jones, John C.; Jones, John A.; Jones, John P.

9. The one of the following which lists the names of the companies in the CORRECT alphabetical order is

    A. Blane Co., Blake Co., Block Co., Blear Co.
    B. Blake Co., Blane Co., Blear Co., Block Co.
    C. Block Co., Blear Co., Blane Co., Blake Co.
    D. Blear Co., Blake Co., Blane Co., Block Co.

10. You are to return to the file an index card on *Barry C. Wayne Materials and Supplies Co.* Of the following, the CORRECT alphabetical group that you should return the index card to is

    A. A to G
    B. H to M
    C. N to S
    D. T to Z

11. If 75 crates of food were ordered and 100 crates were delivered, then the shipment is larger than the number ordered by _____ crates.

    A. 10 B. 15 C. 25 D. 35

12. If 200 boxes of merchandise were ordered and 100 boxes are delivered, then the shipment is short by _____ boxes.

    A. 50 B. 100 C. 150 D. 175

13. You should be careful when storing food items which give off odors.
    Of the following, the food item which is MOST likely to give off a strong odor is

    A. baking powder   B. butter
    C. garlic   D. starch

14. Of the following, the one which is NOT an example of equipment generally used in preventing or fighting fires is a(n)

    A. extinguisher
    B. smoke alarm
    C. overhead sprinkler
    D. air pump

Questions 15-17.

DIRECTIONS: Questions 15 through 17 are to be answered on the basis of the information given below.

You are instructed to pack several items in a large shipping box. You are to pack the items as follows: items weighing 9 to 12 pounds are to be packed at the bottom of the box; items weighing 5 to 8 pounds are to be packed in the middle of the box; items weighing up to 4 pounds are to be packed at the top of the box. Any item weighing more than 12 pounds is to be packed in a separate box.

15. Based on the above instructions, an item weighing 3 pounds should be packed _____ box.

    A. at the bottom of the
    B. in the middle of the
    C. at the top of the
    D. in a separate

16. Based on the above instructions, an item weighing 10 pounds should be packed _____ box.

    A. at the bottom of the
    B. in the middle of the
    C. at the top of the
    D. in a separate

17. Based on the above instructions, an item weighing 13 pounds should be packed _____ box.

    A. at the bottom of the
    B. in the middle of the
    C. at the top of the
    D. in a separate

18. The color that BEST indicates DANGER and which generally appears on emergency stop buttons of electrical equipment is

    A. green   B. black   C. red   D. brown

19. Of the following, the material that would be MOST easily damaged if it becomes wet is

    A. plastic   B. rubber   C. glass   D. wood

20. The length of time for which whole milk can be stored under refrigeration without becoming spoiled is MOST NEARLY one

    A. day   B. week   C. month   D. year

21. You are told by your supervisor to unpack and check a box of 100 glass jars. While unwrapping the glass jars, you find that two of them are broken.
    The BEST action for you to take FIRST is to

    A. rewrap the broken glass jars and put them back in the box
    B. get rid of the broken glass jars
    C. report the breakage to your supervisor
    D. try to repair the broken glass jars

22. For safety reasons, the BEST kind of shoes to wear while working in a warehouse are   22.____

   A. medium-heeled, slip-on loafers with smooth leather soles
   B. low-heeled, slip-on moccasins
   C. high-heeled, dressy lace-up shoes
   D. low-heeled, lace-up shoes with non-skid soles

23. Your supervisor tells you to put an item back in its proper storage place. However, you do not know where the item is to be put back.   23.____
   Of the following, the BEST action for you to take is to

   A. put the item somewhere and forget about it
   B. ask your supervisor exactly where the item should be put back
   C. put the item in a separate box on the nearest shelf
   D. give the item to someone else to put back

24. You are to load a hand truck with cartons weighing a total of 200 pounds.   24.____
   If each carton weighs 20 pounds, then the TOTAL number of cartons to be loaded is

   A. 8   B. 9   C. 10   D. 11

25. You are to unpack twelve cartons of paper and place the paper on a storage shelf.   25.____
   If each carton has eight packs of paper, then the number of packs of paper that you will place on the shelf is

   A. 72   B. 84   C. 96   D. 108

26. If floor wax costs $2.90 a gallon, then the TOTAL cost of a carton in which there are six gallons of wax is   26.____

   A. $17.40   B. $19.00   C. $21.40   D. $29.00

27. You know that a storage shelf unit can safely hold items up to a total weight of 300 pounds.   27.____
   If there are already 8 boxes of canned food on the shelves of the unit, all exactly the same, and each box weighs 25 pounds, then the number of the same boxes of canned food that you can safely add to those on the shelves is

   A. 4   B. 5   C. 6   D. 7

28. When lifting a heavy box from the floor, you should place the box as _____ you as possible.   28.____

   A. much to the left of   B. much to the right of
   C. far away from   D. close to

29. You are asked by your supervisor to store some packages on a high shelf, which you will need a ladder to reach. When you find the ladder in your work area, you notice that it is in very bad condition. Some of the steps are very loose and need to be fixed.   29.____
   Of the following, the BEST action for you to take is to

   A. ask a co-worker to hold the ladder while you are using it
   B. tell your supervisor about the ladder and ask where another one can be found
   C. put the ladder aside and try to climb the shelves to store the packages
   D. take a chance and use the ladder to store the packages

Questions 30-35.

DIRECTIONS: Questions 30 through 35 are to be answered by choosing for your answer to each question the classification that BEST fits the stock item.

30. *Eggs* may BEST be classified under 30.____

    A. food and dairy B. metals
    C. chemicals D. paints and brushes

31. *Aspirin* may BEST be classified under 31.____

    A. kitchenware B. drugs
    C. plumbing supplies D. electrical supplies

32. *Oral thermometers* may BEST be classified under 32.____

    A. fire extinguishers B. cleaning equipment
    C. lumber supplies D. hospital supplies

33. *Paper clips* may BEST be classified under 33.____

    A. lighting equipment B. oils and greases
    C. office supplies D. gardening materials

34. *Hammer* may BEST be classified under 34.____

    A. liquids B. food products
    C. tools D. glass products

35. *Carburetors* may BEST be classified under _____ equipment. 35.____

    A. welding B. automotive
    C. laboratory D. building

KEY (CORRECT ANSWERS)

1.	D	16.	A
2.	A	17.	D
3.	B	18.	C
4.	A	19.	D
5.	C	20.	B
6.	D	21.	C
7.	A	22.	D
8.	C	23.	B
9.	B	24.	C
10.	D	25.	C
11.	C	26.	A
12.	B	27.	A
13.	C	28.	D
14.	D	29.	B
15.	C	30.	A

31. B
32. D
33. C
34. C
35. B

TEST 2

DIRECTIONS: Each question or incomplete statement is followed by several suggested answers or completions. Select the one that BEST answers the question or completes the statement. *PRINT THE LETTER OF THE CORRECT ANSWER IN THE SPACE AT THE RIGHT.*

1. Your supervisor has told you that food items, as they are received, should be dated on the outside of each package by the receiver. You are also told that you should always take the oldest food items first when you pick items from stock.
   Based on the above information, the BEST way to find the *oldest* stock is to

   A. check the date on each package
   B. open each package and check the items inside
   C. find out from the receiver
   D. ask your supervisor

   1.____

2. Your supervisor assigns you to unload a truck containing 10 cartons of medical supplies. While unloading the truck, you notice that one carton of medical supplies is open. All of the other cartons are sealed.
   Of the following, the BEST action for you to take is to

   A. seal the carton neatly and continue to unload the truck
   B. report this matter to your supervisor
   C. hide the open carton and say nothing about the matter
   D. leave the carton open and store it with the other cartons

   2.____

3. You are told to move an empty 55-gallon drum, which is on its side, a short distance. Of the following, the BEST way to move the drum while keeping control is for you to use your

   A. hands   B. feet   C. shoulder   D. back

   3.____

4. You are told to unpack two boxes which, according to the purchase order and the invoice, are supposed to contain four gallons of paint each. However, you find that there are six gallons of paint in each box.
   Of the following, the MOST reasonable course of action for you to take is to

   A. put all the paint in storage until someone finds out about the error
   B. store only the paint which has been ordered and keep the extra paint for yourself
   C. tell your supervisor about the extra gallons of paint that you found in each box
   D. give the extra gallons of paint to those whom you know can use them

   4.____

5. When receiving a delivery of goods, it will usually be necessary for you to do the following tasks:
   I. Stock the goods on the storage shelf
   II. Unload the goods from the truck
   III. Take the goods to the storage area
   Which one of the following shows the CORRECT order in which you should do the tasks listed above?

   A. I, II, and III
   B. II, III, and I
   C. III, II, and I
   D. II, I, and III

   5.____

6. You are on the top of a 6-foot ladder and are about to put a 30-pound box on a high shelf when the telephone rings. There is no one else around to answer it.
   Of the following, the BEST course of action for you to take is to _____ answer the telephone.

   A. come down off the ladder with the box and
   B. put the box on the shelf and then come down from the ladder to
   C. let the box fall to the floor and then come down from the ladder to
   D. come down off the ladder with the box and see if you can find someone else to

Questions 7-9.

DIRECTIONS: Questions 7 through 9 are to be answered on the basis of the following charts and information.

AREA 1

Section A	Section B
stationery	electrical supplies
office supplies	lighting equipment
kitchenware	dry goods

AREA 2

Section A	Section B
drugs	tools
chemicals	laboratory equipment
cleaning supplies	hospital supplies

The above charts represent a storage room which is separated into two areas, Area 1 and Area 2, and separated within each area into two sections, Section A and Section B. Each section stores the items shown on the charts.

7. According to the above charts, you should find *laboratory equipment* in Area _____, Section _____ .

   A. 1; A   B. 1; B   C. 2; A   D. 2; B

8. According to the above charts, all of the following items are in Area 1, Section A EXCEPT

   A. dry goods   B. stationery
   C. kitchenware   D. office supplies

9. According to the above charts, you should store light bulbs in Area _____, Section _____.

   A. 1; A   B. 1; B   C. 2; A   D. 2;B

Questions 10-12.

DIRECTIONS: Questions 10 through 12 are to be answered on the basis of the information given in the stock listing below.

STOCK LISTING OF BOLTS, NUTS, SCREWS, WASHERS, ETC.

Item No.	Commodity Code	Description
1	43-A00059	Anchor Expansion Mach Screw Type 6/32 inch
2	43-A00061	Anchor Expansion Mach Screw Type 8/32 inch
3	43-B06028	Bolt Carriage Oval HD Hex Nut 3/16 x 1 inch
4	43-B06029	Bolt Carriage Oval HD Hex Nut 3/16 x $1\frac{1}{2}$ inch
5	43-N06033	Nut Mach Screw Brass Hex 4/40 inch
6	43-N04725	Nut Mach Screw Brass Hex 6/40 inch
7	43-S08963	Screw Mach Brass Rnd HD 6/32 x 1 inch
8	43-S08975	Screw Mach Brass Rnd HD 6/32 x 2 inch
9	43-W00700	Washer Brass Round 1 lb Pkg No. 4
10	43-W03024	Washer Brass Round 1 lb Pkg No. 6

10. The type of item which is described as *1 lb Pkg* is a

    A. bolt B. nut C. screw D. washer

11. The Commodity Code which appears in the next row below Commodity Code 43-B06029 is

    A. 43-A00061 B. 43-B06028
    C. 43-N06033 D. 43-N04725

12. The one of the following which does NOT have the complete information taken from the *Description* column of the item is

    A. Anchor Expansion Mach Screw Type 8/32 inch
    B. Bolt Carriage Oval Nut 3/16 x $1\frac{1}{2}$ inch
    C. Nut Mach Screw Brass Hex 6/40 inch
    D. Screw Mach Brass Rnd HD 6/32 x 2 inch

Questions 13-17.

DIRECTIONS: Questions 13 through 17 are to be answered on the basis of the following diagram and information.

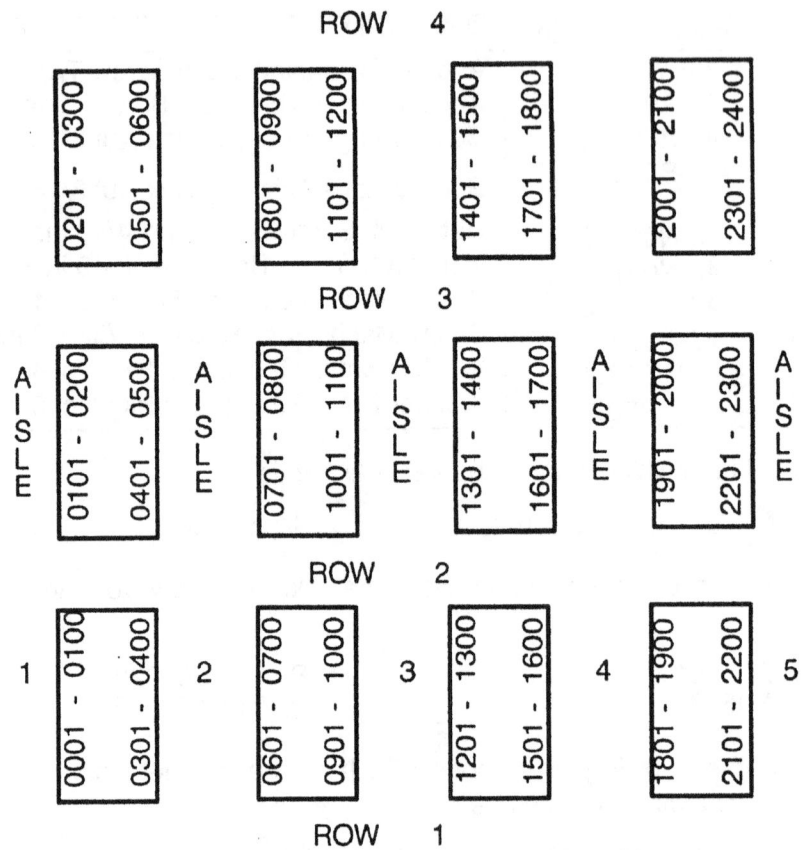

The above diagram represents a warehouse which has 4 Rows and 5 Aisles. Items are stored in this warehouse according to their item numbers which are shown in groups along the sides of the aisles. To find an item, you must go to the aisle and rows between which the item is located. For example, to find item number 0078, you must go to Aisle 1, between Rows 1 and 2, because item number 0078 is in group 0001 - 0100.

13. To find item number 1657, you should go to Aisle _____, between Rows _____.   13.____

    A. 1; 1 and 2
    C. 4; 2 and 3
    B. 2; 2 and 3
    D. 5; 1 and 2

14. To find item number 0723, you should go to Aisle _____, between Rows _____.   14.____

    A. 2; 1 and 2
    C. 4; 2 and 3
    B. 2; 2 and 3
    D. 4; 3 and 4

15. To find item number 1445, you should go to Aisle _____, between Rows _____. 15.____

    A. 1; 3 and 4   B. 2; 3 and 4
    C. 3; 3 and 4   D. 4; 3 and 4

16. To find item number 1201, you should go to Aisle _____, between Rows _____. 16.____

    A. 3; 1 and 2   B. 2; 3 and 4
    C. 5; 1 and 2   D. 4; 3 and 4

17. To find item number 2325, you should go to Aisle _____, between Rows _____. 17.____

    A. 2; 1 and 2   B. 3; 3 and 4
    C. 4; 1 and 2   D. 5; 3 and 4

Questions 18-20.

DIRECTIONS: Questions 18 through 20 are to be answered on the basis of the information given in the chart shown below.

Item	Weight
Metal file box	5 pounds
Large desk stapler	2 pounds
Large tape dispenser	1.5 pounds
Hardcover dictionary	3 pounds

18. Based on the figures shown in the chart above, the TOTAL weight of 5 metal file boxes, 3 hardcover dictionaries, and a large tape dispenser is _____ pounds. 18.____

    A. 33.5   B. 34.5   C. 35.5   D. 36.5

19. Of the following, which group of items would weigh a TOTAL of 25 pounds or less? 19.____

    A. 6 metal file boxes and 1 hardcover dictionary
    B. 10 large desk staplers and 1 hardcover dictionary
    C. 8 hardcover dictionaries and 2 large tape dispensers
    D. 10 large tape dispensers and 3 metal file boxes

20. Assume that 5 large desk staplers, 6 metal file boxes, 10 hardcover dictionaries, and 3 large tape dispensers are placed in a shipping container with a weight limit of 100 pounds. 20.____
    When you add up the total weight of the items, the number of pounds under the weight limit would be _____ pounds.

    A. 23.5   B. 24.5   C. 25.5   D. 26.5

Questions 21-25.

DIRECTIONS: Questions 21 through 25 are to be answered on the basis of the information given in the stock listing below.

LISTING OF ENVELOPES IN STOCK

Item No.	Description	Unit of Issue	Amount
1	Envelope Commercial White 3 5/8" x $6\frac{1}{2}$"	1000 per carton	14 cartons
2	Envelope Commercial White $4\frac{1}{2}$" x $9\frac{1}{2}$"	2500 per carton	7 cartons
3	Envelope Open End Metal Clasp 7" x 10"	1000 per carton	16 cartons
4	Envelope Open End Metal Clasp $8\frac{1}{2}$" x $11\frac{1}{2}$"	1000 per carton	15 cartons
5	Envelope Open End Metal Clasp $9\frac{1}{2}$" x $12\frac{1}{2}$"	500 per carton	28 cartons
6	Envelope Open End Metal Clasp $11\frac{1}{2}$" x $4\frac{1}{2}$"	500 per carton	24 cartons

21. The TOTAL number of cartons of envelopes in stock is   21.___

    A. 87   B. 84   C. 100   D. 104

22. The envelopes which all have a unit of issue of 1000 per carton are found in Item Nos.   22.___

    A. 1, 2, and 3   B. 1, 3, and 4
    C. 2, 4, and 5   D. 3, 4, and 6

23. The item for which there is the GREATEST number of envelopes in stock is Item No.   23.___

    A. 2   B. 3   C. 4   D. 5

24. The TOTAL number of envelopes in stock for all of the items listed above is   24.___

    A. 74,000   B. 81,000   C. 88,500   D. 104,500

25. You receive an order for the following items: Item No. 1, 2000 envelopes; Item No. 2, 5000 envelopes; Item No. 4, 2000 envelopes; Item No. 6, 1000 envelopes.
    The TOTAL number of cartons that you will have to pick from stock in filling the order is   25.___

    A. 6   B. 7   C. 8   D. 9

Questions 26-33.

DIRECTIONS: Questions 26 through 33 are to be answered on the basis of the following blank ORDER FOR SUPPLIES form and information.

ORDER FOR SUPPLIES

Agency 1	Date 2	Agency Order No. 3
Expected Date of Delivery 4	Unit 5	Agency Address 6
Item No 7	Description of Item 8	No. of Items Ordered 9
Line 1 _____	_____	_____
Line 2 _____	_____	_____
Line 3 _____	_____	_____
Line 4 _____	_____	_____
Line 5 _____	_____	_____
Items Picked By 10 Name_____ Date_____	Items Packed By 11 Name_____ Date_____	Items Received By 12 Name_____ Date_____

On September 3, Agency A, located at 220 Reade Street in Manhattan, orders the following items:

Item No.	Description of Item	No. of Items Ordered
65	Large roll of scotch tape	50
21	Desk calendar refill	73
20	Desk blotter	40
18	12-inch wooden ruler	36
17	Desk stapler	15

The agency order number is 000177A. The expected date of delivery is November 5. The items are ordered by the Accounting Unit of Agency A. The items are picked by J. Hines on October 20. The items are packed by L. Warren on October 21. The items are received by G. Westerly on November 3.

26. The date which should appear in Box 10 on the form is

    A. October 20   B. October 21
    C. November 3   D. November 5

27. The agency order number which should appear in Box 3 is

    A. 00117A   B. 00017A   C. 00177A   D. 000177A

28. The date of November 5 should appear in Box

    A. 2   B. 4   C. 11   D. 12

29. If the item numbers are written in Box 7 on Lines 1 through 5, from the lowest to the highest number, then the Item No. that should appear on Line 3 is

    A. 17   B. 20   C. 21   D. 65

30. The person whose name should appear in Box 11 is

    A. L. Warren   B. J. Hines
    C. G. Westerly   D. A. Haynes

31. For which one of the following is the number of items ordered the SMALLEST?

    A. Large roll of scotch tape
    B. Desk calendar refill
    C. 12-inch wooden ruler
    D. Desk stapler

32. The one of the following which is the CORRECT street address that should appear in Box 6 is _____ Street.

    A. 220 Reade   B. 202 Read
    C. 220 Reed   D. 202 Rade

33. The time from the date the items were ordered to the date the items were received was MOST NEARLY

    A. 2 days   B. 6 weeks   C. 2 months   D. 6 months

34. A storeroom has 12 rows of boxes with 8 boxes in each row. Each box contains 14 cartons of juice.
    The TOTAL number of cartons of juice in the storeroom is

    A. 112   B. 168   C. 672   D. 1344

35. There is shelf space available that measures 60 inches wide, 20 inches deep, and 20 inches high.
    If you have a carton that measures 18 inches wide, 18 inches deep, and 18 inches high, then the number of cartons you can put on the shelf is MOST NEARLY

    A. 2   B. 3   C. 4   D. 5

KEY (CORRECT ANSWERS)

1.	A	11.	C	21.	D	31.	D
2.	B	12.	B	22.	B	32.	A
3.	A	13.	C	23.	A	33.	C
4.	C	14.	B	24.	C	34.	D
5.	B	15.	C	25.	C	35.	B
6.	B	16.	A	26.	A		
7.	D	17.	D	27.	D		
8.	A	18.	C	28.	B		
9.	B	19.	B	29.	B		
10.	D	20.	C	30.	A		

EXAMINATION SECTION
TEST 1

DIRECTIONS: Each question or incomplete statement is followed by several suggested answers or completions. Select the one that BEST answers the question or completes the statement. *PRINT THE LETTER OF THE CORRECT ANSWER IN THE SPACE AT THE RIGHT.*

1. The stock items on the purchase order should be the same as those on the shipment receipt at time of delivery. In general, it is BEST to check this at the time that the stock items are

    A. received in the storehouse
    B. ordered by the agency using the material
    C. issued by the storehouse personnel
    D. certified for payment

    1.____

2. Sawdust and shredded paper are materials that are generally used in *which one* of the following operations?

    A. Packing   B. Inventory   C. Spraying   D. Transporting

    2.____

3. Storage areas with good air circulation and ventilation are generally considered

    A. *good;* only in hot and humid weather
    B. *good;* to retard mold growth
    C. *poor;* due to danger of fire
    D. *poor;* because of cleaning costs

    3.____

4. To get the best use from storage areas, it is usually *desirable* to use high ceilinged areas for storing

    A. heavy bulky stock items
    B. light-weight stock items
    C. loose stock items in small bins
    D. extremely large sized stock items

    4.____

5. The section of the storeroom that can carry the least weight should generally *NOT* be used for storing stock items that

    A. have a large size
    B. have a small size
    C. are very heavy
    D. are very light

    5.____

6. Where should you store unusually large and heavy stock items, that are used very often?

    A. As close to the shipping and receiving areas as possible
    B. Away from work areas such as shipping and receiving
    C. On hand trucks until the using agency asks for the item
    D. Only in storage areas which are outside the storehouse

    6.____

7. Which of the following would be MOST important in deciding how wide the space should be between cartons stacked in a storage area?

    A. Type of equipment that will be used to handle the stock
    B. Size of the storage area
    C. Number of employees in the storage area
    D. How far the storage area is away from the receiving area

    7.____

8. Stock items that might break, chip, or be crushed should be packed

   A. *tightly* with items touching each other
   B. *loosely* in a heavy wood container
   C. *tightly* with little movement allowed between items
   D. *tightly* with cushioning material between items

9. Suppose that some stock items delivered by truck are found to tie damaged before they are unloaded. Which of the following actions would be BEST to take?

   A. Take the damaged stock and then give it out first to prevent further damage
   B. Refuse to take any damaged items
   C. Tell the driver of the truck to return the entire shipment
   D. Tell your supervisor about the damage so that he can take the necessary steps

10. It is dangerous to store gasoline because

    A. it can only be stored in specially constructed rooms in a storehouse
    B. it gives off vapors that can easily burn
    C. it can explode when moved around
    D. no one has found a safe way of storing gasoline

11. Gases are usually stored under pressure in steel cans. Which of the following is the *LEAST* dangerous practice?

    A. Allowing the cans to come in contact with electrical circuits
    B. Lifting the cans by their valves
    C. Allowing the cans to touch each other
    D. Keeping the valves on the cans open after the gas has been used up

12. Acids are a danger in storage because leakage may result in a sudden fire if contact is made with other chemicals.
    When storing acids, the *one* of the following practices which is *INCORRECT* is to

    A. keep them in heavy duty metal cans
    B. store them in isolated areas
    C. protect the containers against breakage
    D. keep flames or lit matches out of areas where acids are stored

13. Tape with a cellophane backing will become wrinkled and lumpy if stored in an area that is

    A. warm   B. cool   C. damp   D. very dry

14. To keep wooden furniture from warping and twisting, it should be stored in an area that is

    A. warm and dry   B. warm and damp
    C. cool and dry   D. cool and damp

15. Which one of the following items should *NOT* be stored in a very dry storage area?

    A. Soup cubes   B. Baking soda
    C. Tea leaves   D. Lettuce

16. Suppose that a stockroom started the week with an initial supply of 3 gross of pencils and that one gross equals 144 pencils. After orders were filled, the stockroom had an inventory at the end of the week as follows: 2 gross of 4H pencils; 3 dozen 2B pencils, 1 1/2 dozen HB pencils, and 15 H pencils.
    How many pencils were ordered?

    A. 22 pencils   B. 45 pencils   C. 75 pencils   D. 97 pencils

17. How many 18-inch pieces can be cut from 10 lengths of 8-foot glass tubing?

    A. 47 pieces   B. 50 pieces   C. 53 pieces   D. 56 pieces

18. Suppose a roll of wire is 27 feet 3 inches long. A piece of wire measuring 18 feet 9 inches in length is cut from the roll.
    What is the length of wire left on the roll?

    A. 7 feet 3 inches   B. 7 feet 6 inches
    C. 8 feet 3 inches   D. 8 feet 6 inches

19. Suppose that 25% of a delivery of canned peaches was spoiled. If 36 cans were spoiled, then the delivery had a total of

    A. 9 cans   B. 25 cans   C. 144 cans   D. 180 cans

20. Suppose that a one-quart can of white flat ceiling paint weighs 5 pounds. What is the GREATEST number of quart cans that can be stored on a shelf that supports 167 pounds?

    A. 5 quart cans   B. 33 quart cans
    C. 41 quart cans   D. 67 quart cans

Questions 21-25.

DIRECTIONS: Answer Questions 21 through 25 on the basis of the formation given below.

LISTING OF PAPER				
Description	Quantity Ordered by Stockroom A (In dozen reams)	Quantity in Stock Before Delivery (In dozen reams)	Cost Per Ream	Location of Stock in Stockroom
8 1/2"x11" Blue	17	5	$ .94	Bin A7
8 1/2"x11" Buff	8	3	$ .93	Bin A7
8 1/2"x11" Green	11	4	$ .95	Bin B4
8 1/2"x11" Pink	10	4	$ .93	Bin B4
8 1/2"x11" White	80	15	$ .86	Bin A8
8 1/2"x13" White	76	12	$1.02	Bin A8
8 1/2"x14" Blue	7	2	$1.19	Bin A7
8 1/2"x14" Buff	7	3	$1.18	Bin A7
8 1/2"x14" Green	5	2	$1.20	Bin B4
8 1/2"x14" Pink	8	4	$1.18	Bin B4
8 1/2"x14" White	110	28	$1.15	Bin A8
8 1/2"x14" Yellow	2	1	$1.23	Bin C6

21. How many reams of 8 1/2"x13" paper will there be in stock if only one-half of the amount ordered is delivered?   21.____

    A. 456 reams   B. 600 reams   C. 912 reams   D. 1056 reams

22. Suppose all ordered material is delivered. The bin that will have the MOST reams of paper is   22.____

    A. A7   B. A8   C. B4   D. C6

23. Suppose all ordered material has been delivered. What is the approximate value of all 8 1/2"x11" paper which is in Bin B4?   23.____

    A. $27   B. $171   C. $198   D. $327

24. How many reams of white paper of all sizes were ordered?   24.____

    A. 55 reams   B. 266 reams   C. 660 reams   D. 3192 reams

25. Before any of the orders were delivered, the following requests were filled and removed from the stockroom: 25.____
    2 dozen reams 8 1/2" X 11" Blue; 2 dozen reams 8 1/2" X 11" Green;
    7 dozen reams 8 1/2" X 11" White; 5 dozen reams 8 1/2" x13" White;
    1 dozen reams 8 1/2" X 14" Green; 13 dozen reams 8 1/2" X14" Whit.
    How many reams of paper were left in the stockroom after the above requests were filled?

    A. 30   B. 53   C. 636   D. 996

KEY (CORRECT ANSWERS)

1. A	11. C
2. A	12. A
3. B	13. C
4. B	14. C
5. C	15. D
6. A	16. C
7. A	17. B
8. D	18. D
9. D	19. C
10. B	20. B

21. B
22. B
23. D
24. D
25. C

TEST 2

DIRECTIONS: Each question or incomplete statement is followed by several suggested answers or completions. Select the one that *BEST* answers the question or completes the statement. *PRINT THE LETTER OF THE CORRECT ANSWER IN THE SPACE AT THE RIGHT.*

Questions 1-10.

DIRECTIONS: Each of Questions 1 through 10 presents a stock item followed by 4 classes of things. For each question choose the class of things in which the given item is *MOST* likely to be found.

1. *Pliers* may *BEST* be classified under

    A. food products B. tools
    C. office supplies D. machinery

    1.____

2. *White Pine lumber* may *BEST* be classified under

    A. building materials B. laboratory materials
    C. safety materials D. seeds and plants

    2.____

3. *Linseed oil* may *BEST* be classified under

    A. drugs and chemicals B. painters' supplies
    C. building materials D. fuel and fuel oils

    3.____

4. *Ceiling tiles* may *BEST* be classified under

    A. office supplies B. hardware
    C. electrical supplies D. building materials

    4.____

5. *Floor finish remover* may *BEST* be classified under

    A. insecticides B. drugs
    C. machinery D. cleaning supplies

    5.____

6. *Arm slings* may *BEST* be classified under

    A. hospital supplies B. clothing
    C. school supplies D. office supplies

    6.____

7. *Staplers* may *BEST* be classified under

    A. office supplies B. laboratory supplies
    C. machinery and metals D. engineering supplies

    7.____

8. *Canvas stretcher* may *BEST* be classified under

    A. laboratory apparatus B. hospital supplies C. clothing

    8.____

9. *Switches* may *BEST* be classified under

    A. camera supplies B. vehicles
    C. electrical supplies D. pipes and pipe fittings

    9.____

23

10. *Bandages* may *BEST* be classified under

    A. laboratory equipment B. surgical instruments
    C. hospital supplies   D. hose and belting

11. Employees who must lift and carry stock items should be careful to avoid injury. When an employee lifts or carries stock items, which of the following is the LEAST safe practice?

    A. Keep the legs straight and lift with the back muscles
    B. Keep the load as close to the body as possible
    C. Get a good grip on the object to be carried
    D. First determine if the item can be lifted and carried safely

12. For warning and protection, the color red is *usually* used for

    A. indicating high temperature stockroom areas
    B. floor markings
    C. location of first-aid supplies
    D. stop buttons, lights for barricades and other dangerous locations

13. Reporting rattles, squeaks, or other noises in equipment to your maintenance supervisor is

    A. *bad;* too much attention to squeaks like these keep important safety problems from being noticed
    B. *bad;* each person should oil and care for his own equipment
    C. *good;* these sounds may mean that the equipment should be fixed
    D. *good;* it shows the supervisor that you are a good worker

14. If you often get cuts on your hands from handling different kinds of cartons and boxes, the *BEST* thing for you to do is to

    A. keep from handling those kinds of cartons and boxes
    B. ask that better boxes and cartons be used
    C. toughen up your hands
    D. wear protective gloves

15. A low, movable platform used for stacking materials in a warehouse is called a "pallet". When lifting and moving "pallets" with a forklift, how should a stockman place the forks?

    A. As wide apart as possible
    B. As close together as possible
    C. Close together and tilted forward
    D. Wide apart and tilted forward

16. Suppose that 3-foot-high boxes are to be stacked in one pile on a 4-inch platform. In addition, 4-inch thick separators are placed between each layer of boxes. Suppose that the ceiling is 22 feet high and there must be at least 1 1/2 feet of space between the ceiling and the stacked boxes.
    What is the GREATEST number of boxes that can be stacked?

    A. 4   B. 5   C. 6   D. 7

17. A part of a storeroom measures 14 1/2 feet by 6 1/4 feet. The number of square feet in this part is 17.____

    A. 8 1/4 square feet   B. 20 3/4 square feet
    C. 90 5/8 square feet   D. 94 3/4 square feet

18. How many cubic feet of storage space would be taken up by 20 boxes, when each box measures 2 feet high, 2 feet wide, and 3 feet long? 18.____

    A. 12 cubic feet   B. 27 cubic feet
    C. 140 cubic feet   D. 240 cubic feet

19. Suppose that a truckload of canned items has been unloaded. There are six rows of boxes with seven boxes in each row. Each box has two dozen cans in it.
How many cans are there all together? 19.____

    A. 24   B. 144   C. 510   D. 1008

20. Suppose that the average weekly use of tissue amounts to 180 rolls.
At least how many boxes must be ordered for a 4-week period if there are 144 rolls in each box? 20.____

    A. 2   B. 3   C. 4   D. 5

Questions 21-25.

DIRECTIONS: Answer Questions 21 through 25 *SOLELY* on the basis of the information given in the table on the next page.

CONTROLLED DRUG A					
Time Period	Purchase Order Number and	Quantity Ordered	*Quantity Delivered by Vendor	Quantity Distributed during 2-Wk Period	Inventory Balance at end of 2-Wk period
April 23-May 6	110,327	105 ounces	135 ounces	27 ounces	108 ounces
May 7-May 20	111,437	42 ounces	40 ounces	39 ounces	109 ounces
May 21-June 3	112,347	37 ounces	27 ounces	32 ounces	104 ounces
June 4-June 17	112,473	35 ounces	35 ounces	45 ounces	94 ounces
June 18-July 1	114,029	40 ounces	40 ounces	37 ounces	97 ounces

*Delivery is made on first day of time period.

21. The difference between Quantity Ordered and Quantity Delivered was *GREATEST* on Purchase Order Number 21.____

    A. 110,327   B. 111,437   C. 112,347   D. 112,473

22. The *difference* between the total number of ounces ordered and the total number of ounces delivered on April 23 through June 18 is 22.____

    A. 17 ounces   B. 18 ounces   C. 19 ounces   D. 20 ounces

4 (#2)

23. Suppose that average weekly usage was expected to be 26 ounces per week. Your supervisor has asked you to tell him whenever inventory balances get below a four-week level. Under these conditions, you should have told your supervisor during the two-week period beginning

    A. April 23, May 21, June 4, June 18
    B. May 21, June 4, June 18
    C. May 21, June 18
    D. June 4, June 18

24. The *GREATEST* decreases in inventory balances happened between the two-week periods beginning

    A. April 23 and May 7   B. May 7 and May 21
    C. May 21 and June 4   D. June 4 and June 18

25. Suppose a new program has been started at your hospital and the weekly usage of Drug A is expected to be 52 ounces per week. If your supervisor must keep on hand a four-week supply, then the amount that should be delivered for the two-week period beginning on July 2 is

    A. 52 ounces   B. 111 ounces   C. 208 ounces   D. 211 ounces

KEY (CORRECT ANSWERS)

1. B		11. B	
2. A		12. D	
3. B		13. C	
4. D		14. D	
5. D		15. A	
6. A		16. C	
7. A		17. C	
8. B		18. D	
9. C		19. D	
10. C		20. D	

21. A
22. C
23. D
24. C
25. B

CLERICAL ABILITIES TEST

Clerical aptitude involves the ability to perceive pertinent detail in verbal or tabular material, to observe differences in copy, to proofread words and numbers, and to avoid perceptual errors in arithmetic computation.

NATURE OF THE TEST

Four types of clerical aptitude questions are presented in the Clerical Abilities Test. There are 120 questions with a short time limit. The test contains 30 questions on name and number checking, 30 on the arrangement of names in correct alphabetical order, 30 on simple arithmetic, and 30 on inspecting groups of letters and numbers. The questions have been arranged in groups or cycles of five questions of each type. The Clerical Abilities Test is primarily a test of speed in carrying out relatively simple clerical tasks. While accuracy on these tasks is important and will be taken into account in the scoring, experience has shown that many persons are so concerned about accuracy that they do the test more slowly than they should. Competitors should be cautioned that speed as well as accuracy is important to achieve a good score.

HOW THE TEST IS ADMINISTERED

Each competitor should be given a copy of the test booklet with sample questions on the cover page, an answer sheet, and a medium No. 2 pencil. Ten minutes are allowed to study the directions and sample questions and to answer the questions in the proper boxes on the two pages.

The separate answer sheet should be used for the test proper. Fifteen minutes are allowed for the test.

HOW THE TEST IS SCORED

The correct answers should be counted and recorded. The number of incorrect answers must also be counted because one-fourth of the number of incorrect answers is subtracted from the number of right answers. An omission is considered as neither a right nor a wrong answer. The score on this test is the number of right answers minus one-fourth of the number of wrong answers (fractions of one-half or less are dropped). For example, if an applicant had answered 89 questions correctly and 10 questions incorrectly, and had omitted 1 question, his score would be 87.

EXAMINATION SECTION

DIRECTIONS: This test contains four kinds of questions. There are some of each kind on each page in the booklet. The time limit for the test will be announced by the examiner.
Use the special pencil furnished by the examiner in marking your answers on the separate answer sheet. For each question, there are five suggested answers. Decide which answer is correct, find the number of the question on the answer sheet, and make a solid black mark between the dotted lines just below the letter of your answer. If you wish to change your answer, erase the first mark completely, do not merely cross it out.

SAMPLE QUESTIONS

In each line across the page there are three names or numbers that are much alike. Compare the three names or numbers and decide which ones are exactly alike. On the Sample Answer Sheet at the right, mark the answer
  A. if ALL THREE names or numbers are exactly ALIKE
  B. if only the FIRST and SECOND names or numbers are exactly ALIKE
  C. if only the FIRST and THIRD names or numbers are exactly ALIKE
  D. if only the SECOND and THIRD names or numbers are exactly ALIKE
  E. if ALL THREE names or numbers are DIFFERENT

I.	Davis Hazen	David Hozen	David Hazen
II.	Lois Appel	Lois Appel	Lois Apfel
III.	June Allan	Jane Allan	Jane Allan
IV.	10235	10235	10235
V.	32614	32164	32614

It will be to your advantage to learn what A, B, C, D, and E stand for. If you finish the sample questions before you are told to turn to the test, study them.

In the next group of sample questions, there is a name in a box at the left, and four other names in alphabetical order at the right. Find the correct space for the boxed name so that it will be in alphabetical order with the others, and mark the letter of that space as your answer.

VI. | Jones, Jane |

A. →
   Goodyear, G.L.
B. →
   Haddon, Harry
C. →
   Jackson, Mary
D. →
   Jenkins, William
E. →

VII. | Kessler, Neilson |

A. →
   Kessel, Carl
B. →
   Kessinger, D.J.
C. →
   Kessler, Karl
D. →
   Kessner, Lewis
E. →

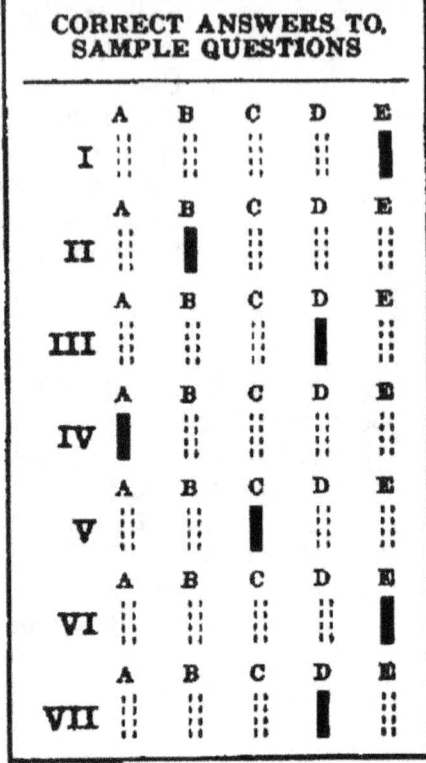

DIRECTIONS: In the following questions, complete the equation and find your answer among the list of suggested answers. Mark the Sample Answer Sheet A, B, C, or D for the answer you obtained; or if your answer is not among these, mark E for that question.

VIII. Add: 22
         +33

   A. 44   B. 45   C. 54   D. 55   E. None of these

IX. Subtract: 24
            - 3

   A. 20   B. 21   C. 27   D. 29   E. None of these

X. Multiply: 25
           x 5

   A. 100   B. 115   C. 125   D. 135   E. None of these

XI. Divide: 6/126̄

    A. 20   B. 22   C. 24   D. 26   E. None of these

DIRECTIONS: There is one set of suggested answers for the next group of sample questions. Do not try to memorize these answers, because there will be a different set on each age in the test.

To find the answer to a question, find which suggested answer contains numbers and letters, all of which appear in the question. If no suggested answer fits, mark E for that question.

XII. 8 N K 9 G T 4 6

XIII. T 9 7 Z 6 L 3 K

XIV. Z 7 G K 3 9 8 N

XV. 3 K 9 4 6 G Z L

XVI. Z N 7 3 8 K T 9

Suggested Answers
A = 7, 9, G, K
B = 8, 9, T, Z
C = 6, 7, K, Z
D = 6, 8, G, T
E = None of the above

After you have marked your answers to all the questions on the Sample Answer Sheets on this page and on the front page of the booklet, check them with the answers in the boxes marked Correct Answers To Sample Questions.

Questions 1-5.

In Questions 1 through 5, compare the three names or numbers, and mark
    A. if ALL THREE names or numbers are exactly ALIKE
    B. if only the FIRST and SECOND names or numbers are exactly ALIKE
    C. if only the FIRST and THIRD names or numbers are exactly ALIKE
    D. if only the SECOND and THIRD names or numbers are exactly ALIKE
    E. if ALL THREE names or numbers are DIFFERENT

1.	5261383	5261383	5261338
2.	8125690	8126690	8125609
3.	W.E. Johnston	W.E. Johnson	W.E. Johnson
4.	Vergil L. Muller	Vergil L. Muller	Vergil L. Muller

5.   Atherton R. Warde   Asheton R. Warde   Atherton P. Warde

Questions 6-10.

In Questions 6 through 10, find the correct place for the name in the box

6. | Hackett, Gerald |

   A. →
      Habert, James
   B. →
      Hachett, J.J.
   C. →
      Hachetts, K. Larson
   D. →
      Hachettson, Leroy
   E. →

7. | Margenroth, Alvin |

   A. →
      Margeroth, Albert
   B. →
      Margestein, Dan
   C. →
      Margestein, David
   D. →
      Margue, Edgar
   E. →

8. | Bobbitt, Olivier E. |

   A. →
      Bobbitt, D. Olivier
   B. →
      Bobbitt, Olivia B
   C. →
      Bobbitt, Olivia H.
   D. →
      Bobbitt, R. Olivia
   E. →

9. | Mosley, Werner |

   A. →
      Mosely, Albert J.
   B. →
      Mosley, Alvin
   C. →
      Mosley, S.M.
   D. →
      Mozley, Vinson N.
   E. →

10. | Youmuns, Frank L. | A. →
                             Youmons, Frank G.
                          B. →
                             Youmons, Frank H.
                          C. →
                             Youmons, Frank K.
                          D. →
                             Youmons, Frank M.
                          E. →

Questions 11-15.

11. Add: 43
          +32

    A. 55   B. 65   C. 66   D. 75   E. None of these

12. Subtract: 83
              - 4

    A. 73   B. 79   C. 80   D. 89   E. None of these

13. Multiply: 41
              x 7

    A. 281   B. 287   C. 291   D. 297   E. None of these

14. Divide: 6/306

    A. 44   B. 51   C. 52   D. 60   E. None of these

15. Add: 37
          +15

    A. 42   B. 52   C. 53   D. 62   E. None of these

Questions 16-20.

In Questions 16 through 20, find which one of the suggested answers appears in that question.

16. 6 2 5 K 4 P T G

17. L 4 7 2 T 6 V K

18. 3 5 4 L 9 V T G

19. G 4 K 7 L 3 5 Z

SUGGESTED ANSWERS
A = 4, 5, K, T
B = 4, 7, G, K
C = 2, 5, G, L
D = 2, 7, L, T
E = None of the above

20. 4 K 2 9 N 5 T G

Questions 21-25.

In Questions 21 through 25, compare the three names or numbers, and mark
   A. if ALL THREE names or numbers are exactly ALIKE
   B. if only the FIRST and SECOND names or numbers are exactly ALIKE
   C. if only the FIRST and THIRD names or numbers are exactly ALIKE
   D. if only the SECOND and THIRD names or numbers are exactly ALIKE
   E. if ALL THREE names or numbers are DIFFERENT

21.	2395890	2395890	2395890
22.	1926341	1926347	1926314
23.	E. Owens McVey	E. Owen McVey	E. Owen McVay
24.	Emily Neal Rouse	Emily Neal Rowse	Emily Neal Rowse
25.	H. Merritt Audubon	H. Merriott Audubon	H. Merritt Audubon

Questions 26-30.

In Questions 26 through 30, find the correct place for the name in the box.

26. Watters, N.O.

   A. →
      Waters, Charles L.
   B. →
      Waterson, Nina P.
   C. →
      Watson, Nora J.
   D. →
      Wattwood, Paul A.
   E. →

27. Johnston, Edward

   A. →
      Johnston, Edgar R.
   B. →
      Johnston, Edmond
   C. →
      Johnston, Edmund
   D. →
      Johnstone, Edmund A.
   E. →

28. Rensch, Adeline

   A. →
      Ramsay, Amos
   B. →
      Remschel, Augusta
   C. →
      Renshaw, Austin
   D. →
      Rentzel, Becky
   E. →

29. Schnyder, Maurice

   A. →
      Schneider, Martin
   B. →
      Schneider, Mertens
   C. →
      Schnyder, Newman
   D. →
      Schreibner, Norman
   E. →

30. Freedenburg, C. Erma

   A. →
      Freedenberg, Emerson
   B. →
      Freedenberg, Erma
   C. →
      Freedenberg, Erma E.
   D. →
      Freedinberg, Erma F.
   E. →

Questions 31-35.

31. Subtract: 68
             - 47

   A. 10   B. 11   C. 20   D. 22   E. None of these

32. Multiply: 50
              x 8

   A. 400   B. 408   C. 450   D. 458   E. None of these

33. Divide: 9/180

   A. 20   B. 29   C. 30   D. 39   E. None of these

34. Add: 78
         + 63

   A. 131   B. 140   C. 141   D. 151   E. None of these

35. Add: 89
    -70

    A. 9   B. 18   C. 19   D. 29   E. None of these

Questions 36-40.

In Questions 36 through 40, find which one of the suggested answers appears in that question.

36. 9 G Z 3 L 4 6 N

37. L 5 N K 4 3 9 V

38. 8 2 V P 9 L Z 5

39. V P 9 Z 5 L 8 7

40. 5 T 8 N 2 9 V L

SUGGESTED ANSWERS
A = 4, 9, L, V
B = 4, 5, N, Z
C = 5, 8, L, Z
D = 8, 9, N, V
E = None of the above

Questions 41-45.

In Questions 41 through 45, compare the three names or numbers, and mark
- A. if ALL THREE names or numbers are exactly ALIKE
- B. if only the FIRST and SECOND names or numbers are exactly ALIKE
- C. if only the FIRST and THIRD names or numbers are exactly ALIKE
- D. if only the SECOND and THIRD names or numbers are exactly ALIKE
- E. if ALL THREE names or numbers are DIFFERENT

41.	6219354	621354	6219354
42.	2312793	2312793	2312793
43.	1065407	1065407	1065047
44.	Francis Ransdell	Frances Ramsdell	Francis Ramsdell
45.	Cornelius Detwiler	Cornelius Detwiler	Cornelius Detwiler

Questions 46-50.

In Questions 46 through 50, find the correct place for the name in the box.

46. | DeMattia, Jessica |

A. →
   DeLong, Jesse
B. →
   DeMatteo, Jessie
C. →
   Derby, Jessie S.
D. →
   DeShazo, L.M.
E. →

47. | Theriault, Louis |

A. →
   Therien, Annette
B. →
   Therien, Elaine
C. →
   Thibeault, Gerald
D. →
   Thiebeault, Pierre
E. →

48. | Gaston, M. Hubert |

A. →
   Gaston, Dorothy M.
B. →
   Gaston, Henry N.
C. →
   Gaston, Isabel
D. →
   Gaston, M. Melvin
E. →

49. | SanMiguel, Carlos |

A. →
   SanLuis, Juana
B. →
   Santilli, Laura
C. →
   Stinnett, Nellie
D. →
   Stoddard, Victor
E. →

50. | DeLaTour, Hall F. |

A. →
DeLargy, Harold
B. →
DeLathouder, Hilda
C. →
Lathrop, Hillary
D. →
LaTour, Hulbert E.
E. →

Questions 51-55.

51. Multiply: 62
    x 5

   A. 300   B. 310   C. 315   D. 360   E. None of these

52. Divide: 3√153

   A. 41   B. 43   C. 51   D. 53   E. None of these

53. Add: 47
       +21

   A. 58   B. 59   C. 67   D. 68   E. None of these

54. Subtract: 87
           - 42

   A. 34   B. 35   C. 44   D. 45   E. None of these

55. Multiply: 37
             x 3

   A. 91   B. 101   C. 104   D. 114   E. None of these

Questions 56-60.

For Questions 56 through 60, find which one of the suggested answers appears in that question.

56. N 5 4 7 T K 3 Z

57. 8 5 3 V L 2 Z N

58. 7 2 5 N 9 K L V

59. 9 8 L 2 5 Z K V

60. Z 6 5 V 9 3 P N

SUGGESTED ANSWERS
A = 3, 8, K, N
B = 5, 8, N, V
C = 3, 9, V, Z
D = 5, 9, K, Z
E = None of the above

Questions 61-65.

In Questions 61 through 65, compare the three names or numbers, and mark
- A. if ALL THREE names or numbers are exactly ALIKE
- B. if only the FIRST and SECOND names or numbers are exactly ALIKE
- C. if only the FIRST and THIRD names or numbers are exactly ALIKE
- D. if only the SECOND and THIRD names or numbers are exactly ALIKE
- E. if ALL THREE names or numbers are DIFFERENT

61. 6452054   6452654   6452054

62. 8501268   8501268   8501286

63. Ella Burk Newham Ella Burk Newnham Elena Burk Newnham

64. Jno. K. Ravencroft Jno. H. Ravencroft Jno. H. Ravencoft

65. Martin Wills Pullen Martin Wills Pulen Martin Wills Pullen

Questions 66-70.

In Questions 66 through 70, find the correct place for the name in the box.

66. | O'Bannon, M.J. |

 A. →
    O'Beirne, B.B.
 B. →
    Oberlin, E.L.
 C. →
    Oberneir, L.P.
 D. →
    O'Brian, S.F.
 E. →

67. | Entsminger, Jacob |

 A. →
    Ensminger, J.
 B. →
    Entsminger, J.A.
 C. →
    Entsminger, Jack
 D. →
    Entsminger, James
 E. →

68. Iacone, Pete R.

A. →
Iacone, Pedro
B. →
Iacone, Pedro M.
C. →
Iacone, Peter F.
D. →
Iascone, Peter W.
E. →

69. Sheppard, Gladys

A. →
Shepard, Dwight
B. →
Shepard, F.H.
C. →
Shephard, Louise
D. →
Shepperd, Stella
E. →

70. Thackton, Melvin T.

A. →
Thackston, Milton G.
B. →
Thackston, Milton W.
C. →
Thackston, Theodore
D. →
Thackston, Thomas G.
E. →

Questions 71-75.

71. Divide: $7\overline{)357}$

   A. 51   B. 52   C. 53   D. 54   E. None of these

72. Add: 58
        +27

   A. 75   B. 84   C. 85   D. 95   E. None of these

73. Subtract: 86
           - 57

   A. 18   B. 29   C. 38   D. 39   E. None of these

74. Multiply: 68
    x 4

    A. 242   B. 264   C. 272   D. 274   E. None of these

75. Divide: 9/639

    A. 71   B. 73   C. 81   D. 83   E. None of these

Questions 76-80.

For Questions 76 through 80, find which one of the suggested answers appears in that question.

76. 6 Z T N 8 7 4 V

77. V 7 8 6 N 5 P L

78. N 7 P V 8 4 2 L

79. 7 8 G 4 3 V L T

80. 4 8 G 2 T N 6 L

SUGGESTED ANSWERS
A = 2, 7, L, N
B = 2, 8, T, V
C = 6, 8, L, T
D = 6, 7, N, V
E = None of the above

Questions 81-85.

In Questions 81 through 85, compare the three names or numbers, and mark
- A. if ALL THREE names or numbers are exactly ALIKE
- B. if only the FIRST and SECOND names or numbers are exactly ALIKE
- C. if only the FIRST and THIRD names or numbers are exactly ALIKE
- D. if only the SECOND and THIRD names or numbers are exactly ALIKE
- E. if ALL THREE names or numbers are DIFFERENT

81.	3457988	3457986	3457986
82.	4695682	4695862	4695682
83.	Stricklund Kanedy	Stricklund Kanedy	Stricklund Kanedy
84.	Joy Harbor Witner	Joy Harloe Witner	Joy Harloe Witner
85.	R.M.O. Uberroth	R.M.O. Uberroth	R.N.O. Uberroth

Questions 86-90.

In Questions 86 through 90, find the correct place for the name in the box.

86. | Dunlavey, M. Hilary |

A. →
Dunleavy, Hilary G.
B. →
Dunleavy, Hilary K.
C. →
Dunleavy, Hilary S.
D. →
Dunleavy, Hilery W.
E. →

87. | Yarbrough, Maria |

A. →
Yabroudy, Margy
B. →
Yarboro, Marie
C. →
Yarborough, Marina
D. →
Yarborough, Mary
E. →

88. | Prouty, Martha |

A. →
Proutey, Margaret
B. →
Proutey, Maude
C. →
Prouty, Myra
D. →
Prouty, Naomi
E. →

89. | Pawlowicz, Ruth M. |

A. →
Pawalek, Edward
B. →
Pawelek, Flora G.
C. →
Pawlowski, Joan M.
D. →
Pawtowski, Wanda
E. →

90. | Vanstory, George |

    A. →
       Vanover, Eva
    B. →
       VanSwinderen, Floyd
    C. →
       VanSyckle, Harry
    D. →
       Vanture, Laurence
    E. →

Questions 91-95

91. Add: 28
     +35

   A. 53   B. 62   C. 64   D. 73   E. None of these

92. Subtract: 78
         -69

   A. 7   B. 8   C. 18   D. 19   E. None of these

93. Multiply: 86
        x 6

   A. 492   B. 506   C. 516   D. 526   E. None of these

94. Divide: 8/648

   A. 71   B. 76   C. 81   D. 89   E. None of these

95. Add: 97
     +34

   A. 131   B. 132   C. 140   D. 141   E. None of these

Questions 96-100.

For Questions 96 through 100, find which one of the suggested answers appears in that question.

96. V 5 7 Z N 9 4 T

97. 4 6 P T 2 N K 9

98. 6 4 N 2 P 8 Z K

99. 7 P 5 2 4 N K T

100. K T 8 5 4 N 2 P

SUGGESTED ANSWERS
A = 2, 5, N, Z
B = 4, 5, N, P
C = 2, 9, P, T
D = 4, 9, T, Z
E = None of the above

Questions 101-105.

In Questions 101 through 105, compare the three names or numbers, and mark
    A. if ALL THREE names or numbers are exactly ALIKE
    B. if only the FIRST and SECOND names or numbers are exactly ALIKE
    C. if only the FIRST and THIRD names or numbers are exactly ALIKE
    D. if only the SECOND and THIRD names or numbers are exactly ALIKE
    E. if ALL THREE names or numbers are DIFFERENT

101. 1592514   1592574   1592574

102. 2010202   2010202   2010220

103. 6177396   6177936   6177396

104. Drusilla S. Ridgeley   Drusilla S. Ridgeley   Drusilla S. Ridgeley

105. Andrei I. Toumantzev   Andrei I. Tourmantzev   Andrei I. Toumantzov

Questions 106-110.

In Questions 106 through 110, find the correct place for the name in the box.

106. | Fitzsimmons, Hugh |

    A. →
        Fitts, Harold
    B. →
        Fitzgerald, June
    C. →
        FitzGibbon, Junius
    D. →
        FitzSimons, Martin
    E. →

107. | D'Amato, Vincent |

    A. →
        Daly, Steven
    B. →
        D'Amboise, S. Vincent
    C. →
        Daniel, Vail
    D. →
        DeAlba, Valentina
    E. →

108. Schaeffer, Roger D.

A. →
   Schaffert, Evelyn M.
B. →
   Schaffner, Margaret M.
C. →
   Schafhirt, Milton G.
D. →
   Shafer, Richard E.
E. →

109. White-Lewis, Cecil

A. →
   Whitelaw, Cordelia
B. →
   White-Leigh, Nancy
C. →
   Whitely, Rodney
D. →
   Whitlock, Warren
E. →

110. VanDerHeggen, Don

A. →
   VanDemark, Doris
B. →
   Vandenberg, H.E.
C. →
   VanDercook, Marie
D. →
   vanderLinden, Robert
E. →

Questions 111-115.

111. Add: 75
         +49

   A. 124   B. 125   C. 134   D. 225   E. None of these

112. Subtract: 69
              - 45

   A. 14   B. 23   C. 24   D. 26   E. None of these

113. Multiply: 36
              x 8

   A. 246   B. 262   C. 288   D. 368   E. None of these

114. Divide: 8/328̄

    A. 31   B. 41   C. 42   D. 48   E. None of these

115. Multiply: 58
               x 9

    A. 472   B. 513   C. 521   D. 522   E. None of these

Questions 116-120.

For Questions 116 through 120, find which one of the suggested answers appears in that question.

116. Z 3 N P G 5 4 2

117. 6 N 2 8 G 4 P T

118. 6 N 4 T V G 8 2

119. T 3 P 4 N 8 G 2

120. 6 7 K G N 2 L 5

SUGGESTED ANSWERS:
A = 2, 3, G, N
B = 2, 6, N, T
C = 3, 4, G, K
D = 4, 6, K, T
E = None of the above

KEY (CORRECT ANSWERS)

1. B	21. A	41. A	61. C	81. D	101. D
2. E	22. E	42. A	62. B	82. C	102. B
3. D	23. E	43. B	63. E	83. A	103. C
4. A	24. D	44. E	64. E	84. D	104. A
5. E	25. C	45. A	65. C	85. B	105. E
6. E	26. D	46. C	66. A	86. A	106. D
7. A	27. D	47. A	667. D	87. E	107. B
8. D	28. C	48. D	68. C	88. C	108. A
9. B	29. C	49. B	69. D	89. C	109. C
10. E	30. D	50. C	70. E	90. B	110. D
11. D	31. E	51. B	71. A	91. E	111. A
12. B	32. A	52. C	72. C	92. E	112. C
13. B	33. A	53. D	73. B	93. C	113. C
14. B	34. C	54. D	74. C	94. C	114. B
15. B	35. C	55. E	75. A	95. A	115. D
16. A	36. E	56. E	76. D	96. D	116. A
17. D	37. A	57. B	77. D	97. C	117. B
18. E	38. C	58. E	78. A	98. E	118. B
19. B	39. C	59. D	79. E	99. B	119. A
20. A	40. D	60. C	80. C	100. B	120. E

CLERICAL ABILITIES TEST
EXAMINATION SECTION
TEST 1

DIRECTIONS: Each question or incomplete statement is followed by several suggested answers or completions. Select the one that BEST answers the question or completes the statement. *PRINT THE LETTER OF THE CORRECT ANSWER IN THE SPACE AT THE RIGHT.*

Questions 1-10.

DIRECTIONS: Questions 1 through 10 consist of lines of names, dates, and numbers. For each question, you are to choose the option (A, B, C, or D) in Column II which EXACTLY matches the information in Column I. *PRINT THE LETTER OF THE CORRECT ANSWER IN THE SPACE AT THE RIGHT.*

SAMPLE QUESTION

Column I
Schneider 11/16/75 581932

Column II
A. Schneider 11/16/75 518932
B. Schneider 11/16/75 581932
C. Schnieder 11/16/75 581932
D. Shnieder   11/16/75 518932

The correct answer is B. Only Option B shows the name, date, and number exactly as they are in Column I. Option A has a mistake in the number. Option C has a mistake in the name. Option D has a mistake in the name and in the number. Now answer Questions 1 through 10 in the same manner.

Column I
1. Johnston 12/26/74 659251

   Column II
   A. Johnson   12/23/74 659251
   B. Johston   12/26/74 659251
   C. Johnston 12/26/74 695251
   D. Johnston 12/26/74 659251

   1.____

2. Allison 1/26/75 9939256

   A. Allison 1/26/75 9939256
   B. Alisson 1/26/75 9939256
   C. Allison 1/26/76 9399256
   D. Allison 1/26/75 9993356

   2.____

3. Farrell 2/12/75 361251

   A. Farell   2/21/75 361251
   B. Farrell 2/12/75 361251
   C. Farrell 2/21/75 361251
   D. Farrell 2/12/75 361151

   3.____

4. Guerrero 4/28/72 105689
    A. Guererro 4/28/72 105689
    B. Guererro 4/28/72 105986
    C. Guerrero 4/28/72 105869
    D. Guerrero 4/28/72 105689

4.____

5. McDonnell 6/05/73 478215
    A. McDonnell 6/15/73 478215
    B. McDonnell 6/05/73 478215
    C. McDonnell 6/05/73 472815
    D. MacDonell 6/05/73 478215

5.____

6. Shepard 3/31/71 075421
    A. Sheperd 3/31/71 075421
    B. Shepard 3/13/71 075421
    C. Shepard 3/31/71 075421
    D. Shepard 3/13/71 075241

6.____

7. Russell 4/01/69 031429
    A. Russell 4/01/69 031429
    B. Russell 4/10/69 034129
    C. Russell 4/10/69 031429
    D. Russell 4/01/69 034129

7.____

8. Phillips 10/16/68 961042
    A. Philipps 10/16/68 961042
    B. Phillips 10/16/68 960142
    C. Phillips 10/16/68 961042
    D. Philipps 10/16/68 916042

8.____

9. Campbell 11/21/72 624856
    A. Campbell 11/21/72 624856
    B. Campbell 11/21/72 624586
    C. Campbell 11/21/72 624686
    D. Campbel 11/21/72 624856

9.____

10. Patterson 9/18/71 76199176
    A. Patterson 9/18/72 76191976
    B. Patterson 9/18/71 76199176
    C. Patterson 9/18/72 76199176
    D. Patterson 9/18/71 76919176

10.____

Questions 11-15.

DIRECTIONS: Questions 11 through 15 consist of groups of numbers and letters which you are to compare. For each question, you are to choose the option (A, B,C, or D) in Column I which EXACTLY matches the group of numbers and letters given in Column I.

SAMPLE QUESTION

<u>Column I</u>
B92466

<u>Column II</u>
A. B92644
B. B94266
C. A92466
D. B92466

The correct answer is D. Only Option D in Column II shows the group of numbers and letters EXACTLY as it appears in Column I. Now answer Questions 11 through 15 in the same manner.

	Column I		Column II	
11.	925AC5	A. B. C. D.	952CA5 925AC5 952AC5 925CA6	11.____
12.	Y006925	A. B. C. D.	Y060925 Y006295 Y006529 Y006925	12.____
13.	J236956	A. B. C. D.	J236956 J326965 J239656 J932656	13.____
14.	AB6952	A. B. C. D.	AB6952 AB9625 AB9652 AB6925	14.____
15.	X259361	A. B. C. D.	X529361 X259631 X523961 X259361	15.____

Questions 16-25.

DIRECTIONS: Each of questions 16 through 25 consists of three lines of code letters and three lines of numbers. The numbers on each line should correspond with the code letters on the same line in accordance with the table below.

Code Letter	S	V	W	A	Q	M	X	E	G	K
Corresponding Number	0	1	2	3	4	5	5	7	8	9

On some of the lines, an error exists in the coding. Compare the letters and numbers in each question carefully. If you find an error or errors on:
    only one of the lines in the question, mark your answer A;
    any two lines in the question, mark your answer B;
    all three lines in the question, mark your answer C;
    none of the lines in the question, mark your answer D.

SAMPLE QUESTION

    WQGKSXG   2489068
    XEKVQMA   6591453
    KMAESXV   9527061

In the above sample, the first line is correct since each code letter listed has the correct corresponding number. On the second line, an error exists because code letter E should have the number 7 instead of the number 5. On the third line, an error exists because the code letter A should have the number 3 instead of the number 2. Since there are errors in two of the three lines, the correct answer is B. Now answer Questions 16 through 25 in the same manner.

16. SWQEKGA 0247983   16.____
   KEAVSXM 9731065
   SSAXGKQ 0036894

17. QAMKMVS 4259510   17.____
   MGGEASX 5897306
   KSWMKWS 9125920

18. WKXQWVE 2964217   18.____
   QKXXQVA 4966413
   AWMXGVS 3253810

19. GMMKASE 8559307   19.____
   AWVSKSW 3210902
   QAVSVGK 4310189

20. XGKQSMK 6894049   20.____
   QSVKEAS 4019730
   GSMXKMV 8057951

21. AEKMWSG 3195208   21.____
   MKQSVQK 5940149
   XGQAEVW 6843712

22. XGMKAVS 6858310   22.____
   SKMAWEQ 0953174
   GVMEQSA 8167403

23. VQSKAVE 1489317   23.____
   WQGKAEM 2489375
   MEGKAWQ 5689324

24. XMQVSKG 6541098   24.____
   QMEKEWS 4579720
   KMEVGKG 9571983

25. GKVAMEW   88912572   25.____
     AXMVKAE   3651937
     KWAGMAV   9238531

Questions 26-35.

DIRECTIONS: Each of Questions 26 through 35 consists of a column of figures. For each question, add the column of figures and choose the correct answer from the four choices given.

26. 5,665.43   26.____
     2,356.69
     6,447.24
     7,239.65

   A. 20,698.01   B. 21,709.01
   C. 21,718.01   D. 22,609.01

27. 817,209.55   27.____
     264,354.29
      82,368.76
     849,964.89

   A. 1,893.977.49   B. 1,989,988.39
   C. 2,009,077.39   D. 2,013,897.49

28. 156,366.89   28.____
     249,973.23
     823,229.49
      56,869.45

   A. 1,286,439.06   B. 1,287,521.06
   C. 1,297,539.06   D. 1,296,421.06

29.   23,422.15   29.____
     149,696.24
     238,377.53
      86,289.79
     505,533.63

   A. 989,229.34   B. 999,879.34
   C. 1,003,330.34   D. 1,023,329.34

6 (#1)

30. 2,468,926.70
     656,842.28
     49,723.15
     832,369.59

     A. 3,218,062.72   B. 3,808,092.72
     C. 4,007,861.72   D. 4,818,192.72

30._____

31.   524,201.52
      7,775,678.51
      8,345,299.63
     40,628,898.08
     31,374,670.07

     A. 88,646,647.81   B. 88,646,747.91
     C. 88,648,647.91   D. 88,648,747.81

31._____

32. 6,824,829.40
       682,482.94
     5,542,015.27
       775,678.51
     7,732,507.25

     A. 21,557,513.37   B. 21,567,513.37
     C. 22,567,503.37   D. 22,567,513.37

32._____

33. 22,109,405.58
      6,097,093.43
      5,050,073.99
      8,118,050.05
      4,313,980.82

     A. 45,688,593.87   B. 45,688,603.87
     C. 45,689,593.87   D. 45,689,603.87

33._____

34. 79,324,114.19
     99,848,129.74
     43,331,653.31
     41,610,207.14

     A. 264,114,104.38   B. 264,114,114.38
     C. 265,114,114.38   D. 265,214,104.38

34._____

35. 33,729,653.94
    5,959,342.58
    26,052,715.47
    4,452,669.52
    7,079,953.59

    A. 76,374,334.10   B. 76,375,334.10
    C. 77,274,335.10   D. 77,275,335.10

35.____

Questions 36-40.

DIRECTIONS: Each of Questions 36 through 40 consists of a single number in Column I and four options in Column II. For each question, you are to choose the option (A, B, C, or D) in Column II which EXACTLY matches the number in Column I.

SAMPLE QUESTION

Column I
5965121

Column II
A. 5956121
B. 5965121
C. 5966121
D. 5965211

The correct answer is B. Only Option B shows the number EXACTLY as it appears in Column I. Now answer Questions 36 through 40 in the same manner.

Column I
36. 9643242

Column II
A. 9643242
B. 9462342
C. 9642442
D. 9463242

36.____

37. 3572477

A. 3752477
B. 3725477
C. 3572477
D. 3574277

37.____

38. 5276101

A. 5267101
B. 5726011
C. 5271601
D. 5276101

38.____

39. 4469329

A. 4496329
B. 4469329
C. 4496239
D. 4469239

39.____

40. 2326308

A. 2236308
B. 2233608
C. 2326308
D. 2323608

40._____

KEY (CORRECT ANSWERS)

1.	D	11.	B	21.	A	31.	D
2.	A	12.	D	22.	C	32.	A
3.	B	13.	A	23.	B	33.	B
4.	D	14.	A	24.	D	34.	A
5.	B	15.	D	25.	A	35.	C
6.	C	16.	D	26.	B	36.	A
7.	A	17.	C	27.	D	37.	C
8.	C	18.	A	28.	A	38.	D
9.	A	19.	D	29.	C	39.	B
10.	B	20.	B	30.	C	40.	C

TEST 2

DIRECTIONS: Each question or incomplete statement is followed by several suggested answers or completions. Select the one that BEST answers the question or completes the statement. *PRINT THE LETTER OF THE CORRECT ANSWER IN THE SPACE AT THE RIGHT.*

Questions 1-5.

DIRECTIONS: Each of Questions 1 through 5 consists of a name and a dollar amount. In each question, the name and dollar amount in Column II should be an EXACT copy of the name and dollar amount in Column I. If there is:
    a mistake only in the name, mark your answer A;
    a mistake only in the dollar amount, mark your answer B;
    a mistake in both the name and the dollar amount, mark your answer C;
    no mistake in either the name or the dollar amount, mark your answer D.

SAMPLE QUESTION

Column I	Column II
George Peterson	George Petersson
$125.50	$125.50

Compare the name and dollar amount in Column II with the name and dollar amount in Column I. The name *Petersson* in Column II is spelled *Peterson* in Column I. The amount is the same in both columns. Since there is a mistake only in the name, the answer to the sample question is A. Now answer Questions 1 through 5 in the same manner.

	Column I	Column II	
1.	Susanne Shultz $3440	Susanne Schultz $3440	1.____
2.	Anibal P. Contrucci $2121.61	Anibel P. Contrucci $2112.61	2.____
3.	Eugenio Mendoza $12.45	Eugenio Mendozza $12.45	3.____
4.	Maurice Gluckstadt $4297	Maurice Gluckstadt $4297	4.____
5.	John Pampellonne $4656.94	John Pammpellonne $4566.94	5.____

Questions 6-11.

DIRECTIONS: Each of Questions 6 through 11 consist of a set of names and addresses, which you are to compare. In each question, the name and addresses in Column II should be an EXACT copy of the name and address in Column I. If there is:
- a mistake only in the name, mark your answer A;
- a mistake only in the address, mark your answer B;
- a mistake in both the name and address, mark your answer C;
- no mistake in either the name or address, mark your answer D.

SAMPLE QUESTION

Column I
Michael Filbert
456 Reade Street
New York, N.Y. 10013

Column II
Michael Filbert
645 Reade Street
New York, N.Y. 10013

Since there is a mistake only in the address (the street number should be 456 instead of 645), the answer to the sample question is B. Now answer Questions 6 through 11 in the same manner.

Column I

6. Hilda Goettelmann
55 Lenox Rd.
Brooklyn, N.Y. 11226

7. Arthur Sherman
2522 Batchelder St.
Brooklyn, N.Y. 11235

8. Ralph Barnett
300 West 28 Street
New York, New York 10001

9. George Goodwin
135 Palmer Avenue
Staten Island, New York 10302

10. Alonso Ramirez
232 West 79 Street
New York, N.Y. 10024

11. Cynthia Graham
149-34 83 Street
Howard Beach, N.Y. 11414

Column II

Hilda Goettelman
55 Lenox Ave.
Brooklyn, N.Y. 11226

Arthur Sharman
2522 Batcheder St.
Brooklyn, N.Y. 11253

Ralph Barnett
300 West 28 Street
New York, New York 10001

George Godwin
135 Palmer Avenue
Staten Island, New York 10302

Alonso Ramirez
223 West 79 Street
New York, N.Y. 10024

Cynthia Graham
149-35 83 Street
Howard Beach, N.Y. 11414

6._____
7._____
8._____
9._____
10._____
11._____

Questions 12-20.

DIRECTIONS: Questions 12 through 20 are problems in subtraction. For each question do the subtraction and select your answer from the four choices given.

12. 232,921.85
    -179,587.68

    A. 52,433.17   B. 52,434.17
    C. 53,334.17   D. 53,343,17

    12.____

13. 5,531,876.29
    -3,897,158.36

    A. 1,634,717.93   B. 1,644,718.93
    C. 1,734,717.93   D. 1,7234,718.93

    13.____

14. 1,482,658.22
    -937,925.76

    A. 544,633.46   B. 544,732.46
    C. 545,632.46   D. 545,732.46

    14.____

15. 937,828.17
    -259,673.88

    A. 678,154.29   B. 679,154.29
    C. 688,155.39   D. 699,155.39

    15.____

16. 760,412.38
    -263,465.95

    A. 496,046.43   B. 496,946.43
    C. 496,956.43   D. 497,046.43

    16.____

17. 3,203,902.26
    -2,933,087.96

    A. 260,814.30   B. 269,824.30
    C. 270,814.30   D. 270,824.30

    17.____

18. 1,023,468.71
    -934,678.88

    A. 88,780.83   B. 88,789.83
    C. 88,880.83   D. 88,889.83

    18.____

19. 831,549.47
     -772,814.78

   A. 58,734.69   B. 58,834.69
   C. 59,735.69   D. 59,834.69

20. 6,306,181.74
     -3,617,376.99

   A. 2,687,904.99   B. 2,688,904.99
   C. 2,689,804.99   D. 2,799,905.99

Questions 21-30.

DIRECTIONS: Each of Questions 21 through 30 consists of three lines of code letters and three lines of numbers. The numbers on each line should correspond with the code letters on the same line in accordance with the table below.

Code Letter	J	U	B	T	Y	D	K	R	L	P
Corresponding Number	0	1	2	3	4	5	5	7	8	9

On some of the lines, an error exists in the coding. Compare the letters and numbers in each question carefully. If you find an error or errors on:
  only *one* of the lines in the question, mark your answer A;
  any *two* lines in the question, mark your answer B;
  all *three* lines in the question, mark your answer C;
  none of the lines in the question, mark your answer D.

SAMPLE QUESTION

    BJRPYUR   2079417
    DTBPYKJ   5328460
    YKLDBLT   4685283

In the above sample, the first line is correct since each code letter listed has the correct corresponding number. On the second line, an error exists because code letter P should have the number 9 instead of the number 8. The third line is correct since each code letter listed has the correct corresponding number. Since there is an error in *one* of the three lines, the correct answer is A. Now answer Questions 21 through 30 in the same manner.

21. BYPDTJL   2495308
     PLRDTJU   9815301
     DTJRYLK   5207486

22. RPBYRJK   7934706
     PKTYLBU   9624821
     KDLPJYR   6489047

23. TPYBUJR   3942107   23.____
    BYRKPTU   2476931
    DUKPYDL   5169458

24. KBYDLPL   6345898   24.____
    BLRKBRU   2876261
    JTULDYB   0318542

25. LDPYDKR   8594567   25.____
    BDKDRJL   2565708
    BDRPLUJ   2679810

26. PLRLBPU   9858291   26.____
    LPYKRDJ   88936750
    TDKPDTR   3569527

27. RKURPBY   7617924   27.____
    RYUKPTJ   7426930
    RTKPTJD   7369305

28. DYKPBJT   5469203   28.____
    KLPJBTL   6890238
    TKPLBJP   3698209

29. BTPRJYL   2397148   29.____
    LDKUTYR   8561347
    YDBLRPJ   4528190

30. ULPBKYT   1892643   30.____
    KPDTRBJ   6953720
    YLKJPTB   4860932

KEY (CORRECT ANSWERS)

1.	A	11.	D	21.	B
2.	C	12.	C	22.	C
3.	A	13.	A	23.	D
4.	D	14.	B	24.	B
5.	C	15.	A	25.	A
6.	C	16.	B	26.	C
7.	C	17.	C	27.	A
8.	D	18.	B	28.	D
9.	A	19.	A	29.	B
10.	B	20.	B	30.	D

RECORD KEEPING
EXAMINATION SECTION
TEST 1

DIRECTIONS: Each question or incomplete statement is followed by several suggested answers or completions. Select the one that BEST answers the question or completes the statement. *PRINT THE LETTER OF THE CORRECT ANSWER IN THE SPACE AT THE RIGHT.*

Questions 1-7.

DIRECTIONS: In answering Questions 1 through 7, use the following master list. For each question, determine where the name would fit on the master list. Each answer choice indicates right before or after the name in the answer choice.

    Aaron, Jane
    Armstead, Brendan
    Bailey, Charles
    Dent, Ricardo
    Grant, Mark
    Mars, Justin
    Methieu, Justine
    Parker, Cathy
    Sampson, Suzy
    Thomas, Heather

1. Schmidt, William
   A. Right before Cathy Parker
   B. Right after Heather Thomas
   C. Right after Suzy Sampson
   D. Right before Ricardo Dent

2. Asanti, Kendall
   A. Right before Jane Aaron
   B. Right after Charles Bailey
   C. Right before Justine Methieu
   D. Right after Brendan Armstead

3. O'Brien, Daniel
   A. Right after Justine Methieu
   B. Right before Jane Aaron
   C. Right after Mark Grant
   D. Right before Suzy Sampson

4. Marrow, Alison
   A. Right before Cathy Parker
   B. Right before Justin Mars
   C. Right before Mark Grant
   D. Right after Heather Thomas

5. Grantt, Marissa
   A. Right before Mark Grant
   B. Right after Mark Grant
   C. Right after Justin Mars
   D. Right before Suzy Sampson

1.____

2.____

3.____

4.____

5.____

6. Thompson, Heath   6._____
   A. Right after Justin Mars   B. Right before Suzy Sampson
   C. Right after Heather Thomas   D. Right before Cathy Parker

DIRECTIONS: Before answering Question 7, add in all of the names from Questions 1 through 6. Then fit the name in alphabetical order based on the new list.

7. Francisco, Mildred   7._____
   A. Right before Mark Grant   B. Right after Marissa Grantt
   C. Right before Alison Marrow   D. Right after Kendall Asanti

Questions 8-10.

DIRECTIONS: In answering Questions 8 through 10, compare each pair of names and addresses. Indicate whether they are the same or different in any way.

8. William H. Pratt, J.D.   William H. Pratt, J.D.   8._____
   Attourney at Law   Attorney at Law
   A. No differences   B. 1 difference
   C. 2 differences   D. 3 differences

9. 1303 Theater Drive,; Apt. 3-B   1330 Theatre Drive,; Apt. 3-B   9._____
   A. No differences   B. 1 difference
   C. 2 differences   D. 3 differences

10. Petersdorff, Briana and Mary   Petersdorff, Briana and Mary   10._____
    A. No differences   B. 1 difference
    C. 2 differences   D. 3 differences

11. Which of the following words, if any, are misspelled?   11._____
    A. Affordable   B. Circumstansial
    C. Legalese   D. None of the above

Questions 12-13.

DIRECTIONS: Questions 12 and 13 are to be answered on the basis of the following table.

Standardized Test Results for High School Students in District #1230

	English	Math	Science	Reading
High School 1	21	22	15	18
High School 2	12	16	13	15
High School 3	16	18	21	17
High School 4	19	14	15	16

The scores for each high school in the district were averaged out and listed for each subject tested. Scores of 0-10 are significantly below College Readiness Standards. 11-15 are below College Readiness, 16-20 meet College Readiness, and 21-25 are above College Readiness.

12. If the high schools need to meet or exceed in at least half the categories in order to NOT be considered "at risk," which schools are considered "at risk"? 12.____
    A. High School 2   B. High School 3
    C. High School 4   D. Both A and C

13. What percentage of subjects did the district as a whole meet or exceed College Readiness standards? 13.____
    A. 25%   B. 50%   C. 75%   D. 100%

Questions 14-15.

DIRECTIONS: Questions 14 and 15 are to be answered on the basis of the following information.

You have seven employees working as a part of your team: Austin, Emily, Jeremy, Christina, Martin, Harriet, and Steve. You have just sent an e-mail informing them that there will be a mandatory training session next week. To ensure that work still gets done, you are offering the training twice during the week: once on Tuesday and also on Thursday. This way half the employees will still be working while the other half attend the training. The only other issue is that Jeremy doesn't work on Tuesdays and Harriet doesn't work on Thursdays due to compressed work schedules.

14. Which of the following is a possible attendance roster for the first training session? 14.____
    A. Emily, Jeremy, Steve   B. Steve, Christina, Harriet
    C. Harriet, Jeremy, Austin   D. Steve, Martin, Jeremy

15. If Harriet, Christina, and Steve attend the training session on Tuesday, which of the following is a possible roster for Thursday's training session? 15.____
    A. Jeremy, Emily, and Austin   B. Emily, Martin, and Harriet
    C. Austin, Christina, and Emily   D. Jeremy, Emily, and Steve

Questions 16-20.

DIRECTIONS: In answering Questions 16 through 20, you will be given a word and will need to choose the answer choice that is MOST similar or different to the word.

16. Which word means the SAME as *annual*? 16.____
    A. Monthly   B. Usually   C. Yearly   D. Constantly

17. Which word means the SAME as *effort*? 17.____
    A. Energy   B. Equate   C. Cherish   D. Commence

18. Which word means the OPPOSITE of *forlorn*? 18.____
    A. Neglected   B. Lethargy   C. Optimistic   D. Astonished

19. Which word means the SAME as *risk*? 19.____
    A. Admire   B. Hazard   C. Limit   D. Hesitant

20. Which word means the OPPOSITE of *translucent*?
    A. Opaque B. Transparent C. Luminous D. Introverted

    20.____

21. Last year, Jamie's annual salary was $50,000. Her boss called her today to inform her that she would receive a 20% raise for the upcoming year. How much more money will Jamie receive next year?
    A. $60,000 B. $10,000 C. $1,000 D. $51,000

    21.____

22. You and a co-worker work for a temp hiring agency as part of their office staff. You both are given 6 days off per month. How many days off are you and your co-worker given in a year?
    A. 24 B. 72 C. 144 D. 48

    22.____

23. If Margot makes $34,000 per year and she works 40 hours per week for all 52 weeks, what is her hourly rate?
    A. $16.34/hour B. $17.00/hour C. $15.54/hour D. $13.23/hour

    23.____

24. How many dimes are there in $175.00?
    A. 175 B. 1,750 C. 3,500 D. 17,500

    24.____

25. If Janey is three times as old as Emily, and Emily is 3, how old is Janey?
    A. 6 B. 9 C. 12 D. 15

    25.____

KEY (CORRECT ANSWERS)

1.	C	11.	B
2.	D	12.	A
3.	A	13.	D
4.	B	14.	B
5.	B	15.	A
6.	C	16.	C
7.	A	17.	A
8.	B	18.	C
9.	C	19.	B
10.	A	20.	A

21.	B
22.	C
23.	A
24.	B
25.	B

TEST 2

DIRECTIONS: Each question or incomplete statement is followed by several suggested answers or completions. Select the one that BEST answers the question or completes the statement. *PRINT THE LETTER OF THE CORRECT ANSWER IN THE SPACE AT THE RIGHT.*

Questions 1-6.

DIRECTIONS: Questions 1 through 6 are to be answered on the basis of the following information.

item	name of item to be ordered
quantity	minimum number that can be ordered
beginning amount	amount in stock at start of month
amount received	amount receiving during month
ending amount	amount in stock at end of month
amount used	amount used during month
amount to order	will need at least as much of each item as used in the previous month
unit price	cost of each unit of an item
total price	total price for the order

Item	Quantity	Beginning	Received	Ending	Amount Used	Amount to Order	Unit Price	Total Price
Pens	10	22	10	8	24	20	$0.11	$2.20
Spiral notebooks	8	30	13	12			$0.25	
Binder clips	2 boxes	3 boxes	1 box	1 box			$1.79	
Sticky notes	3 packs	12 packs	4 packs	2 packs			$1.29	
Dry erase markers	1 pack (dozen)	34 markers	8 markers	40 markers			$16.49	
Ink cartridges (printer)	1 cartridge	3 cartridges	1 cartridge	2 cartridges			$79.99	
Folders	10 folders	25 folders	15 folders	10 folders			$1.08	

1. How many packs of sticky notes were used during the month?   1.____
   A. 16   B. 10   C. 12   D. 14

2. How many folders need to be ordered for next month?   2.____
   A. 15   B. 20   C. 30   D. 40

3. What is the total price of notebooks that you will need to order?   3.____
   A. $6.00   B. $0.25   C. $4.50   D. $2.75

4. Which of the following will you spend the second most money on?   4.____
   A. Ink cartridges   B. Dry erase markers
   C. Sticky notes   D. Binder clips

5. How many packs of dry erase markers should you order?   5.____
   A. 1   B. 8   C. 12   D. 0

6. What will be the total price of the file folders you order? 6.____
   A. $20.16   B. $21.60   C. $10.80   D. $4.32

Questions 7-11.

DIRECTIONS: Questions 7 through 11 are to be answered on the basis of the following table.

Number of Car Accidents, By Location and Cause, for 2014						
	Location 1		Location 2		Location 3	
Cause	Number	Percent	Number	Percent	Number	Percent
Severe Weather	10		25		30	
Excessive Speeding	20	40	5		10	
Impaired Driving	15		15	25	8	
Miscellaneous	5		15		2	4
TOTALS	50	100	60	100	50	100

7. Which of the following is the third highest cause of accidents for all three locations? 7.____
   A. Severe Weather
   B. Impaired Driving
   C. Miscellaneous
   D. Excessive Speeding

8. The average number of Severe Weather accidents per week at Location 3 for the year (52 weeks) was MOST NEARLY 8.____
   A. 0.57   B. 30   C. 1   D. 1.25

9. Which location had the LARGEST percentage of accidents caused by Impaired Driving? 9.____
   A. 1   B. 2   C. 3   D. Both A and B

10. If one-third of the accidents at all three locations resulted in at least one fatality, what is the LEAST amount of deaths caused by accidents last year? 10.____
    A. 60   B. 106   C. 66   D. 53

11. What is the percentage of accidents caused by miscellaneous means from all three locations in 2014? 11.____
    A. 5%   B. 10%   C. 13%   D. 25%

12. How many pairs of the following groups of letters are exactly alike? 12.____
    ACDOBJ   ACDBOJ
    HEWBWR   HEWRWB
    DEERVS   DEERVS
    BRFQSX   BRFQSX
    WEYRVB   WEYRVB
    SPQRZA   SQRPZA

    A. 2   B. 3   C. 4   D. 5

3 (#2)

Questions 13-19.

DIRECTIONS: Questions 13 through 19 are to be answered on the basis of the following information.

In 2012, the most current information on the American population was finished. The information was compiled by 200 volunteers in each of the 50 states. The territory of Puerto Rico, a sovereign of the United States, had 25 people assigned to compile data. In February of 2010, volunteers in each state and sovereign began collecting information. In Puerto Rico, data collection finished by January 31st, 2011, while work in the United States was completed on June 30, 2012. Each volunteer gathered data on the population of their state or sovereign. When the information was compiled, volunteers sent reports to the nation's capital, Washington, D.C. Each volunteer worked 20 hours per month and put together 10 reports per month. After the data was compiled in total, 50 people reviewed the data and worked from January 2012 to December 2012.

13. How many reports were generated from February 2010 to April 2010 in Illinois and Ohio? 13.____
 A. 3,000 B. 6,000 C. 12,000 D. 15,000

14. How many volunteers in total collected population data in January 2012? 14.____
 A. 10,000 B. 2,000 C. 225 D. 200

15. How many reports were put together in May 2012? 15.____
 A. 2,000 B. 50,000 C. 100,000 D. 100,250

16. How many hours did the Puerto Rican volunteers work in the fall (September-November)? 16.____
 A. 60 B. 500 C. 1,500 D. 0

17. How many workers were compiling or reviewing data in July 2012? 17.____
 A. 25 B. 50 C. 200 D. 250

18. What was the total amount of hours worked by Nevada volunteers in July 2010? 18.____
 A. 500 B. 4,000 C. 4,500 D. 5,000

19. How many reviewers worked in January 2013? 19.____
 A. 75 B. 50 C. 0 D. 25

20. John has to file 10 documents per shelf. How many documents would it take for John to fill 40 shelves? 20.____
 A. 40 B. 400 C. 4,500 D. 5,000

21. Jill wants to travel from New York City to Los Angeles by bike, which is approximately 2,772 miles. How many miles per day would Jill need to average if she wanted to complete the trip in 4 weeks? 21.____
 A. 100 B. 89 C. 99 D. 94

22. If there are 24 CPU's and only 7 monitors, how many more monitors do you need to have the same amount of monitors as CPU's?

22.____

    A. Not enough information   B. 17
    C. 31   D. 0

23. If Gerry works 5 days a week and 8 hours each day, and John works 3 days a week and 10 hours each day, how many more hours per year will Gerry work than John?

23.____

    A. They work the same amount of hours.
    B. 450
    C. 520
    D. 832

24. Jimmy gets transferred to a new office. The new office has 25 employees, but only 16 are there due to a blizzard. How many coworkers was Jimmy able to meet on his first day?

24.____

    A. 16   B. 25   C. 9   D. 7

25. If you do a fundraiser for charities in your area and raise $500 total, how much would you give to each charity if you were donating equal amounts to 3 of them?

25.____

    A. $250.00   B. $167.77   C. $50.00   D. $111.11

KEY (CORRECT ANSWERS)

#	Ans		#	Ans
1.	D		11.	C
2.	B		12.	B
3.	A		13.	C
4.	C		14.	A
5.	D		15.	C
6.	B		16.	C
7.	D		17.	B
8.	A		18.	B
9.	A		19.	C
10.	D		20.	B

#	Ans
21.	C
22.	B
23.	C
24.	A
25.	B

TEST 3

DIRECTIONS: Each question or incomplete statement is followed by several suggested answers or completions. Select the one that BEST answers the question or completes the statement. *PRINT THE LETTER OF THE CORRECT ANSWER IN THE SPACE AT THE RIGHT.*

Questions 1-3.

DIRECTIONS: In answering Questions 1 through 3, choose the correctly spelled word.

1. A. allusion B. alusion C. allusien D. allution 1.____

2. A. altitude B. alltitude C. atlitude D. altlitude 2.____

3. A. althogh B. allthough C. althrough D. although 3.____

Questions 4-9.

DIRECTIONS: In answering Questions 4 through 9, choose the answer that BEST completes the analogy.

4. Odometer is to mileage as compass is to 4.____
   A. speed B. needle C. hiking D. direction

5. Marathon is to race as hibernation is to 5.____
   A. winter B. dream C. sleep D. bear

6. Cup is to coffee as bowl is to 6.____
   A. dish B. spoon C. food D. soup

7. Flow is to river as stagnant is to 7.____
   A. pool B. rain C. stream D. canal

8. Paw is to cat as hoof is to 8.____
   A. lamb B. horse C. lion D. elephant

9. Architect is to building as sculptor is to 9.____
   A. museum B. chisel C. stone D. statue

Questions 10-14.

DIRECTIONS: Questions 10 through 14 are to be answered on the basis of the following graph.

Population of Carroll City Broken Down by Age and Gender (in Thousands)			
Age	Female	Male	Total
Under 15	60	60	120
15-23		22	
24-33		20	44
34-43	13	18	31
44-53	20		67
64 and Over	65	65	130
TOTAL	230	232	462

10. How many people in the city are between the ages of 15-23?
    A. 70 B. 46,000 C. 70,000 D. 225,000

11. Approximately what percentage of the total population of the city was female aged 24-33?
    A. 10% B. 5% C. 15% D. 25%

12. If 33% of the males have a job and 55% of females don't have a job, which of the following statements is TRUE?
    A. Males have approximately 2,600 more jobs than females.
    B. Females have approximately 49,000 more jobs than males.
    C. Females have approximately 26,000 more jobs than males.
    D. None of the above statements are true.

13. How many females between the ages of 15-23 live in Carroll City?
    A. 67,000 B. 24,000 C. 48,000 D. 91,000

14. Assume all males 44-53 living in Carroll City are employed. If two-thirds of males age 44-53 work jobs outside of Carroll City, how many work within city limits?
    A. 31,333
    B. 15,667
    C. 47,000
    D. Cannot answer the question with the information provided

Questions 15-16.

DIRECTIONS: Questions 15 and 16 are labeled as shown. Alphabetize them for filing. Choose the answer that correctly shows the order.

15. (1) AED
    (2) OOS
    (3) FOA
    (4) DOM
    (5) COB

    A. 2-5-4-3-2   B. 1-4-5-2-3   C. 1-5-4-2-3   D. 1-5-4-3-2

15.____

16. Alphabetize the names of the people. Last names are given last.
    (1) Lindsey Jamestown
    (2) Jane Alberta
    (3) Ally Jamestown
    (4) Allison Johnston
    (5) Lyle Moreno

    A. 2-1-3-4-5   B. 3-4-2-1-5   C. 2-3-1-4-5   D. 4-3-2-1-5

16.____

17. Which of the following words is misspelled?
    A. disgust   B. whisper
    C. locale   D. none of the above

17.____

Questions 18-21.

DIRECTIONS: Questions 18 through 21 are to be answered on the basis of the following list of employees.

   Robertson, Aaron
   Bacon, Gina
   Jerimiah, Trace
   Gillette, Stanley
   Jacks, Sharon

18. Which employee name would come in third in alphabetized list?
    A. Robertson, Aaron   B. Jerimiah, Trace
    C. Gillette, Stanley   D. Jacks, Sharon

18.____

19. Which employee's first name starts with the letter in the alphabet that is five letters after the first letter of their last name?
    A. Jerimiah, Trace   B. Bacon, Gina
    C. Jacks, Sharon   D. Gillette, Stanley

19.____

20. How many employees have last names that are exactly five letters long?
    A. 1   B. 2   C. 3   D. 4

20.____

21. How many of the employees have either a first or last name that starts with the letter "G"?
    A. 1   B. 2   C. 4   D. 5

Questions 22-25.

DIRECTIONS: Questions 22 through 25 are to be answered on the basis of the following chart.

Bicycle Sales (Model #34JA32)							
Country	May	June	July	August	September	October	Total
Germany	34	47	45	54	56	60	296
Britain	40	44	36	47	47	46	260
Ireland	37	32	32	32	34	33	200
Portugal	14	14	14	16	17	14	89
Italy	29	29	28	31	29	31	177
Belgium	22	24	24	26	25	23	144
Total	176	198	179	206	208	207	1166

22. What percentage of the overall total was sold to the German importer?
    A. 25.3%   B. 22%   C. 24.1%   D. 23%

23. What percentage of the overall total was sold in September?
    A. 24.1%   B. 25.6%   C. 17.9%   D. 24.6%

24. What is the average number of units per month imported into Belgium over the first four months shown?
    A. 26   B. 20   C. 24   D. 31

25. If you look at the three smallest importers, what is their total import percentage?
    A. 35.1%   B. 37.1%   C. 40%   D. 28%

KEY (CORRECT ANSWERS)

1.	A		11.	B
2.	A		12.	C
3.	D		13.	C
4.	D		14.	B
5.	C		15.	D
6.	D		16.	C
7.	A		17.	D
8.	B		18.	D
9.	D		19.	B
10.	C		20.	B

21. B
22. A
23. C
24. C
25. A

TEST 4

DIRECTIONS: Each question or incomplete statement is followed by several suggested answers or completions. Select the one that BEST answers the question or completes the statement. *PRINT THE LETTER OF THE CORRECT ANSWER IN THE SPACE AT THE RIGHT.*

Questions 1-6.

DIRECTIONS: In answering Questions 1 through 6, choose the sentence that represents the BEST example of English grammar.

1. A. Joey and me want to go on a vacation next week.
   B. Gary told Jim he would need to take some time off.
   C. If turning six years old, Jim's uncle would teach Spanish to him.
   D. Fax a copy of your resume to Ms. Perez and me.

   1.____

2. A. Jerry stood in line for almost two hours.
   B. The reaction to my engagement was less exciting than I thought it would be.
   C. Carlos and me have done great work on this project.
   D. Two parts of the speech needs to be revised before tomorrow.

   2.____

3. A. Arriving home, the alarm was tripped.
   B. Jonny is regarded as a stand up guy, a responsible parent, and he doesn't give up until a task is finished.
   C. Each employee must submit a drug test each month.
   D. One of the documents was incinerated in the explosion.

   3.____

4. A. As soon as my parents get home, I told them I finished all of my chores.
   B. I asked my teacher to send me my missing work, check my absences, and how did I do on my test.
   C. Matt attempted to keep it concealed from Jenny and me.
   D. If Mary or him cannot get work done on time, I will have to split them up.

   4.____

5. A. Driving to work, the traffic report warned him of an accident on Highway 47.
   B. Jimmy has performed well this season.
   C. Since finishing her degree, several job offers have been given to Cam.
   D. Our boss is creating unstable conditions for we employees.

   5.____

6. A. The thief was described as a tall man with a wiry mustache weighing approximately 150 pounds.
   B. She gave Patrick and I some more time to finish our work.
   C. One of the books that he ordered was damaged in shipping.
   D. While talking on the rotary phone, the car Jim was driving skidded off the road.

   6.____

Questions 7-9.

DIRECTIONS: Questions 7 through 9 are to be answered on the basis of the following graph.

Ice Lake Frozen Flight (2002-2013)		
Year	Number of Participants	Temperature (Fahrenheit)
2002	22	4°
2003	50	33°
2004	69	18°
2005	104	22°
2006	108	24°
2007	288	33°
2008	173	9°
2009	598	39°
2010	698	26°
2011	696	30°
2012	777	28°
2013	578	32°

7. Which two year span had the LARGEST difference between temperatures?   7.____
   A. 2002 and 2003
   B. 2011 and 2012
   C. 2008 and 2009
   D. 2003 and 2004

8. How many total people participated in the years after the temperature reached at least 29°?   8.____
   A. 2,295   B. 1,717   C. 2,210   D. 4,543

9. In 2007, the event saw 288 participants, while in 2008 that number dropped to 173. Which of the following reasons BEST explains the drop in participants?   9.____
   A. The event had not been going on that long and people didn't know about it.
   B. The lake water wasn't cold enough to have people jump in.
   C. The temperature was too cold for many people who would have normally participated.
   D. None of the above reasons explain the drop in participants.

10. In the following list of numbers, how many times does 4 come just after 2 when 2 comes just after an odd number?   10.____
    2365247653898632488572486392424
    A. 2   B. 3   C. 4   D. 5

11. Which choice below lists the letter that is as far after B as S is after N in the alphabet?   11.____
    A. G   B. H   C. I   D. J

Questions 12-15.

DIRECTIONS: Questions 12 through 15 are to be answered on the basis of the following directory and list of changes.

Directory		
Name	Emp. Type	Position
Julie Taylor	Warehouse	Packer
James King	Office	Administrative Assistant
John Williams	Office	Salesperson
Ray Moore	Warehouse	Maintenance
Kathleen Byrne	Warehouse	Supervisor
Amy Jones	Office	Salesperson
Paul Jonas	Office	Salesperson
Lisa Wong	Warehouse	Loader
Eugene Lee	Office	Accountant
Bruce Lavine	Office	Manager
Adam Gates	Warehouse	Packer
Will Suter	Warehouse	Packer
Gary Lorper	Office	Accountant
Jon Adams	Office	Salesperson
Susannah Harper	Office	Salesperson

Directory Updates:
- Employee e-mail addresses will adhere to the following guidelines: lastnamefirstname@apexindustries.com (ex. Susannah Harper is harpersusannah@apexindustries.com). Currently, employees in the warehouse share one e-mail, distribution@apexindustries.com.
- The "Loader" position will now be referred to as "Specialist I"
- Adam Gates has accepted a Supervisor position within the Warehouse and is no longer a Packer. All warehouse employees report to the two Supervisors and all office employees report to the Manager.

12. Amy Jones tried to send an e-mail to Adam Gates, but it wouldn't send. Which of the following offers the BEST explanation?
    A. Amy put Adam's first name first and then his last name.
    B. Adam doesn't check his e-mail, so he wouldn't know if he received the e-mail or not.
    C. Adam does not have his own e-mail.
    D. Office employees are not allowed to send e-mails to each other.

13. How many Packers currently work for Apex Industries?
    A. 2   B. 3   C. 4   D. 5

14. What position does Lisa Wong currently hold?
    A. Specialist I   B. Secretary
    C. Administrative Assistant   D. Loader

15. If an employee wanted to contact the office manager, which of the following e-mails should the e-mail be sent to?
   A. officemanager@apexindustries.com
   B. brucelavine@apexindustries.com
   C. lavinebruce@apexindustries.com
   D. distribution@apexindustries.com

15.____

Questions 16-19.

DIRECTIONS: In answering Questions 16 through 19, compare the three names, numbers or addresses.

16. Smiley Yarnell   Smiley Yarnel   Smily Yarnell   16.____
   A. All three are exactly alike.
   B. The first and second are exactly alike.
   C. The second and third are exactly alike.
   D. All three are different.

17. 1583 Theater Drive   1583 Theater Drive   1583 Theatre Drive   17.____
   A. All three are exactly alike.
   B. The first and second are exactly alike.
   C. The second and third are exactly alike.
   D. All three are different.

18. 3341893212   3341893212   3341893212   18.____
   A. All three are exactly alike.
   B. The first and second are exactly alike.
   C. The second and third are exactly alike.
   D. All three are different.

19. Douglass Watkins   Douglas Watkins   Douglass Watkins   19.____
   A. All three are exactly alike.
   B. The first and third are exactly alike.
   C. The second and third are exactly alike.
   D. All three are different.

Questions 20-24.

DIRECTIONS: In answering Questions 20 through 24, you will be presented with a word. Choose the synonym that BEST represents the word in question.

20. Flexible   20.____
   A. delicate   B. inflammable   C. strong   D. pliable

21. Alternative   21.____
   A. choice   B. moderate   C. lazy   D. value

22. Corroborate
    A. examine   B. explain   C. verify   D. explain   22.____

23. Respiration
    A. recovery   B. breathing   C. sweating   D. selfish   23.____

24. Negligent
    A. lazy   B. moderate   C. hopeless   D. lax   24.____

25. Plumber is to Wrench as Painter is to   25.____
    A. pipe   B. shop   C. hammer   D. brush

KEY (CORRECT ANSWERS)

1.	D	11.	A
2.	A	12.	C
3.	D	13.	A
4.	C	14.	A
5.	B	15.	C
6.	C	16.	D
7.	C	17.	B
8.	B	18.	A
9.	C	19.	B
10.	C	20.	D

21. A
22. C
23. B
24. D
25. D

NAME AND NUMBER CHECKING
EXAMINATION SECTION
TEST 1

DIRECTIONS: This test is designed to measure your speed/and accuracy. You are urged to work both quickly and accurately and to do correctly as many lists as you can in the time allowed. The test consists of lists or pairs of names and numbers. Count the number of IDENTICAL pairs in each list. Then, select the correct number, 1, 2, 3, 4, 5, and indicate your choice in the space at the right. Two sample questions are presented for your guidance, together with the correct solutions.

SAMPLE LIST A
Adelphi College – Adelphia College
Braxton Corp – Braxeton Corp.
Wassaic State School – Wassaic State School
Central Islip State Hospital – Central Isllip State Hospital
Greenwich House – Greenwich House

NOTE: There are only two correct pairs—Wassaic State School and Greenwich House. Therefore, the CORRECT answer is 2.

SAMPLE LIST B
78453694 – 78453684
784530 – 784530
533 – 534
67845 – 67845
2368745 – 2368755

NOTE: There are only two correct pairs—784530 and 67845. Therefore, the CORRECT answer is 2.

LIST 1   1.____
    Diagnostic Clinic   – Diagnostic Clinic
    Yorkville Health   – Yorkville Health
    Meinhard Clinic   – Meinhart Clinic
    Corlears Clinic   – Carlears Clinic
    Tremont Diagnostic – Tremont Diagnostic

LIST 2   2.____
    73526   – 73526
    7283627198   – 7283627198
    627   – 637
    728352617283   – 7283526178282
    6281   – 6281

LIST 3
    Jefferson Clinic   – Jeffersen Clinic
    Mott Haven Center   – Mott Havan Center
    Bronx Hospital   – Bronx Hospital
    Montefiore Hospital   – Montifeore Hospital
    Beth Isreal Hospital   – Beth Israel Hospital

3._____

LIST 4
    936271826   – 936371826
    5271   – 5291
    82637192037   – 82637192037
    527182   – 5271882
    726354256   - 72635456

4._____

LIST 5
    Trinity Hospital   – Trinity Hospital
    Central Harlem   – Centrel Harlem
    St. Luke's Hospital   – St. Lukes' Hospital
    Mt. Sinai Hospital   – Mt. Sinia Hospital
    N.Y. Dispensery   – N.Y. Dispensary

5._____

LIST 6
    725361552637   – 725361555637
    7526378   – 7526377
    6975   – 6975
    82637481028   – 82637481028
    3427   – 3429

6._____

LIST 7
    Misericordia Hospital   – Miseracordia Hospital
    Lebonan Hospital   – Lebanon Hospital
    Gouverneur Hospital   – Gouverner Hospital
    German Polyclinic   – German Policlinic
    French Hospital   – French Hospital

7._____

LIST 8
    8277364933251   – 827364933351
    63728   – 63728
    367281   – 367281
    62733846273   – 6273846293
    62836   - 6283

8._____

LIST 9
    King's County Hospital   – Kings County Hospital
    St. Johns Long Island   – St. John's Long Island
    Bellevue Hospital   – Bellvue Hospital
    Beth David Hospital   – Beth David Hospital
    Samaritan Hospital   – Samariton Hospital

9._____

3 (#1)

LIST 10   10._____
   62836454   – 62836455
   42738267   – 42738369
   573829   – 573829
   738291627874   – 738291627874
   725   - 735

LIST 11   11._____
   Bloomingdal Clinic   – Bloomingdale Clinic
   Communitty Hospital   – Community Hospital
   Metroplitan Hospital   – Metropoliton Hospital
   Lenox Hill Hospital   – Lonex Hill Hospital
   Lincoln Hospital   – Lincoln Hospital

LIST 12   12._____
   6283364728   – 6283648
   627385   – 627383
   54283902   – 54283602
   63354   – 63354
   7283562781   - 7283562781

LIST 13   13._____
   Sydenham Hospital   – Sydanham Hospital
   Roosevalt Hospital   – Roosevelt Hospital
   Vanderbilt Clinic   – Vanderbild Clinic
   Women's Hospital   – Woman's Hospital
   Flushing Hospital   – Flushing Hospital

LIST 14   14._____
   62738   – 62738
   727355542321   – 72735542321
   263849332   – 263849332
   262837   – 263837
   47382912   - 47382922

LIST 15   15._____
   Episcopal Hospital   – Episcapal Hospital
   Flower Hospital   – Flouer Hospital
   Stuyvesent Clinic   – Stuyvesant Clinic
   Jamaica Clinic   – Jamaica Clinic
   Ridgwood Clinic   – Ridgewood Clinic

LIST 16   16._____
   628367299   – 628367399
   111   – 111
   118293304829   – 1182839489
   4448   – 4448
   333693678   - 333693678

LIST 17
    Arietta Crane Farm   – Areitta Crane Farm
    Bikur Chilim Home   – Bikur Chilom Home
    Burke Foundation   – Burke Foundation
    Blythedale Home   – Blythdale Home
    Campbell Cottages   – Cambell Cottages

17.____

LIST 18
    32123   – 32132
    273893326783   – 27389326783
    473829   – 473829
    7382937   – 7383937
    3628890122332   - 36289012332

18.____

LIST 19
    Caraline Rest   – Caroline Rest
    Loreto Rest   – Loretto Rest
    Edgewater Creche   – Edgwater Creche
    Holiday Farm   – Holiday Farm
    House of St. Giles   – House of st. Giles

19.____

LIST 20
    557286777   – 55728677
    3678902   – 3678892
    1567839   – 1567839
    7865434712   – 7865344712
    9927382   - 9927382

20.____

LIST 21
    Isabella Home   – Isabela Home
    James A. Moore Home   – James A. More Home
    The Robin's Nest   – The Roben's Nest
    Pelham Home   – Pelam Home
    St. Eleanora's Home   – St. Eleanora's Home

21.____

LIST 22
    273648293048   – 273648293048
    334   – 334
    7362536478   – 7362536478
    7362819273   – 7362819273
    7362   - 7363

22.____

LIST 23
    St. Pheobe's Mission   – St. Phebe's Mission
    Seaside Home   – Seaside Home
    Speedwell Society   – Speedwell Society
    Valeria Home   – Valera Home
    Wiltwyck   - Wildwyck

23.____

5 (#1)

LIST 24
    63728   – 63738
    63728192736   – 63728192738
    428   – 458
    62738291527   – 62738291529
    63728192   - 63728192

24.____

LIST 25
    McGaffin   – McGafin
    David Ardslee   – David Ardslee
    Axton Supply   – Axeton Supply Co
    Alice Russell   – Alice Russell
    Dobson Mfg. Co. – Dobsen Mfg. Co.

25.____

KEY (CORRECT ANSWERS)

1.	3		11.	1
2.	3		12.	2
3.	1		13.	1
4.	1		14.	2
5.	1		15.	1
6.	2		16.	3
7.	1		17.	1
8.	2		18.	1
9.	1		19.	1
10.	2		20.	2

    21. 1
    22. 4
    23. 2
    24. 1
    25. 2

TEST 2

DIRECTIONS: This test is designed to measure your speed/and accuracy. You are urged to work both quickly and accurately and to do correctly as many lists as you can in the time allowed. The test consists of lists or pairs of names and numbers. Count the number of IDENTICAL pairs in each list. Then, select the correct number, 1, 2, 3, 4, 5, and indicate your choice in the space at the right.

LIST 1   1.____
    82637381028   – 82637281028
    928   – 928
    72937281028   – 72937281028
    7362   – 7362
    927382615   – 927382615

LIST 2   2.____
    Albee Theatre   – Albee Theatre
    Lapland Lumber Co.   – Laplund Lumber Co.
    Adelphi College   – Adelphi College
    Jones & Son Inc.   – Jones & Sons Inc.
    S.W. Ponds Co.   – S.W. Ponds Co.

LIST 3   3.____
    85345   – 85345
    895643278   – 895643277
    726352   – 726353
    632685   – 632685
    7263524   – 7236524

LIST 4   4.____
    Eagle Library   – Eagle Library
    Dodge Ltd.   – Dodge Co.
    Stromberg Carlson   – Stromberg Carlsen
    Clairice Ling   – Clairice Linng
    Mason Book Co.   – Matson Book Co.

LIST 5   5.____
    66273   – 66273
    629   – 629
    7382517283   – 7382517283
    637281   – 639281
    2738261   – 2788261

LIST 6   6.____
    Robert MacColl   – Robert McColl
    Buick Motor   – Buck Motors
    Murray Bay & Co. Ltd. – Murray Bay Co. Ltd.
    L.T. Ltyle   – L.T. Lyttle
    A.S. Landas   – A.S. Landas

LIST 7
 6271526374890   – 627152637490
 73526189   – 73526189
 5372   – 5392
 637281142   – 63728124
 4783946   – 4783046

7.____

LIST 8
 Tyndall Burke   – Tyndell Burke
 W. Briehl   – W. Briehl
 Burritt Publishing Co.   – Buritt Publishing Co.
 Frederick Breyer & Co.   – Frederick Breyer Co.
 Bailey Buulard   – Bailey Bullard

8.____

LIST 9
 634   – 634
 16837   – 163837
 273892223678   – 27389223678
 527182   – 527782
 3628901223   – 3629002223

9.____

LIST 10
 Ernest Boas   – Ernest Boas
 Rankin Barne   – Rankin Barnes
 Edward Appley   – Edward Appely
 Camel   – Camel
 Caiger Food Co.   – Caiger Food Co.

10.____

LIST 11
 6273   – 6273
 322   – 332
 15672839   – 15672839
 63728192637   – 63728192639
 738   – 738

11.____

LIST 12
 Wells Fargo Co.   – Wells Fargo Co.
 W.D. Brett   – W.D. Britt
 Tassco Co.   – Tassko Co.
 Republic Mills   – Republic Mill
 R.W. Burnham   – R.W. Burhnam

12.____

LIST 13
 7253529152   – 7283529152
 6283   – 6383
 52839102738   – 5283910238
 308   – 398
 82637201927   – 8263720127

13.____

LIST 14
    Schumacker Co.   – Shumacker Co.
    C.H. Caiger   – C.H. Caiger
    Abraham Strauss   – Abram Straus
    B.F. Boettjer   – B.F. Boettijer
    Cut-Rate Store   – Cut-Rate Stores

14. ____

LIST 15
    15273826   – 15273826
    72537   – 73537
    726391027384   – 62639107384
    637389   – 627399
    725382910   – 725382910

15. ____

LIST 16
    Hixby Ltd.   – Hixby Lt'd.
    S. Reiner   – S. Riener
    Reynard Co.   – Reynord Co.
    Esso Gassoline Co. – Esso Gasolene Co.
    Belle Brock   – Belle Brock

16. ____

LIST 17
    7245   – 7245
    819263728192   – 819263728172
    682537289   – 682537298
    789   – 789
    82936542891   – 82936542891

17. ____

LIST 18
    Joseph Cartwright   – Joseph Cartwrite
    Foote Food Co.   – Foot Food Co.
    Weiman & Held   – Weiman & Held
    Sanderson Shoe Co. – Sandersen Shoe Co.
    A.M. Byrne   – A.N. Byrne

18. ____

LIST 19
    4738267   – 4738277
    63728   – 63729
    6283628901   – 6283628991
    918264   – 918264
    263728192037   – 2637728192073

19. ____

LIST 20
    Exray Laboratories – Exray Labratories
    Curley Toy Co.   – Curly Toy Co.
    J. Lauer & Cross   – J. Laeur & Cross
    Mireco Brands   – Mireco Brands
    Sandor Lorand   – Sandor Larand

20. ____

4 (#2)

LIST 21   21.____
   607   – 609
   6405   – 6403
   976   – 996
   101267   – 101267
   2065432   – 20965432

LIST 22   22.____
   John Macy & Sons   – John Macy & Son
   Venus Pencil Co.   – Venus Pencil Co.
   Nell McGinnis   – Nell McGinnis
   McCutcheon & Co.   – McCutcheon & Co.
   Sun-Tan Oil   – Sun-Tan Oil

LIST 23   23.____
   703345700   – 703345700
   46754   – 466754
   3367490   – 3367490
   3379   – 3778
   47384   – 47394

LIST 24   24.____
   arthritis   – arthritis
   asthma   – asthma
   endocrine   – endocrene
   gastro-enterological   – gastrol-enteralogical
   orthopedic   – orthopedic

LIST 25   25.____
   743829432   – 743828432
   998   – 998
   732816253902 – 732816252902
   46829   – 46830
   7439120249   – 7439210249

KEY (CORRECT ANSWERS)

1.	4		11.	3
2.	3		12.	1
3.	2		13.	1
4.	1		14.	1
5.	2		15.	2
6.	1		16.	1
7.	2		17.	3
8.	1		18.	1
9.	1		19.	1
10.	3		20.	1

21. 1
22. 4
23. 2
24. 3
25. 1

NAME AND NUMBER CHECKING
EXAMINATION SECTION
TEST 1

DIRECTIONS: Questions 1 through 17 consist of sets of names and addresses. In each question, the name and address in Column II should be an exact copy of the name and address in Column I.
If there is:
a mistake only in the name, mark your answer A;
a mistake only in the address, mark your answer B;
a mistake in both name and address, mark your answer C;
No mistake in either name or address, mark your answer D.

Sample Question

Column I
Christina Magnusson
288 Greene Street
New York, N.Y. 10003

Column II
Christina Magnusson
288 Greene Street
New York, N.Y. 10013

Since there is a mistake only in the address (the zip code should be 10003 instead of 10013), the answer to the sample question is B.

COLUMN I

1. Ms. Joan Kelly
   313 Franklin Avenue
   Brooklyn, N.Y. 11202

2. Mrs. Eileen Engel
   47-24 86 Road
   Queens, N.Y. 11122

3. Marcia Michaels
   213 E. 81 St.
   New York, N.Y. 10012

4. Rev. Edward J. Smyth
   1401 Brandeis Street
   San Francisco, Calif. 96201

5. Alicia Rodriguez
   24-68 82 St.
   Elmhurst, N.Y. 11122

COLUMN II

Ms. Joan Kielly
318 Franklin Ave.
Brooklyn, N.Y. 11202

Mrs. Ellen Engel
47-24 86 Road
Queens, New York 11122

Marcia Michaels
213 E. 81 St.
New York, N.Y. 10012

Rev. Edward J. Smyth
1401 Brandies Street
San Francisco, Calif. 96201

Alicia Rodriguez
2468 81 St.
Elmhurst, N.Y. 11122

1.____

2.____

3.____

4.____

5.____

COLUMN I	COLUMN II	
6. Ernest Eisemann 21 Columbia St. New York, N.Y. 10007	Ernest Eisermann 21 Columbia St. New York, N.Y. 10007	6.____
7. Mr. & Mrs. George Petersson 87-11 91st Avenue Woodhaven, N.Y. 11421	Mr. & Mrs. George Peterson 87-11 91st Avenue Woodhaven, N.Y. 11421	7.____
8. Mr. Ivan Klebnikov 1848 Newkirk Avenue Brooklyn, N.Y. 11226	Mr. Ivan Klebikov 1848 Newkirk Avenue Brooklyn, N.Y. 11622	8.____
9. Mr. Samuel Rothfleisch 71 Pine Street New York, N.Y. 10005	Samuel Rothfleisch 71 Pine Street New York, N.Y. 100005	9.____
10. Mrs. Isabel Tonnessen 198 East 185th Street Bronx, N.Y. 10458	Mrs. Isabel Tonnessen 189 East 185th Street Bronx, N.Y. 10348	10.____
11. Esteban Perez 173 Eighth Street Staten Island, N.Y. 10306	Estaban Perez 173 Eighth Street Staten Island, N.Y. 10306	11.____
12. Esta Wong 141 West 68 St. New York, N.Y. 10023	Esta Wang 141 West 68 St. New York, N.Y. 10023	12.____
13. Dr. Alberto Grosso 3475 12th Avenue Brooklyn, N.Y. 11218	Dr. Alberto Grosso 3475 12th Avenue Brooklyn, N.Y. 11218	13.____
14. Mrs. Ruth Bortias 482 Theresa Ct. Far Rockaway, N.Y. 11691	Ms. Ruth Bortlas 482 Theresa Ct. Far Rockaway, N.Y. 11169	14.____
15. Mr. & Mrs. Howard Fox 2301 Sedgwick Ave. Bronx, N.Y. 10468	Mr. & Mrs. Howard Fox 231 Sedgwick Ave. Bronx, N.Y. 10468	15.____
16. Miss Marjorie Black 223 East 23 Street New York, N.Y. 10010	Miss Margorie Black 223 East 23 Street New York, N.Y. 10010	16.____

COLUMN I | COLUMN II

17. Michelle Herman Michelle Hermann 17.____
    806 Valley Rd. 806 Valley Dr.
    Old Tappan, N.J. 07675 Old Tappan, N.J. 07675

KEY (CORRECT ANSWERS)

1.	C	7.	A	13.	D
2.	A	8.	C	14.	C
3.	D	9.	D	15.	B
4.	B	10.	B	16.	A
5.	B	11.	A	17.	C
6.	A	12.	D		

TEST 2

DIRECTIONS: Questions 1 through 15 are to be answered SOLELY on the instructions given below. *PRINT THE LETTER OF THE CORRECT ANSWER IN THE SPACE AT THE RIGHT.*

INSTRUCTIONS

In each of the following questions, the 3-line name and address in Column I is the master-list entry, and the 3-line entry in Column II is the information to be checked against the master list. If there is one line that does not match, mark your answer A; if there are two lines that do not match, mark your answer B; if all three lines do not match, mark your answer C; if the lines all match exactly, mark your answer D.

Sample Question

Column I
Mark L. Field
11-09 Price Park Blvd.
Bronx, N.Y. 11402

Column II
Mark L. Field
11-99 Prince Park Way
Bronx, N.Y. 11401

The first lines in each column match exactly. The second lines do not match since 11-09 does not match 11-99; and Blvd. does not match Way. The third lines do not match either since 11402 does not match 11401. Therefore, there are two lines that do not match, and the CORRECT answer is B.

COLUMN I | COLUMN II

1. Jerome A. Jackson
   1243 14th Avenue
   New York, N.Y. 10023

   Jerome A. Johnson
   1234 14th Avenue
   New York, N.Y. 10023

2. Sophie Strachtheim
   33-28 Connecticut Ave.
   Far Rockaway, N.Y. 11697

   Sophie Strachtheim
   33-28 Connecticut Ave.
   Far Rockaway, N.Y. 11697

3. Elisabeth N.T. Gorrell
   256 Exchange St.
   New York, N.Y. 10013

   Elizabeth N.T. Gorrell
   256 Exchange St.
   New York, N.Y. 10013

4. Maria J. Gonzalez
   7516 E. Sheepshead Rd.
   Brooklyn, N.Y. 11240

   Maria J. Gonzalez
   7516 N. Shepshead Rd.
   Brooklyn, N.Y. 11240

5. Leslie B. Brautenweiler
   21 57A Seiler Terr.
   Flushing, N.Y. 11367

   Leslie B. Brautenwieler
   21-75A Seiler Terr.
   Flushing, N.J. 11367

2 (#2)

COLUMN I	COLUMN II	
6. Rigoberto J. Peredes 157 Twin Towers, #18F Tottenville, S. I., N.Y,	Rigoberto J. Peredes 157 Twin Towers, #18F Tottenville, S.I., N.Y.	6.____
7. Pietro F. Albino P.O. Box 7548 Floral Park, N.Y. 11005	Pietro F. Albina P.O. Box 7458 Floral Park, N.Y. 11005	7.____
8. Joanne Zimmerman Bldg. SW, Room 314 532-4601	Joanne Zimmermann Bldg. SW, Room 314 532-4601	8.____
9. Carlyle Whetstone Payroll Div. –A, Room 212A 262-5000, ext. 471	Carlyle Whetstone Payroll Div. –A, Room 212A 262-5000, ext. 417	9.____
10. Kenneth Chiang Legal Council, Room 9745 (201) 416-9100, ext. 17	Kenneth Chiang Legal Counsel, Room 9745 (201) 416-9100, Ext. 17	10.____
11. Ethel Koenig Personnel Services Division, Room 433; 635-7572	Ethel Hoenig Personal Services Division, Room 433; 635-7527	11.____
12. Joyce Ehrhardt Office of the Administrator, Room W56; 387-8706	Joyce Ehrhart Office of the Administrator, Room W56; 387-7806	12.____
13. Ruth Lang EAM Bldg., Room C101 625-2000, ext. 765	Ruth Lang EAM Bldg., Room C110 625-2000, ext. 765	13.____
14. Anne Marie Ionozzi Investigations, Room 827 576-4000, ext. 832	Anna Marie Ionozzi Investigation, Room 827 566-4000, ext. 832	14.____
15. Willard Jameson Fm C Bldg., Room 687 454-3010	Willard Jamieson Fm C Bldg., Room 687 454-3010	15.____

KEY (CORRECT ANSWERS)

1.	B	6.	D		C	C
2.	D	7.	B	12.	B	
3.	A	8.	D	13.	A	
4.	A	9.	B	14.	C	
5.	C	10.	A	15.	A	

TEST 3

DIRECTIONS: Questions 1 through 10 are to be answered on the basis of the following instructions. *PRINT THE LETTER OF THE CORRECT ANSWER IN THE SPACE AT THE RIGHT.*

INSTRUCTIONS

For each such set of names, addresses, and numbers listed in Columns I and II, select your answer from the following options:
  The names in Columns I and II are different,
  The addresses in Columns I and II are different,
  The numbers in Columns I and II are different,
  The names, addresses, and numbers in Columns I and II are identical.

COLUMN I | COLUMN II

1. Francis Jones
   62 Stately Avenue
   96-12446

   Francis Jones
   62 Stately Avenue
   96-21446

   1.____

2. Julio Montez
   19 Ponderosa Road
   56-73161

   Julio Montez
   19 Ponderosa Road
   56-71361

   2.____

3. Mary Mitchell
   2314 Melbourne Drive
   68-92172

   Mary Mitchell
   2314 Melbourne Drive
   68-92172

   3.____

4. Harry Patterson
   25 Dunne Street
   14-33430

   Harry Patterson
   25 Dunne Street
   14-34330

   4.____

5. Patrick Murphy
   171 West Hosmer Street
   93-81214

   Patrick Murphy
   171 West Hosmer Street
   93-18214

   5.____

6. August Schultz
   816 St. Clair Avenue
   53-40149

   August Schultz
   816 St. Claire Avenue
   53-40149

   6.____

7. George Taft
   72 Runnymede Street
   47-04033

   George Taft
   72 Runnymede Street
   47-04023

   7.____

8. Angus Henderson
   1418 Madison Street
   81-76375

   Angus Henderson
   1318 Madison Street
   81-76375

   8.____

COLUMN I   COLUMN II

9. Carolyn Mazur   Carolyn Mazur   9.____
    12 Riverview Road   12 Rivervane Road
    38-99615   38-99615

10. Adele Russell   Adela Russell   10.____
    1725 Lansing Lane   1725 Lansing Lane
    72-91962   72-91962

KEY (CORRECT ANSWERS)

1.	C	6.	B
2.	C	7.	C
3.	D	8.	D
4.	C	9.	B
5.	C	10.	A

TEST 4

DIRECTIONS: Questions 1 through 20 test how good you are at catching mistakes in typing or printing. In each question, the name and address in Column II should be an exact copy of the name and address in Column I. Mark your answer
A. If there is no mistake in either name or address;
B. If there is a mistake in both name and address;
C. If there is a mistake only in the name;
D. If there is a mistake only in the address.
PRINT THE LETTER OF THE CORRECT ANSWER IN THE SPACE AT THE RIGHT.

COLUMN I								COLUMN II

1. Milos Yanocek							Milos Yanocek							1.____
   33-60 14 Street							33-60 14 Street
   Long Island City, N.Y. 11011					Long Island City, N.Y. 11001

2. Alphonse Sabattelo						Alphonse Sabbattelo						2.____
   24 Minnetta Lane							24 Minetta Lane
   New York, N.Y. 10006						New York, N.Y. 10006

3. Helen Steam							Helene Stearn							3.____
   5 Metropolitan Oval						5 Metropolitan Oval
   Bronx, N.Y. 10462						Bronx, N.Y. 10462

4. Jacob Weisman							Jacob Weisman							4.____
   231 Francis Lewis Boulevard					231 Francis Lewis Boulevard
   Forest Hills, N.Y. 11325					Forest Hills, N.Y. 11325

5. Riccardo Fuente							Riccardo Fuentes						5.____
   134 West 83 Street						134 West 88 Street
   New York, N.Y. 10024						New York, N.Y. 10024

6. Dennis Lauber							Dennis Lauder							6.____
   52 Avenue D								52 Avenue D
   Brooklyn, N.Y. 11216						Brooklyn, N.Y. 11216

7. Paul Cutter							Paul Cutter							7.____
   195 Galloway Avenue						175 Galloway Avenue
   Staten Island, N.Y. 10356					Staten Island, N.Y. 10365

8. Sean Donnelly							Sean Donnelly							8.____
   45-58 41 Avenue							45-58 41 Avenue
   Woodside, N.Y. 11168						Woodside, N.Y. 11168

9. Clyde Willot							Clyde Willat							9.____
   1483 Rockaway Avenue						1483 Rockaway Avenue
   Brooklyn, N.Y. 11238						Brooklyn, N.Y. 11238

2 (#4)

COLUMN I	COLUMN II	
10. Michael Stanakis 419 Sheriden Avenue Staten Island, N.Y. 10363	Michael Stanakis 419 Sheraden Avenue Staten Island, N.Y. 10363	10.____
11. Joseph DiSilva 63-84 Saunders Road Rego Park, N.Y. 11431	Joseph Disilva 64-83 Saunders Road Rego Park, N.Y. 11431	11.____
12. Linda Polansky 2224 Fendon Avenue Bronx, N.Y. 20464	Linda Polansky 2255 Fenton Avenue Bronx, N.Y. 10464	12.____
13. Alfred Klein 260 Hillside Terrace Staten Island, N.Y. 15545	Alfred Klein 260 Hillside Terrace Staten Island, N.Y. 15545	13.____
14. William McDonnell 504 E. 55 Street New York, N.Y. 10103	William McConnell 504 E. 55 Street New York, N.Y. 10108	14.____
15. Angela Cipolla 41-11 Parson Avenue Flushing, N.Y. 11446	Angela Cipola 41-11 Parsons Avenue Flushing, N.Y. 11446	15.____
16. Julie Sheridan 1212 Ocean Avenue Brooklyn, N.Y. 11237	Julia Sheridan 1212 Ocean Avenue Brooklyn, N.Y. 11237	16.____
17. Arturo Rodriguez 2156 Cruger Avenue Bronx, N.Y. 10446	Arturo Rodrigues 2156 Cruger Avenue Bronx, N.Y. 10446	17.____
18. Helen McCabe 2044 East 19 Street Brooklyn, N.Y. 11204	Helen McCabe 2040 East 19 Street Brooklyn, N.Y. 11204	18.____
19. Charles Martin 526 West 160 Street New York, N.Y. 10022	Charles Martin 526 West 160 Street New York, N.Y. 10022	19.____
20. Morris Rabinowitz 31 Avenue M Brooklyn, N.Y. 11216	Morris Rabinowitz 31 Avenue N Brooklyn, N.Y. 11216	20.____

KEY (CORRECT ANSWERS)

1.	D	11.	B
2.	B	12.	D
3.	C	13.	A
4.	A	14.	B
5.	B	15.	B
6.	C	16.	C
7.	D	17.	C
8.	A	18.	D
9.	B	19.	A
10.	D	20.	D

TEST 5

DIRECTIONS: In copying the addresses below from Column A to the same line in Column B, an Agent-in-Training made some errors. For Questions 1 through 5, if you find that the agent made an error in
only one line, mark your answer A;
only two lines, mark your answer B;
only three lines, mark your answer C;
all four lines, mark your answer D.

EXAMPLE

COLUMN A	COLUMN B
24 Third Avenue	24 Third Avenue
5 Lincoln Road	5 Lincoln Street
50 Central Park West	6 Central Park West
37-21 Queens Boulevard	21-37 Queens Boulevard

Since errors were made on only three lines, namely the second, third, and fourth, the CORRECT answer is C.
PRINT THE LETTER OF THE CORRECT ANSWER IN THE SPACE AT THE RIGHT.

	COLUMN A	COLUMN B	
1.	57-22 Springfield Boulevard 94 Gun Hill Road 8 New Dorp Lane 36 Bedford Avenue	75-22 Springfield Boulevard 94 Gun Hill Avenue 8 New Drop Lane 36 Bedford Avenue	1.____
2.	538 Castle Hill Avenue 54-15 Beach Channel Drive 21 Ralph Avenue 162 Madison Avenue	538 Castle Hill Avenue 54-15 Beach Channel Drive 21 Ralph Avenue 162 Morrison Avenue	2.____
3.	49 Thomas Street 27-21 Northern Blvd. 86 125th Street 872 Atlantic Ave.	49 Thomas Street 21-27 Northern Blvd. 86 125th Street 872 Baltic Ave,	3.____
4.	261-17 Horace Harding Expwy. 191 Fordham Road 6 Victory Blvd. 552 Oceanic Ave.	261-17 Horace Harding Pkwy. 191 Fordham Road 6 Victoria Blvd. 552 Ocean Ave.	4.____
5.	90-05 38th Avenue 19 Central Park West 9281 Avenue X 22 West Farms Square	90-05 36th Avenue 19 Central Park East 9281 Avenue X 22 West Farms Square	5.____

KEY (CORRECT ANSWERS)

1. C
2. A
3. B
4. C
5. B

TEST 6

DIRECTIONS: For Questions 1 through 10, choose the letter in Column II next to the number which EXACTLY matches the number in Column I. *PRINT THE LETTER OF THE CORRECT ANSWER IN THE SPACE AT THE RIGHT.*

	COLUMN I		COLUMN II	
1.	14235	A. B. C. D.	13254 12435 13245 14235	1.____
2.	70698	A. B. C. D.	90768 60978 70698] 70968	2.____
3.	11698	A. B. C. D.	11689 11986 11968 11698	3.____
4.	50497	A. B. C. D.	50947 50497 50749 54097	4.____
5.	69635	A. B. C. D.	60653 69630 69365 69635	5.____
6.	1201022011	A. B. C. D.	1201022011 1201020211 1202012011 1021202011	6.____
7.	3893981389	A. B. C. D.	3893891389 3983981389 3983891389 3893981389	7.____
8.	4765476589	A. B. C. D.	4765476598 4765476588 4765476589 4765746589	8.____

2 (#6)

9. 8679678938
   - A. 8679687938
   - B. 8679678938
   - C. 8697678938
   - D. 8678678938

   9.____

10. 6834836932
    - A. 6834386932
    - B. 6834836923
    - C. 6843836932
    - D. 6834836932

    10.____

Questions 11-15.

DIRECTIONS: For Questions 11 through 15, determine how many of the symbols in Column Z are exactly the same as the symbol in Column Y.
If none is exactly the same, answer A;
If only one symbol is exactly the same, answer B;
If two symbols are exactly the same, answer C;
If three symbols are exactly the same, answer D.

COLUMN Y	COLUMN Z	
11. A123B1266	A123B1366 A123B1266 A133B1366 A123B1266	11.____
12. CC28D3377	CD22D3377 CC38D3377 CC28C3377 CC28D2277	12.____
13. M21AB201X	M12AB201X M21AB201X M21AB201Y M21BA201X	13.____
14. PA383Y744	AP383Y744 PA338Y744 PA388Y744 PA383Y774	14.____
15. PB2Y8893	PB2Y8893 PB2Y8893 PB3Y8898 PB2Y8893	15.____

KEY (CORRECT ANSWERS)

1.	D	6.	A	11.	C
2.	C	7.	D	12.	A
3.	D	8.	C	13.	B
4.	B	9.	B	14.	A
5.	D	10.	D	15.	D

DRUG LAWS OF THE UNITED STATES

CONTENTS

		Page
1.	Laws governing pharmacy	1
2.	The Federal Food, Drug, and Cosmetic Act	1
	a. Adulterated drugs	1
	b. Misbranded drugs	1
	c. Labeling	2
	d. Coal tar colors	2
	e. New drugs	2
3.	The Durham-Humphrey Act	2
	a. Prescription legend drugs	2
	b. Telephone prescriptions	2
	c. Renewing legend drug prescriptions	3
	d. Enforcement of the acts	3
4.	The drug efficacy studies	3
5.	Controlled substances	4
	a. General	4
	b. Schedule substances	4
	c. Code R and Code K items	5
	d. Ordering	5
	e. Record keeping	5
	f. Filing	6
	g. Inventorying	6
	h. Security	6
	i. Dispensing	6
	j. Destruction	8
6.	UCMJ	8
7.	Prescription ownership	8
8.	Confidentiality of prescriptions	8

DRUG LAWS OF THE UNITED STATES

1. Laws governing pharmacy. There are Federal laws pertaining to pharmacy which must be followed by everyone practicing pharmacy who is associated with the U.S. Government. There are also State laws which pertain to the practice of pharmacy in a particular state. Any State law may be more stringent or strict than the Federal law, but it may not be less so. The practice of Army pharmacy is also governed by Army Regulations such as AR 40-2, AR 40-4, AR 40-7, AR 40-18, and AR 40-61. In the Army, we must abide by the Federal pharmacy laws and Army Regulations, but we do not have to abide by the State laws. It is a matter of local policy whether a particular installation will also abide by the pharmacy laws of the state in which the installation is located.

2. The Federal Food, Drug, and Cosmetic Act. The Federal Food, Drug, and Cosmetic Act first became law in 1906, followed by revision, amendment, and final emergence as our present law in 1965. This act is intended to protect the consumer from adulterated and misbranded food, drugs, devices, and cosmetics, and for other purposes. It directly prohibits adulterated or misbranded items from movement across state lines (interstate commerce).

a. Adulterated drugs. By provision of the Federal Food, Drug, and Cosmetic Act, a drug or device is construed as being adulterated under the following conditions if:

(1) It contains any filthy, putrid, or decomposed substance, or is packed under conditions which would result in its contamination; if it is a drug and its container is composed of any poisonous or injurious substance which could be passed on to the contents; or if it contains a coal tar color not certified by regulations.

(2) It is said or advertised to be a drug of official nature and differs from or is not the same quality as the official standard.

(3) Its strength differs from or the purity and quality fall below that indicated on the label.

(4) It is a drug and any other drug has been substituted for it or mixed with it to reduce its quality or strength.

b. Misbranded drugs. A drug or device is misbranded if—

(1) The labeling is not truthful or is misleading.

(2) It is in a package and does not contain the name and address of the manufacturer, packager, or distributor, and an accurate statement of the weight, measure, or numerical count of the contents.

(3) Any word or information required by the Act to appear on the label is not prominently placed (in comparison with the rest of the label) so that it is likely to be read and understood by ordinary individuals.

(4) It is intended for human use and contains any quantity of a substance which is habit-forming, unless the label shows the name and quantity of that substance and adjacent to it, the statement "Warning: May be habit-forming."

(5) It is a drug and is not labeled by a name official in our compendia (USP and NF), unless it bears the common name, if one exists; and if it is made of two or more ingredients, the common or usual name of each active ingredient.

(6) It is a drug of one or more active ingredients and the name, quantity, and proportion of any alcohol contained is not specified on the label.

(7) It is a drug and the label does not specify the name and quantity or proportion of any bromides, ether, chloroform, acetanilid, acetophenetidin, aminopyrine, antipyrine, atropine, hyoscine, hyoscyamus, arsenic, digitalis, digitalis glucosides, mercury, ouabain, strophanthin, strychnine, thyroid, or any derivative or preparation of any such substances. If compliance with this item or items (5) and (6) above is impracticable, exemptions may be established by regulation.

(8) The labeling does not bear adequate directions for use and appropriate warnings against use under specific circumstances (for example, laxatives where abdominal pain is present).

(9) It is stated or advertised to be an official preparation and is not packaged and labeled according to the official directions in the monograph.

(10) The packaging is such that it is misleading; it is an imitation of another drug; or it is offered under the name of another drug.

(11) It is dangerous to health when used as recommended by the label on it.

(12) It is, or is stated to be, made of or in part of insulin or antibiotic unless it be from a batch certified by this law.

    c. Labeling. All drugs leaving the pharmacy must be labeled adequately.

    (1) Labeling drugs dispensed on prescription. Drugs dispensed on prescription must bear the proper information on a prescription-type label—including the name and location of the facility, the name of the patient, the date of issuance, the number assigned to the prescription, the directions for use, the prescriber's name, and the initials of the person typing the label. In the Army, AR 40-2 also requires us to place the name and strength of the drug on the label, except when the prescriber directs otherwise, and also the legend "KEEP OUT OF THE REACH OF CHILDREN" in boldface type on all prescription labels. In addition, the labels for controlled substances must contain the legend, "CAUTION: FEDERAL LAW PROHIBITS THE TRANSFER OF THIS DRUG TO ANY PERSON OTHER THAN THE PATIENT FOR WHOM IT WAS PRESCRIBED" in boldface type.

    (2) Labeling drugs dispensed to patients without a prescription. Drugs dispensed by the pharmacy without a prescription as provided in AR 40-2 must be properly labeled. According to law, the label must show the name of the medication; adequate directions for use; the quantity contained; the name of the facility and location; special notes or warnings; and if any habit-forming drugs are contained in any amount, the name of such drug and the amount per unit must be stated on the label as well as the statement—"Warning: May be habit-forming." Items which have an expiration date or deteriorate after mixing must bear a label stating such information. AR 40-2 also states that the legend "KEEP OUT OF THE REACH OF CHILDREN" must appear in boldface type on the label.

    (3) Labels of drug stock in using activities. It is the duty of pharmacy personnel to insure that the stock in wards and in treatment rooms is labeled properly. A little bottle on the shelf in a treatment room marked "Achromycin—250 mg" is not adequate and is in direct violation of the law. When possible, drugs dispensed for ward stock should remain in their original container and with their original labeling. If labeled by pharmacy personnel, the label should contain such things as the name of the drug; trade name, if applicable; strength; quantity; date; name of manufacturer and manufacturer's lot number; and expiration date.

    d. Coal tar colors. A list of certified coal tar colors for the purpose of coloring foods or drugs is set forth in this law. These coloring agents must be proved harmless and suitable for the purpose for which they are intended. A list of these coal tar colors can be found in *Remington's Practice of Pharmacy.*

    e. New drugs. Before being introduced into interstate commerce, all new drugs must be first approved by the Secretary of the Department of Health, Education, and Welfare. Only "approved" drugs will be procured, prescribed, or dispensed except those unapproved drugs authorized by The Surgeon General to save life or prevent suffering. Investigational drugs may be used within the provisions of AR 40-2 (sec. 15) and AR 40-7.

    3. The Durham-Humphrey Act. The Durham-Humphrey Act (Durham-Humphrey Amendment) is nothing more than a set of changes to the Food, Drug, and Cosmetic Act. This amendment groups drugs into two main classes—those which may be dispensed only on prescription, and those which may be sold over-the-counter (OTC); that is, without a prescription.

    a. Prescription legend drugs. The Durham-Humphrey Act rules that drugs which by their nature are unsafe, or require medical supervision or advice with their use, must bear the legend "Caution: Federal Law Prohibits Dispensing Without a Prescription." Any drug so labeled is known as a prescription legend drug (sometimes called a legend drug) and cannot be sold without a prescription. Conversely, all drugs considered safe to use without medical supervision must not bear the caution and may be sold OTC.

    b. Telephoned prescriptions. The Durham-Humphrey Amendment permits a physician to prescribe medication in the legend category by telephone. The pharmacist must reduce the prescription to writing and include the medication, strength, dose or directions for use, the name of the patient, and all other data given him by the physician. AR 40-2 states that all prescriptions will be signed by an authorized prescriber and that prescriptions for potentially harmful drugs (legend drugs) will be dispensed only upon receipt of a *written* prescription.

    c. Renewing legend drug prescriptions. One of the most important stipulations of the Durham-Humphrey Act is that prescriptions for legend drugs may not be renewed (refilled), except when authorized by the prescriber. Such authorization may be made at the time of writing the prescription by stating the number of times the prescription may be refilled. The interpretation of this act, like all the others, must be in accordance with good professional judgment and good faith.

    d. Enforcement of the acts. The Food, Drug, and Cosmetic Act and the Durham-Humphrey Act are enforced by the Food and Drug Administration (FDA) of the Department of Health, Education, and Welfare. Violations of the acts are misdemeanors and are punishable by "imprisonment for not more than one year, or a fine of not more than $1,000, or both."

4. The drug efficacy studies

    a. As a result of the 1962 Kefauver-Harris New Drug Amendments to the Food, Drug, and Cosmetics Act of 1938, it was ruled that *drugs must not only have proof of "safety," but also proof of "effectiveness."* This was the basis for the commissioner of the Food and Drug Administration (FDA) requesting the National Academy of Sciences/National Research Council (NAS/NRC) to make a comprehensive survey of effectiveness for all drugs marketed under new drug applications (NDA) approved between 1938 and October 1962. Their findings are called the *Drug Efficacy Study.* Each drug after review is classified in one of four categories:

    (1) Effective. The drug is effective for the presented indications.

    (2) Probably effective. The effectiveness of the drug is probable for the indications presented but additional evidence of effectiveness is required of the manufacturer within 12 months before it can be classified *effective*.

    (3) Possibly effective. There is little evidence of effectiveness for presented indications; however, the manufacturer is allowed 6 months to submit additional data to provide substantial evidence of effectiveness.

    (4) Ineffective. There is no acceptable evidence to support a claim of effectiveness, and immediate administrative action by the FDA is justified in withdrawing the drug from the market or deleting the claimed indication(s) from the label. The manufacturer has 30 days to submit pertinent data bearing on this regulatory proposal.

    b. As a direct result of the Drug Efficacy Study and FDA enforcement and regulatory action, the Department of Defense established the following policy regarding the procurement and prescribing of three of the above categories of drugs:

    (1) Category 1A, "Ineffective" drugs.
- These drugs have definitely been determined to be ineffective by the FDA.
- No further procurement or issue is authorized for those items that have been withdrawn from the market.
- Remaining stocks of standard and nonstandard items will be destroyed or other appropriate action taken.

    (2) Category 1B, "Ineffective" drugs.
- These drugs have been determined to be ineffective by the FDA; however, manufacturers have been given time to refute the FDA decision.
- Authorization for central or local procurement is suspended until final action is taken by FDA.
- These drugs will be suspended from use and issue until final status of drug is resolved.

    (3) Category 2, "Possibly Effective" drugs.
- Standard and local procurement of these items are no longer authorized. Remaining stocks may be used until exhausted. Exception: continued therapeutic use of these drugs will depend upon the decision of the medical facility Therapeutic Agents Board (TAB). Local procurement is authorized if the TAB decides no alternate means of therapy are available.
- Requisitioning of "possibly effective" drugs (if approved by TAB) is minimized to no more than 60 days stock on hand in the medical facility.

    (4) Category 3, "Probably Effective" drugs.
- All central and local procurement of these items

is minimized so that there is no more than 60 days stock on hand in the medical facility.

• Continued issue and use is authorized until further change in classification by FDA.

   c. Information concerning the classification of a drug within these categories is not specifically included in this manual. If further information is needed, a consolidated listing of drugs classified as "Ineffective," "Possibly Effective," or "Probably Effective" was summarized in SB 8-75-4, 18 January 1972. An updating of this list and current "Drug Safety and Effectiveness Information" will be published periodically in the SB 8-75 series.

5. Controlled substances

   a. *General.* The ordering, dispensing, and destruction of controlled substances in the United States is governed by the "Comprehensive Drug Abuse Prevention and Control Act of 1970" (also known as the Controlled Substances Act or Public Law (PL) 91-513, October 27, 1970). Essentially, this act combines the control of drugs formerly known as Class A, B, X, and M narcotics and DACA (Drug Abuse Control Amendment of 1965, which identified those drugs that have potential for high abuse) into one statute, with responsibility for enforcement placed on one agency, the Bureau of Narcotics and Dangerous Drugs (BNDD), of the U.S. Department of Justice. Most states have their own laws which supplement the Federal law. Although the practice of pharmacy on a military installation is not governed by the law of the state in which the installation is located, it is subject to the provisions of the "Comprehensive Drug Abuse Prevention and Control Act," PL 91-513. The Army does have regulations governing the handling of controlled substances which, in essence, are comparable to state laws. Army regulations are often more stringent than, or at least parallel to, the Federal law, but they are never less stringent than the Federal law. The question of which law or regulation to follow in a given situation then arises. The following rule of thumb should be followed if Army's regulations and Federal law differ, "the more stringent law or regulation is applicable." Regarding the handling of controlled substances, differences between the Federal law and Army regulation will be seen in several areas, such as labeling requirements and filing and destruction procedures. Where these differences exist, the more stringent requirements will be covered here.

   b. *Schedule substances.* The Controlled Substances Act designated controlled drugs into five schedules based on their potential for abuse. As pharmacy specialists, it is easy for you to determine which schedule a given drug belongs to simply by examining the commercial container in which the drug is supplied. The container will bear an identification symbol indicating the schedule in which the drug belongs. The symbol can appear in either of two ways: a capital C followed by the roman numeral indicating the schedule number (for example, C-II), or a capital C with the Roman numeral inside of it (for example, Ⓒ). The five schedules are defined as follows:

   (1) *Schedule I substances.* Have no accepted medical use in the United States. Some examples are heroin, marihuana, LSD, peyote, mescaline, psilocybin, tetrahydrocannabinols, ketobemidone, levomoramide, racemoramide, benzylmorphine, dihydromorphine, morphine methylsulfonate, nicocodeine, nicomorphine, and others.

   (2) *Schedule II substances.* Have a high abuse potential with severe psychic or physical dependence liability. Many have been known in the past as Class A Narcotic Drugs. Non-narcotic substances are currently included in this schedule. Some examples are: amphetamines, methamphetamines, methylphenidate, phenmetrazine, opium, morphine, codeine, dihydromorphinone, methadone, pantopon, meperidine, cocaine, anileridine, oxymorphone, and any other substance so designated by amendments to the Controlled Substances Act. The first difference between Federal law and Army regulations is encountered with Schedule II substances. By Army regulation, paregoric (which by Federal law is classified in Schedule III) and ethyl alcohol and alcoholic beverages (which by Federal law are not included in any schedule), must be received, dispensed, and accounted for in Army hospitals in the same manner as Schedule II substances. (However, commercial containers of paregoric, alcohol, or alcoholic beverages will *not* be imprinted with the C-II or Ⓒ symbol when you receive them.) You must be aware of the fact that these substances are being controlled by the Army in this manner because the Army Regulation, which in this case is more stringent than the Federal law, has to be followed.

   (3) *Schedule III substances.* Have an abuse potential less than those in Schedules I and II, and includes those drugs formerly known as Class B Narcotics and, in addition, non-narcotic

drugs, such as glutethimide, methyprylon, chlorhexadol, phencyclidine, sulfondiethylmethane, sulfonmethane, nalorphine, and some barbiturates, and any other items so designated by amendments to the Controlled Substances Act.

(4) Schedule IV substances. Have an abuse potential less than those listed in Schedule III and include drugs such as barbital, phenobarbital, methylphenobarbital, chloral betaine, chloral hydrate, ethchloruynol, ethinamate, meprobamate, paraldehyde, pentaetythritol chloral, methohexital, chlordiazepoxide, diazepam, and any other items so designated by amendments to the Controlled Substances Act.

(5) Schedule V substances. Have an abuse potential less than those listed in Schedule IV, and consist of those preparations formerly known as Exempt Narcotics, with the exception of paregoric. Paregoric is now listed as a Schedule III Controlled Substance but, as you have seen in *(2)* above, is received, dispensed, and accounted for in the Army as a Schedule II substance.

c. *Code R and Code K items.* Another method of classifying controlled substances is used in military medical supply channels and the Federal Supply Catalog: classification as Code R or Code K items. To be sure you are fully aware of the relationship between these items and the schedules, each term will be defined.

(1) Code R item is defined as those controlled substances classified in Schedule II, plus ethyl alcohol, alcoholic beverages, and paregoric.

(2) Code K item is defined as those controlled substances classified in Schedules III, IV, and V.

d. *Ordering.*

(1) The Controlled Substances Act outlines general guidelines which must be followed by everyone who orders and dispenses controlled substances. In the Army, the specific methods by which these guidelines are carried out are outlined in AR 40-2.

(2) While a special BNDD order form is used by medical supply to locally purchase Schedule II substances, all schedule substances are normally ordered by the pharmacy from medical supply by using a DA Form 2765-1 (Request for Issue or Turn-In). This policy may vary with installation policy, and other forms may be used.

e. *Record keeping.*

(1) When any controlled substance is received from medical supply, you will also receive a numbered voucher which shows the date and quantity of the substance you received. This voucher must be filed and will serve as your debit record when accounting for that substance. By law, Schedule II vouchers must be filed separately from Schedule III, IV, and V vouchers. The date, quantity received, and voucher number will be entered in the appropriate column of the DA Form 3862 (Controlled Substances Stock Record) which is maintained for that specific item. A separate DA Form 3862 must be maintained for each form in which the controlled substance is supplied. The metric system must be used for all entries where appropriate. When you receive controlled substances from medical supply, you will be required to sign a voucher, which is retained by medical supply, showing that these controlled substances have been delivered to you. Make sure that everything ordered is present, or deleted as appropriate, and that all items received are the exact items ordered before you sign for them.

(2) Individual prescriptions serve as your credit record for subtracting from DA Form 3862 the control substance dispensed. The manner in which specific preparations are accounted for depends on the schedule to which the preparation belongs.

(3) For Schedule II substances, ethyl alcohol, alcoholic beverages, and paregoric, each order for stock expended will be subtracted from the balance on hand shown on the DA Form 3862 maintained for that item. Each entry will show the date expended, the prescription number, and the amount expended. The *last* figure in the "Balance on Hand" column of the DA Form 3862 for that item will always reflect the *actual* amount on hand.

(4) Entries for Code R items will be made on DA Form 3862 on a daily basis with each prescription and/or voucher being recorded.

(5) For Schedule III, IV, and V controlled substances (and any other items designated by the commander), expenditures for each item will be summarized weekly and subtracted from the balance on hand shown on the DA Form 3862 maintained for that item. Concurrently, an inventory of all the stocks on hand will be conducted by pharmacy personnel and the inventory balance compared with the balance shown on DA Form 3862. An adjustment for minor overages and shortages caused by

operational handling or undiscoverable posting errors will be made by posting an inventory adjustment to the stock record since a series of small losses over an extended period of time could result in a major inventory shortage. All major inventory shortages will be investigated immediately and remedial action taken. Records of all investigations and remedial actions should be maintained in the pharmacy records.

(6) In event an error is made in posting, one line must be drawn through the incorrect entry and initialed and the correct entry made.

f. *Filing.*

(1) While the Controlled Substances Act provides three general methods by which persons receiving and dispensing controlled substances may maintain their prescription files, AR 40-2 provides one specific method by which prescriptions will be numbered and filed in Army pharmacies.

(2) At least three series of numbers will be used to number prescriptions filled in Army pharmacies—one for Schedule II substances, ethyl alcohol, alcholic beverages, and paregoric; one for Schedule III, IV, and V substances; and one for all other prescriptions. A corresponding file will be established for each series of numbers.

g. *Inventorying.*

(1) AR 40-2 requires that at least once each month a disinterested officer or senior noncommissioned officer be designated by the commander to inspect the stock records for controlled substances. He will conduct an inventory of each Schedule II substance, and all ethyl alcohol, alcoholic beverages, and paregoric, and verify that the amount of each drug or preparation actually in stock is the same amount show in the "Balance on Hand" column of the DA Form 3862 maintained for that item. At the same time he will verify all other entries. His findings, together with the date of the inspection and action taken, will be noted over his signature and grade immediately below the last entry on the card. Any discrepancies noted will be reported immediately in writing to the commander. Concurrently, he will inspect the stock records for at least 10 percent of the Schedule III, IV, and V items and include in his report to the commander any unusual expenditures or any major inventory discrepancies.

(2) If controlled substances are used in the manufacture of pharmaceutical preparations, a DD Form 1289 (Prescription Form) with the R_x symbol lined out will be used to account for their expenditure. Such orders will be authenticated and signed by the officer in charge of the pharmacy. The quantity expended will be subtracted from the DA Form 3862 maintained for that item, and the order will be filed in the appropriate prescription file.

h. *Security.* The Controlled Substances Act directs that Schedule II substances be stored in at least a securely locked, substantially constructed cabinet, and Schedule III, IV, and V substances be either stored in such a locked cabinet or dispersed throughout the stock of noncontrolled drugs in such a manner as to obstruct their theft or diversion. In the Army, controlled substances must be safeguarded at each storage location within a medical facility by placing stocks in appropriate security devices such as a vault, safe, locked cabinet, or locked cage. At least annually, the installation provost marshal must be requested to survey the adequacy of the security provided, and corrective action must be taken as indicated. In other words, in an Army hospital pharmacy all controlled substances must be securely locked in the pharmacy vault or stored in some other secure area.

i. *Dispensing.*

(1) The dispensing process must be examined from two aspects, inpatient dispensing and outpatient dispensing. The Controlled Substances Act sets guidelines for dispensing controlled substances which deal mostly with the outpatient situation. More specific and stringent guidance on how controlled substances are to be dispensed, labeled, and handled within an Army hospital can be found in AR 40-2.

(2) Controlled substances will be dispensed in bulk to inpatient agencies only upon receipt of a properly written and authenticated prescription (DD Form 1289) with the R_x symbol lined out. This order must be signed by an individual authorized to write prescriptions or by a registered nurse. The order will show the name of the agency receiving the controlled substance and the date. This prescription will be used as a credit voucher to deduct the quantity dispensed from the DA Form 3862 maintained for that item. Labeling requirements for controlled substances issued in bulk to wards, clinics, and other authorized agencies will be prescribed locally by the commander.

(3) While the Controlled Substances Act allows oral-prescription orders for Schedule III and IV substances (and Schedule II substances in an emergency), AR 40-2 states that all prescriptions filled in Army pharmacies will be stamped, typed, or written in ink and will be signed by the prescriber. Thus, no oral prescriptions are authorized in military pharmacies.

(4) Both the Controlled Substances Act and AR 40-2 require prescriptions for schedule drugs to contain the date of issue; name, rank, corps, organization, and address of the patient; and signature of the prescriber. The Controlled Substances Act does state that the physician's BNDD registration number has to appear on prescriptions for schedule drugs. Military physicians are exempt from the requirement to register, but by regulation they must place their service identification number, in lieu of the registration number, on all prescriptions for controlled substances. AR 40-2 also requires that the name of the prescriber be typed, handprinted, or stamped on a controlled prescription in addition to his signature.

(5) Both the Controlled Substances Act and AR 40-2 require that the label on the container of controlled substance dispensed to individual patient will contain:

(a) Prescription number.

(b) Identity of the facility dispensing the controlled substance.

(c) Name of the prescriber.

(d) Name of the patient.

(e) Date of dispensing.

(f) Directions for use and any caution or statement (such as "shake well" or "refrigerate") if needed.

(g) Transfer warning or legend "CAUTION: FEDERAL LAW PROHIBITS THE TRANSFER OF THIS DRUG TO ANY PERSON OTHER THAN THE PATIENT FOR WHOM IT WAS PRESCRIBED" in boldface type.

(6) In addition to these seven requirements, AR 40-2 also requires that all prescription labels contain the name and strength of the drug, except when the prescriber directs otherwise; the initials of the person typing the prescription label; and the legend "KEEP OUT OF REACH OF CHILDREN" in boldface type.

(7) Both by law and by regulation, prescriptions for Schedule II substances cannot be refilled. In addition, AR 40-2 extends this restriction to ethyl alcohol, alcoholic beverages, and paregoric, and prohibits personnel who are authorized to write prescriptions for Code R items from prescribing them for themselves or for members of their family.

(8) If the pharmacy does not have enough of a Schedule II item to fill a prescription order completely, partial filling of the prescription is permitted provided the balance is supplied to the patient within 72 hours. When a prescription for a Schedule II substance is partially filled, a notation of the fact must be made on the prescription and the prescriber must be notified of the action taken.

(9) Prescriptions for Schedules III through V controlled substances (and any other drug designated by the commander) cannot be refilled unless such refilling is authorized by the prescriber on the original prescription. These prescriptions cannot be refilled more than five times and cannot be refilled more than six months after the date of issue. When a prescription for any controlled substance in Schedule III or IV is refilled, the pharmacist will enter his initials, the date of refilling, and the amount of drug refilled on the back of the original prescription form or another appropriate uniformly maintained record which indicates prescription refills.

(10) The partial dispensing of Schedules III, IV, and V controlled substances is authorized provided that each partial dispensing is recorded in the same manner as a renewal, the total quantity dispensed in all partial orders does not exceed the total quantity prescribed, and no dispensing occurs six months after the issuance of the prescription order. Although authorized by law, the partial dispensing of Schedule III through V substances in Army hospitals would be a relatively rare situation such as this: the pharmacy temporarily runs out of stock of the item prescribed and dispenses only enough drug to hold the patient over until new stocks can be obtained from medical supply.

(11) While the Controlled Substances Act authorized the dispensing of Schedule V substances without a prescription provided certain conditions are met, AR 40-2 limits nonprescription dispensing to small quantities of noncontrolled pharmaceuticals suitable for relief of distress due to conditions such as simple headache and mild indigestion. Thus, as a pharmacy technician, you need not become concerned with the details of over-the-counter dispensing of Schedule V drugs.

(12) When a pharmacy does not have a controlled substance required by a patient and the patient has no alternative source of that drug reasonably available to him, the pharmacy may obtain it from a second pharmacy. In such a

situation neither pharmacy need register as a distributor. Records of the transaction must be kept, however, and the amount transferred may not exceed that necessary for immediate dispensing. The transaction is recorded as a dispensing by the pharmacy providing the drug and as a receipt by the pharmacy receiving it. Each must retain a signed receipt of the transaction which, if it involves a Schedule II drug, must be an official order form. Since the Pharmacy Service does not have official order forms for controlled substances, arrangement will have to be through medical supply for the transfer of a Schedule II substance.

    j. *Destruction.* Under the provisions of AR 40-2, whenever controlled substances have deteriorated to the point where they are not usable for the purpose originally intended, are of questionable potency, or have had their identity compromised, they will be reported to the commander for a determination of disposition. Commanders will take such action as may be appropriate and, when indicated, will investigate negligence or carelessness and will direct appropriate disposition of the reported items. If destruction is directed, it will be accomplished in the presence of a witnessing officer and such other officials as may be required by regulations. A record of such destruction, signed by the witnessing officer, will be filed in the controlled substances file as authority for dropping the items from the records of the accounts. (AR 40-61 gives procedures for and documentation of this action.)

    6. **UCMJ.** In addition to the specific Federal Statutes referred to above, pharmacy technicians are subject to the Uniform Code of Military Justice, Article 134, which includes the wrongful possession or use of habit-forming narcotic drugs.

    7. **Prescription ownership.** From the time a patient receives his prescription from the prescriber and surrenders it to the pharmacist for filling, there is no doubt that the patient is the rightful owner of that prescription. Once a prescription has been turned over to the pharmacy for filling and the patient has received his medication, the prescription is a necessary legal document for the pharmacy's records and legally belongs to the pharmacy. The courts also say that if a patient brings a prescription for filling but decides after the medication has been compounded that he does not want it, the written prescription still belongs to him and he may demand that it be returned.

    8. **Confidentiality of prescriptions.** Much confidential and privileged information is contained in the prescription file regarding the people of a given community. The nature of prescriptions must not be discussed with unauthorized persons nor may they be permitted to examine the files. If it is important that a person know the contents of a prescription for legal or other reasons, he can obtain a court order to obtain the necessary information. People must not be allowed to examine the files unless they are acting within their official capacity, such as the issuing physician, inventory officer, auditor, or member of an IG team. From the standpoint of pharmaco-medical ethics, it is bad to let one physician examine the prescriptions of another physician; it may also be an invasion of privacy.

    9. **Prescription copies.** Frequently, a patient will ask for a copy of his prescription when he is moving to a different area or going on vacation. You may legally provide a patient with a copy of his prescription IF you adhere to the following:

    a. All copies must plainly, and in large letters, be marked or stamped "COPY."

    b. Prescriptions which cannot be refilled should, in addition to "COPY," bear the words "NOT TO BE REFILLED." Some pharmacists add the notation "FOR INFORMATION ONLY."

    c. Those prescriptions which can be legally refilled (that is, those which do not require a prescription initially) or those which are marked to be refilled a specified number of times must bear a marking instructing future pharmacists regarding the number of times the medication may still be refilled.

    d. You must be alert for those asking for copies of narcotic, barbiturate, or amphetamine type drugs. It may be wise to ask the prescriber for his consent before doing so. Whenever possible, avoid issuing copies of this type of prescription.

BASIC FUNDAMENTALS OF THE PRESCRIPTION

CONTENTS

Page

SECTION I : PRESCRIPTION LANGUAGE-PHARMACEUTICAL LATIN

1.	Latin in pharmacy and medicine	1
2.	Commonly used Latin abbreviations, words, and translations	1
3.	Common names of drugs and the Latin counterpart	3

SECTION II : THE PRESCRIPTION

3

4.	Superscription	3
5.	Inscription	3
6.	Subscription	4
7.	Signa (signatura)	4
8.	Abbreviation of names of drugs	4
9.	Abbreviation in subscription and signa	4
10.	Prescription examples	4
11.	Importance of pharmaceutical calculations	6
12.	Fractions	7
13.	Rules applying to all fractions	7
14.	Working with fractions	8
15.	Lowest terms	8
16.	Lowest common denomincator (LCD)	8
17.	Adding fractions	9
18.	Subtracting fractions	9
19.	Multiplying fractions	10
20.	Dividing fractions	11
21.	Decimals	12
22.	Adding decimals	12
23.	Subtracting decimals	13
24.	Multiplication of decimals	13
25.	Division of decimals	13
26.	Roman numerals	14
27.	Weights and measures	14
28.	Metric system	15
29.	Apothecary system	17
30.	Avoirdupois system	21
31.	Relationship and approximate equivalents	21
32.	Ratio and proportion	22
33.	Percentage preparations	23
34.	Ratio preparations	25
35.	Specific gravity	26
36.	Specific gravity of liquids	26
37.	Specific gravity of solids	28
38.	Application of specific gravity to pharmaceutical Problems	29
39.	Specific volume	31
40.	Density	31
41.	Temperature	31
42.	Temperature calculation	32
43.	Temperature conversion	32
44.	Dosage	33
45.	Concentration and dilution	36
46.	Alligation	36

BASIC FUNDAMENTALS of the PRESCRIPTION

Section I. PRESCRIPTION LANGUAGE–PHARMACEUTICAL LATIN

1. Latin in pharmacy and medicine. Latin in prescription writing is centuries old. Although more and more of the prescription is being written in English today, most prescriptions are in part written in Latin or use the Latin abbreviations. As long as physicians continue to use Latin and Latin abbreviations in prescription writing, the pharmacist will have to be able to read and fully understand the terms that are used. Latin used in medicine and prescription writing may be intended to conceal the nature of the medication from the patient, to reduce the possibility of a patient's tampering with a prescription, or to make the prescription universally legible to pharmacists regardless of their national language. Probably the most outstanding reason for the use of Latin in medicine and pharmacy is through force of habit. It has been done for so long that it is hard to break away from the trend. Medical and pharmacy colleges teach the physician to write prescriptions in Latin and the pharmacist to be able to interpret them.

2. Commonly used Latin abbreviations, words, and translations. Since it would be extremely time consuming and of doubtful value to present an entire course in Pharmaceutical Latin here, it is strongly suggested that you read, learn, and *memorize* the words, abbreviations, and meanings on the right. This will familiarize you with the more common terms and phrases used in prescription writing and enable you to understand the physician's or other prescriber's orders. Later, when you have time and a desire to improve your command of Latin, as pertinent to pharmacy, procure a copy of an authoritative pharmacy text. With the aid of such a text, the average individual may become familiar with Latin as it applies to the professions of medicine and pharmacy.

Latin	*Abbreviation*	*English Translation*
ad	ad	to; up to
ad libitum	ad lib.	at pleasure
adde, addendus	add.	add, let them be added
agitata ante usum	agit. ant. us.	shake before using
albus	alb.	white
alternus horis	alt. hor.	alternate hours
amplus	amplus	large
ana	aa.	of each
ante	a.	before
ante cibos; ante cibum	a.c.	before meals; before food
ante meridiem	A.M.	before noon
applicandus	applicand.	to be applied
aqua	aq.	water
aqua bullions	aq. bull.	boiling water
aqua destillata	aq. dest.	distilled water
aqua fervens	aq. ferv.	hot water
aqua frigida	aq. frig.	cold water
aqua forte	aq. fort.	nitric acid
aromaticus	arom.	aromatic
argentum	arg.	silver
aurio	aur.	ear
bene	ben.	well
bibe	bib.	drink
bis in die	b.i.d.	twice a day
bolus	bol.	a large pill
capeat	cap.	let him take
capsula	cap.	a capsule
charta	chart.	paper (powder)
charta cerati	chart. cerat.	waxed paper
cibus	cib.; c.	food
cochleare amplum	coch. amp.	tablespoonful
cochleare infans	coch. inf.	teaspoonful
cochleare magnum	coch. mag.	tablespoonful
cochleare maximum	coch. max.	tablespoonful
cochleare medium	coch. med.	dessertspoonful
cochleare minimum	coch. min.	teaspoonful
cochleare modicum	coch. mod.	dessertspoonful
cochleare parvum	coch. parv.	teaspoonful
cochleare paulus	coch. paul.	teaspoonful
cochleare plenum	coch. plen.	tablespoonful
cola, colatus	col.	strain, strained
collunarium	collun.	nasal douche
collutorium	collut.	mouthwash
collyrium	collyr.	eye lotion
compositus	comp.	compound,

Latin	Abbreviation	English Translation	Latin	Abbreviation	English Translation
		compounded	misce	M.	Mix
congius	cong.	gallon	mistura	mist.	mixture
continuentur remedia	cont. rem.	continue the medication	mitte	mitt.	send
			modo praescripto	mod. praes.	in the manner prescribed
creta	cret.	chalk			
cum	c.; c̄	with	mollis	moll.	soft
da	d.	give	nasus	n.	nostril
decem	decem	ten	nebula	nebul.	a spray
dentur	dent.; d.	let be given; give	niger	nig.	black
dentur tales doses	d.t.d.	give of such doses	nocte	noct.	at night
dexter	dext.	right			
dies	d.	day	nocte maneque	noct. maneq.; n. et m.	night and morning
diebus alternis	dieb. alt.	on alternate days			
diebus secundis	dieb. secund.	every second day	non	non	not
diebus tertiis	dieb. tert.	every three days	non repetatur	non rep.	do not repeat
diluo; dilutus	dil.	dilute	octarius	O.; oct.	a pint
dispensa; dispensatur	disp.	dispense; let be dispensed	oculus	ocul.	the eye
			oculo dextro	O.D.; ocul. dext.	the right eye, in the
dividatur	div.	divide	oculo sinistro	O.S.; ocul. sinist.	the left eye, in the
dividatur in partes aequales	div. in par. aeq.	divide into equal parts	oculo laevo	O.L.; ocul. laev.	the left eye, in the
			oculo utro	O.U.; ocul. utro	in each eye
dosis	dos.; d.	a dose	oleum	ol.	oil
drachma	ʒ	a drachm	omnis	omn.	every
dura	dur.	hard	omni altera hora	omn. alt. hor.	every alternate hour
e	e	out of; in			
et	et	and	omni hora	omn. hor.	every hour
e lacte	e lact.	in milk	omni mane	omn. man.	every morning
ex modo praescripto	e.m.p.	in the manner prescribed	omni quarta hora	omn. 4 hor.	every four hours
			parvus	parv.	small
fac; fiat; fiant	ft.	make; let be made	per	per	by means of
ferrum	ferr.	iron	per os	per os	by mouth
filtra	filtra	filter	phiala	phial.; p.	a bottle
flavus	flav.	yellow	phiala fusca	phial. fusc.	a brown bottle
folium; folia	fol.	leaf; leaves	phiala prius agitata	p.p.a.	the bottle first being shaken
fortis; fortior	fort.	strong; stronger			
gargarisma	garg.	a gargle	placebo	placebo	I please
gradatim	grad.	gradually	plumbum	plumb.	lead
grossus	gros.	large	ponderosus	pond.	heavy
gramma	Gm.	gram	post aurum	post aur.	behind the ear
granum	gr.	grain	post cibum; post cibos	p.c.	after food; after meals
gutta; guttae	gtt.	drop; drops			
hora	hor.; h	an hour	post meridiem	P.M.	afternoon
hora somni	h.s.	at bedtime	praecipitatus	ppt.	precipitated
hydrargyrum	hydrarg.	mercury	pro capillis	pro capil.	for the hair
in aurem sinistram	in aur. sinist.	in the left ear	pro recto	pro rect.	rectal
			pro re nata	p.r.n.	as occasion arises
in die	in d.	in a day	pro usu externo	pro us. ext.	for external use
in dies	ind.	daily	pulvis	pulv.	powder
in oculo laevo	in ocul. laev; O.L.	in the left eye	quantitatim sufficientum	q.s.	a sufficient quantity
inter	inter	between			
inter cibos	int. cib.	between meals	quaque	qq.	each, every
inter noctem	int. noct.	during the night	quaque die	q.d.	every day
in vitro	in vit.	in glass	quaque hora	q.h.	every hour
lac	lac	milk	quater in diem	q.i.d.	four times a day
levis	lev.	light	repetatur	rep.	let it be repeated
libra	lb.	pound	recipe	Rx; ℞	take thou
liquor	liq.	liquid; solution	ruber	rub.	red
lotio	lot.	lotion	scrupulus	℈	scruple
luteus	lut.	yellow	secundum artem	s.a.	according to the art
magnus	mag.	large	secundum legem	s.l.	according to law
mane	man.	morning, in the	semi	sem.	one-half
massa	mass.	a mass	semissem	ss	one-half
milligramma	mg.; mgm.	a milligram	sesqui	sesqui	one and a half
minimum	♏	a minim			

Latin	Abbreviation	English Translation
signa	sig.; S.	write
simul	simul	at one time
sine	s̄	without
sine aqua	sin. q.; s̄ aq.	without water
si opus sit	s.o.s.	if there is need
solve	solv.	dissolve
spiritus frumenti	sp. frum.	whiskey
spiritus vini rectificatus	S.V.R.	alcohol
spiritus vini tenuis	S.V.T.	diluted alcohol
spiritus vini vitis	sp. vin. vit.	brandy
statim	stat.	immediately
succus	suc.	juice
syrupus	syr.	syrup
tabella	tab.	tablet
talis	tal.; t.	of such
ter in die	t.i.d.	three times a day
tres; trium	tres; trium	three
tussis	tuss.	cough
uncia	℥	ounce
unguentum	ung.; ungt.	ointment
ut dictum	ut dict.	as directed
viridis	vir.	green

3. Common names of drugs and the Latin counterpart

Common Name	Latin
Acid	Acidum
Alcohol	Spiritus Vini Rectificatus (SVR)
Belladonna Leaf	Belladonna Folium
Belladonna Root	Belladonna Radix
Bitter	Amari
Cascara	Rhamnus Purshiana
Castor Oil	Oleum Ricini
Charcoal	Carbo
Wood Charcoal	Carbo Ligni
Clove Oil	Oleum Caryophylli
Coal Tar	Pix Carbonis
Coal Tar Solution	Liquor Carbonis Detergens; Liquor Picis Carbonis
Cod Liver Oil	Oleum Morrhuae
Corn Oil	Oleum Maydis
Cottonseed Oil	Oleum Gosaypie Seminis
Earth	Terra
Hard Soap	Sapo Duris
Juice	Succus
Lard	Adeps
Lime	Calx
Linseed Oil	Oleum Lini
Medicinal Soft Soap	Sapo Mollis Medicinalis
Oil	Oleum
Ointment	Unguentum
Orange	Aurantium
Peppermint	Mentha Piperita
Peppermint Oil	Oleum Menthal Piperitae
Purified Cotton	Gossypium Purificatum
Rosin	Resina
Seed	Semen
Sherry Wine	Vinum Xericum
Solution	Liquor
Spearmint Oil	Oleum Menthae Viridis
Spermaceti	Cetaceum
Starch	Amylum
Sucrose	Surcrosum; Saccharum
Sweet	Dulcis
Syrup	Syrupus
Turpentine	Terebinthinae
Wax	Cera
Wild Cherry	Prunus Virginiana
Whiskey	Spiritus Frumenti
White Ointment	Ungunentum Alba
White Wax	Cera Alba
Wool Fat	Adeps Lanae
Yellow Ointment	Unguentum Flavum
Yellow Wax	Cera Flava

Section II. THE PRESCRIPTION

The word prescription is a derivation of two Latin words; namely, "prae," meaning "before," and "scribo," meaning "I write." Therefore, the prescription is something written beforehand, hence a rule or direction. It is a written order to the pharmacist by a physician, dentist, veterinarian, or other licensed practitioner, instructing him to compound and/or dispense a specific medication for a specific patient. Through common misuse, the word prescription has also come to mean the completed medication itself. The completed prescription is generally divided into four subdivisions: Superscription, Inscription, Subscription, and Signa. These four parts, in addition to the patient's name, address, and age; the date of writing; and the prescriber's signature, address, and registry number, make up the correct completed prescription.

4. Superscription. The superscription is that which is written above. The superscription always consists of, and is in fact represented by the symbol R_x. This symbol is most frequently printed as part of the prescription blank. R_x is taken from the Latin "recipe," meaning "take thou." It is also thought that the slash across the "R" is a sign for Jupiter and is a carry-down of an invocation to the god.

5. Inscription. The inscription, or what is written within, contains the actual ingredients and their respective amounts. Each ingredient is placed on a separate line, and all important words are capitalized. Quantities are written, as will be seen in section III (Pharmaceutical Calculations), in either the metric or the apothecary system. In the apothecary system, the amount is shown by a symbol followed by a roman numeral, e.g., ℥ viii (eight ounces). In the metric system, a symbol is not used, grams or milliliters being written or understood. The inscription may be further subdivided into base, adjuvant, corrective, and vehicle.

    a. Base. The base is the main or active ingredient or ingredients designed to restore the patient to health.

    b. Adjuvant. The adjuvant is a substance which increases the efficiency of the base.

    c. Corrective. The corrective modifies or counteracts any undesirable effects of the base or adjuvant.

    d. Vehicle. The vehicle may serve several purposes. It may give proper dosage form (producing a liquid, suppository, capsule, etc.). It may dilute so that the patient may take one capsule or one teaspoonful rather than a few grains or a few drops. It may be used to improve taste or appearance. Or it may aid the patient in receiving the proper amount of a potent drug.

6. **Subscription.** The subscription, or that written below, follows the inscription. It tells the pharmacist the manner of compounding and what the finished product shall be. For example: *M. Fiant solutio* means to mix and let a solution be made. The order of the ingredients on the prescription is not necessarily the order in which they are incorporated into the medication. This is up to the pharmacist and is done according to the art of pharmacy. As you will see later in the course, order of mixing has a pronounced effect on many prescriptions and can be the cause of incompatibilities.

7. **Signa (signatura).** The signa follows the subscription and means literally to write. It tells the pharmacist the directions to the patient which will be typed on the label. An example of a signa is: ℨ i t. i. d. Since most individuals have no idea of the meaning of a drachm (ℨ), it must be changed to its approximate equivalent, one teaspoonful. The label would then read: "Take one teaspoonful three times a day." Prescriptions should bear exact instructions to the patient as in figure 2-1 rather than the overused "ut dict," which means "as directed." When directions are specified exactly, there is no doubt that the patient understands how much of the medication he is to take, and at what intervals. Also, by using the directions, the pharmacist is able to check more accurately for excessive dosage. Study figure 2-1 to see the relationship of the superscription, the inscription and its parts, the subscription, and the signa.

8. **Abbreviations of names of drugs.** In writing a prescription, it is always desirable that the official names of agents be used and spelled out completely. Abbreviations or chemical symbols are confusing and can lead to serious error. An abbreviation such as Hyd. Chlor. is not clear. It could be taken for chloral hydrate, for calomel (mercurous chloride), or for mercuric chloride. Chloral hydrate is a hypnotic, used to induce sleep. Calomel is a purgative. Mercuric chloride is a deadly poison even in the smallest doses, and is intended for use as an antiseptic in external preparations to be used on inanimate objects. You can readily see what would happen if one agent were mistaken for another! Imagine the possibilities of confusion with HgCl and $HgCl_2$. HgCl is calomel, the purgative; $HgCl_2$ is mercuric chloride, the poison.

9. **Abbreviations in subscription and signa.** The more important abbreviations for use in the subscription and the signa are given on the preceding pages.

10. **Prescription examples.** Read each of the prescriptions shown in figure 2-2 in English and try to pick out the prescription parts previously described in the text and shown in figure 2-1. Note that the prescriptions in figure 2-2 are written in longhand and use abbreviations. This is the form in which you will most likely see them in the pharmacy.

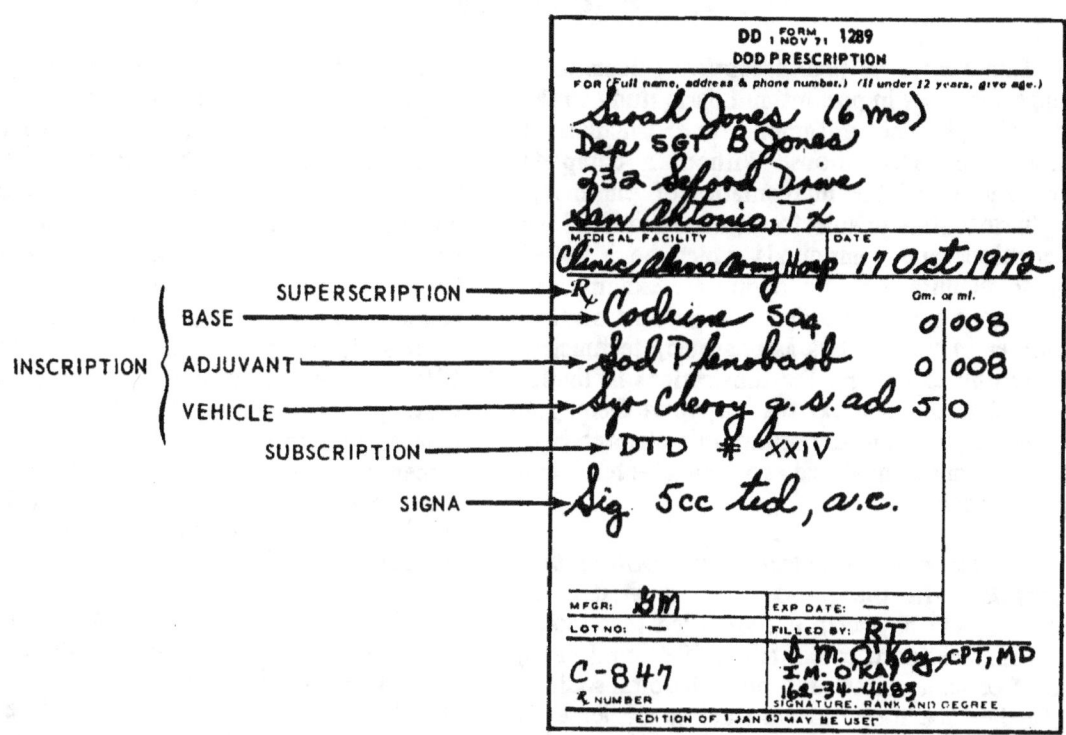

Figure 1. Components of a prescription.

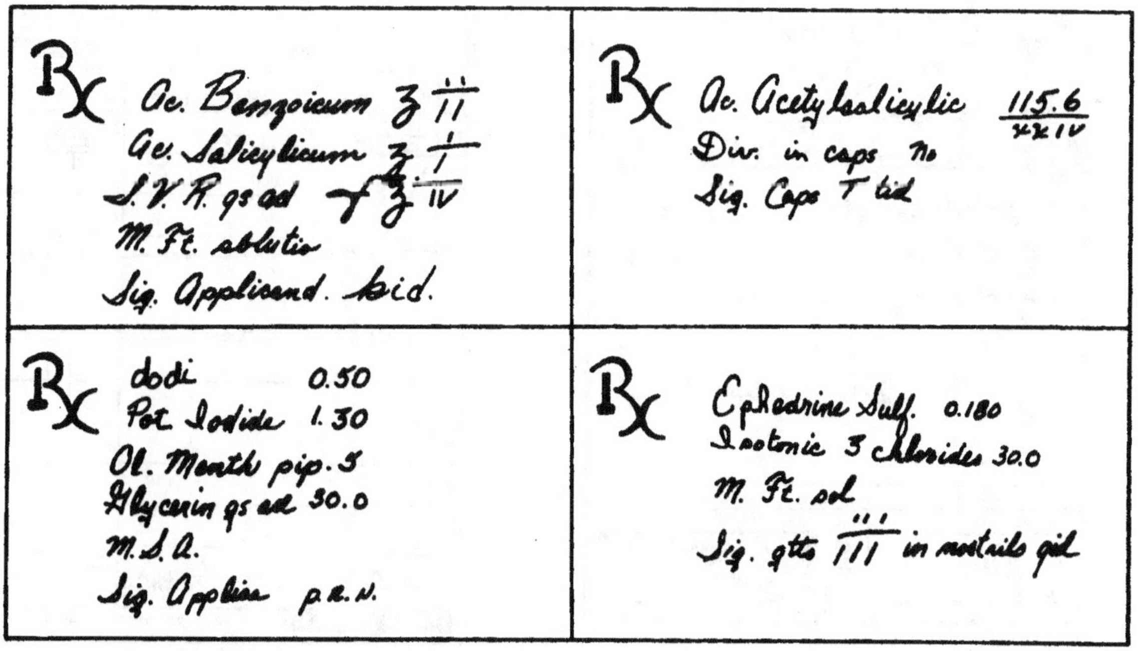

Figure 2. Prescription examples.

Section III. PHARMACEUTICAL CALCULATIONS

11. Importance of pharmaceutical calculations. Perhaps the most important and basic study to the pharmacist is the arithmetic and calculations pertinent to prescriptions. Without a complete understanding of the mathematics of pharmacy, the pharmacist is unable to dispense many of the prescriptions and compounds which he is called upon to manufacture. Following are examples of prescriptions and drug orders which you are apt to encounter in your duties as pharmacy technician. By carefully examining the illustrations in figures 2-3 and 2-4, and the text that supports them, you will realize just how important this chapter is to your becoming qualified to manufacture and dispense medicinals.

a. Example of calculations involved in a prescription. In the prescription illustrated by figure 2-3, the physician has specified that each 5 ml. of medication is to contain 0.008 Gm. (8 mg.) each of codeine sulfate and phenobarbital sodium. He further specifies that you are to dispense 24 doses of this completed medication. How much codeine sulfate, phenobarbital sodium, and cherry syrup will you use in compounding this preparation? What will the total volume of the completed prescription be and what size bottle will be used to contain it? Are the doses of each ingredient safe for this 6-month-old child? When you have completed this chapter, you will readily be able to arrive at the answer: 192 mg. each of codeine sulfate and phenobarbital sodium, and enough cherry syrup to make the product measure 120 ml. are necessary in compounding this prescription correctly. The total volume of the completed prescription will be 120 ml. and will be dispensed in a 4-ounce bottle. The doses are safe for this patient. In addition, you will know that the label for this medication should direct that one teaspoonful be given 3 times a day before meals.

b. Example of calculations involved in a bulk order. Figure 2-4 shows a bulk order for an instrument sterilizer solution. The pharmacist has to calculate how much concentrated benzalkonium chloride solution will be necessary to make 4000

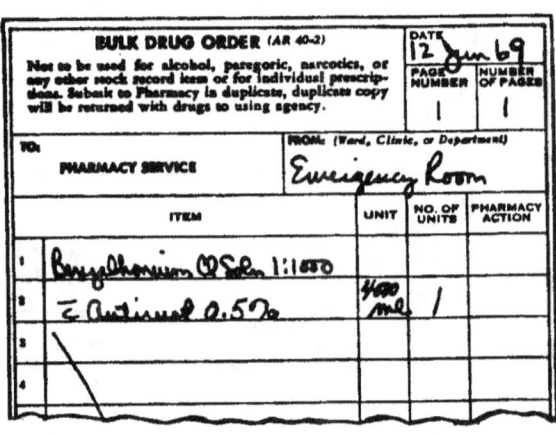

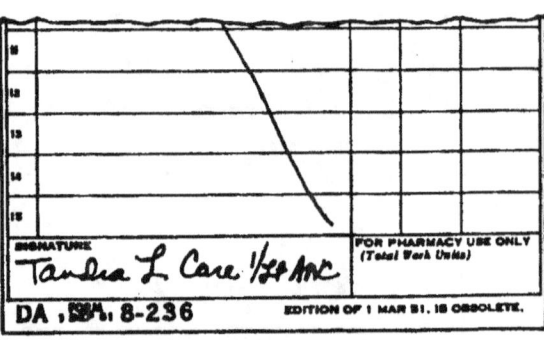

Figure 3. Example of calculations involved in a prescription.

Figure 4. Example of calculations involved in a bulk order.

ml. of a 1:1000 dilution. He will also have to be able to calculate the number of grams of antirust to be used to obtain a 0.5 percent concentration. Upon completing this chapter, it will not be difficult for you to calculate the necessary quantities as being 40 ml. of 10-percent benzalkonium chloride concentrate and 20 Gm. of antirust to make up 4000 ml. of finished solution. These have been but two examples of the absolute necessity of a sound understanding of pharmaceutical arithmetic in pharmacy. As you progress through this chapter, many more will be illustrated and solved.

c. Ground work for pharmaceutical calculations. At first the material that is forthcoming may seem juvenile to you, and you may be inclined to skip over some of the basic aspects. DON'T! Mistakes occur every day in simple addition, subtraction, multiplication, and division. Have you ever caught yourself making such an error? Well, in some places, errors can be allowed for and are not of too much significance, but in pharmacy there is no place for error. First, then, before delving in to the new material, let's begin with a review of fractions and decimals. Here is the place to check yourself on your work. If you work all the problems in fractions and decimals presented in the next few pages, you are well on your way to success in pharmaceutical calculations.

12. Fractions. A fraction represents a simple division problem. It expresses one or more of the equal parts into which a whole number is divided. The fraction $\frac{4}{5}$, then, means five divided into four equal parts of a possible five.

a. Numerator. The number above the separating line is called the numerator. It tells how many parts of the whole are used. In our example $\frac{4}{5}$, four parts of the whole are used.

b. Denominator. The denominator is the number below the separating line and represents the number of parts into which the whole is divided. Again using $\frac{4}{5}$ as an example, the whole (1) is broken into five equal parts, four of which remain.

c. Mixed numbers. Numbers made up of a whole number plus a fraction are called mixed numbers. For example, $1\frac{4}{5}$ has the whole number, 1, and the fraction, $\frac{4}{5}$, and is consequently a mixed number. It means that we have a whole of 1, plus 4 of the 5 parts of another whole.

d. Proper fractions. A fraction having a numerator which is smaller than its denominator is a proper fraction. It always is less than a whole number. Again, $\frac{4}{5}$ is a proper fraction.

e. Improper fractions. A fraction having a numerator larger than or equal to its denominator is an improper fraction, and it is always equal to or greater than a whole number. For example, $\frac{5}{4}$ is an improper fraction. It is the same as $1\frac{1}{4}$ ($\frac{5}{4} = \frac{4}{4}$ and $\frac{1}{4}$; $\frac{4}{4} = 1$).

f. Relative values of fractions. Let's compare the relative values of several fractions. Of $\frac{1}{5}$, $\frac{1}{6}$, $\frac{1}{3}$, and $\frac{1}{4}$, the smallest is $\frac{1}{6}$. Thus, if fractions have the same numerator, but different denominators, the one with the largest denominator is the smallest in value. Comparing $\frac{2}{5}$, $\frac{3}{5}$, and $\frac{4}{5}$; the largest is $\frac{4}{5}$. Thus, in fractions having the same denominator but different numerators, the one with the largest numerator is the largest. To compare fractions with different numerators and different denominators is more difficult.

13. Rules applying to all fractions. Fractions are division problems and follow three basic rules—

a. Value of fractions maintained. If the numerator and denominator are both multiplied or divided by the same number, the value of the fraction is *not* changed. *Example:* Multiplying both the numerator and denominator of $\frac{1}{3}$ by 3, you get $\frac{3}{9}$ which equals $\frac{1}{3}$; $\frac{3}{9}$ divided by 3 (both numerator and denominator) equals $\frac{1}{3}$ which is equal to $\frac{3}{9}$.

b. Multiplying the value of fractions. If the numerator is multiplied or the denominator divided by a number, the value of the fraction is *multiplied* by that number. *Example:* Multiplying the numerator of $\frac{1}{3}$ by 3 you have $\frac{3}{3}$ which is three times as large; or if you divide the denominator of $\frac{3}{3}$ by 3 you have $\frac{1}{1}$ or 1, which is three times as large.

c. Dividing the value of fractions. If the numerator is divided or the denominator multiplied by a number, the value of the fraction is divided by that number. *Example:* Dividing the numerator of $\frac{3}{9}$ by 3 you have $\frac{1}{9}$, or by multiplying the denominator of $\frac{3}{9}$ by 3 you have $\frac{3}{27}$ which is also $\frac{1}{9}$.

14. Working with fractions. When working with fractions, you often have to reduce a whole number to an improper fraction or reduce an improper fraction to a whole or mixed number.

a. Reducing a whole or mixed number to an improper fraction.
 (1) Whole number reduction. To reduce a whole number to an improper fraction, it is necessary to know into how many parts you want to divide the whole (the denominator). If you wish to convert 6, for instance, to an improper fraction having 5 parts, you will have 5 as the denominator. If you reduce 1 to an improper fraction having 5 parts, you would have $\frac{5}{5}$. The whole number, 6, when converted to an improper fraction with 5 as the denominator, would be 6 times as large, or $\frac{5}{5} \times 6 = \frac{30}{5}$.

 (2) Mixed number reduction. A mixed number is handled in the same manner. To reduce $8\frac{2}{10}$ to 10ths: $1 = \frac{10}{10}$; then $\frac{10}{10} \times 8 = \frac{80}{10}$ and $\frac{80}{10}$ plus the original $\frac{2}{10} = \frac{82}{10}$, the number of 10ths in $8\frac{2}{10}$.

b. Reducing an improper fraction to a whole or mixed number. As previously stated, a fraction is simply a division problem. For this reason, by dividing the denominator into the numerator, you will get a whole number if the division is even, or a mixed number (whole number plus a remaining fraction) if the division is not even. *Example:* Reduce $\frac{20}{2}$: $\frac{20}{2} = 20 \div 2 = 10$, a whole number; or reduce $\frac{35}{4}$: $\frac{35}{4} = 35 \div 4 = 8\frac{3}{4}$, a mixed number.

15. Lowest terms. A fraction is said to be in its lowest terms when the numerator and denominator cannot be divided by the same number. To illustrate: $\frac{3}{9}$, $\frac{6}{27}$, and $\frac{9}{36}$ are NOT in their lowest terms, for both the numerator and denominator can be divided by a common number. The 3 and 9 in $\frac{3}{9}$ can each be divided by 3 to give $\frac{1}{3}$ which is the lowest terms; the 6 and 27 in $\frac{6}{27}$ by 3 to give $\frac{2}{9}$, the lowest terms; and the 9 and 36 in $\frac{9}{36}$ by 9 to give $\frac{1}{4}$, the lowest terms. These final numbers, then, $\frac{1}{3}$, $\frac{2}{9}$, and $\frac{1}{4}$ are fractions in their lowest terms.

16. Lowest common denominator (LCD). When you add, subtract, or compare fractions, it is necessary to have them in common terms. As apples cannot be added to oranges or automobiles to airplanes, fractions with different denominators cannot be added. By changing apples and oranges to fruit, their common denominator, they can be added. This is also true of fractions. The common denominator can be found by two methods: by multiplying the denominators together, and by a "visual method."

a. Multiplying denominators to find a common denominator. When all the different denominators of the fractions with which you are dealing are multiplied together, the resulting number is common to all. It is not, however, always the lowest number common to all. For example, to find a denominator common to $\frac{1}{4}$, $\frac{1}{3}$, $\frac{1}{2}$, $\frac{1}{8}$, and $\frac{1}{16}$: Multiply the denominators (all of which are different)— 4 x 3 x 2 x 8 x 16—you get 3072, the common denominator.

   b. Visual method. Visually you can see that 48 is also a denominator common to all the fractions in the preceding example and is much smaller and easier to work with than 3072; 48 is also the *lowest* common denominator. Obtaining the LCD by the visual method is not always easy. The best starting point is to try the denominator which is largest; if it does not work, double it. If doubling the largest denominator does not work, triple it; eventually you will arrive at a common denominator. You must always change the denominators to their LCD before adding, subtracting, or comparing fractions.

   c. Expressing fractions in terms of the LCD. After you have established the lowest common denominator for the fractions with which you are working, you must express each fraction in terms of the LCD. This is accomplished by dividing the denominator of the fraction into the LCD and then multiplying both the numerator and denominator by the resulting number. After this has been done for all the fractions involved, you may proceed to add, subtract, or compare.

17. Adding fractions. In the preceding paragraphs we have defined fractions, stated the rules applying to fractions, and given you the necessary information to work with fractions. Now you will work with examples which have been broken down in step procedures to show how this information is used.

   a. Proper fractions.

   Example: Add $\frac{3}{4}$, $\frac{1}{8}$, and $\frac{5}{6}$.

● *Step 1.* Find the LCD. Visually, you find the LCD to be 24, since 4 will divide into 24, 6 times; 8 will divide into 24, 3 times; and 6 will divide into 24, 4 times.

● *Step 2.* Convert each fraction to similar terms using the LCD. $24 \div 4 = 6$; therefore, $\frac{3}{4} \times \frac{6}{6} = \frac{18}{24}$; $24 \div 8 = 3$; therefore, $\frac{1}{8} \times \frac{3}{3} = \frac{3}{24}$; $24 \div 6 = 4$; therefore, $\frac{5}{6} \times \frac{4}{4} = \frac{20}{24}$.

● *Step 3.* Add the numerators and place the resulting sum over the common denominator. Thus: $18 + 3 + 20 = 41$. Therefore, the sum is $\frac{41}{24}$, which, when reduced to lowest terms, is $1\frac{17}{24}$.

   b. Mixed numbers and fractions.

   Example: Find the sum of $1\frac{1}{3}$, $2\frac{1}{4}$, and $\frac{1}{2}$.

● *Step 1.* When working with mixed numbers, add all the whole numbers first. $1 + 2 = 3$.

● *Step 2.* Find the LCD for the fractions. By the visual method, you arrive at the LCD as being 12. Change the fractions to common terms. $\frac{1}{3} = \frac{4}{12}$; $\frac{1}{4} = \frac{3}{12}$; $\frac{1}{2} = \frac{6}{12}$.

● *Step 3.* Add the numerator. $4 + 3 + 6 = 13$. Place the resulting number (13) over the LCD: $\frac{13}{12}$, which, reduced to lowest terms, is $1\frac{1}{12}$.

● *Step 4.* Add the $1\frac{1}{12}$ to the whole number from step 1: $1\frac{1}{12} + 3 = 4\frac{1}{12}$.

18. Subtracting fractions

   a. Basic method. The procedure for subtracting fractions is basically the same as adding them.

   Example: Subtract $\frac{3}{4}$ from $\frac{9}{10}$.

● *Step 1.* Find the LCD. By the multiplication method you find a common denominator to be 40 (4 x 10). On visual examination, however, you see that 20 is the *lowest* common denominator.

- *Step 2.* Convert each fraction to similar terms using the LCD. Dividing the 4 into 20 you get 5, which when multiplied by the numerator (5 x 3 = 15) gives $\frac{15}{20}$. Doing the same with the $\frac{9}{10}$, 20 divided by 10 = 2; 2 x 9 = 18, therefore, $\frac{18}{20}$.

- *Step 3.* Subtract the two numerators, 18 − 15 = 3. Place this number (3) over the LCD and arrive at the answer: $\frac{3}{20}$.

   b. *Subtracting larger from smaller.* A problem arises in mixed numbers when the fraction portion of the number being subtracted is larger than the fraction portion of the bigger number.

   Example: Subtract $1\frac{2}{3}$ from $3\frac{1}{2}$.

- *Step 1.* Find the LCD. Visually, you see that it is 6.

- *Step 2.* Express both fractions in terms of the LCD. $3\frac{1}{2} = 3\frac{3}{6}$; $1\frac{2}{3} = 1\frac{4}{6}$.

- *Step 3.* Subtract:

$$3\frac{3}{6}$$
$$-1\frac{4}{6}$$

You can't take $\frac{4}{6}$ from $\frac{3}{6}$. Therefore, you will have to convert the whole number (part of it in this case) to a fraction so that you may subtract. By taking 1 from $3\frac{3}{6}$ and changing it to $\frac{6}{6}$ and adding it to the $\frac{3}{6}$ you already have, you get $2\frac{9}{6}$.

You can now subtract:

$$2\frac{9}{6}$$
$$-1\frac{4}{6}$$
$$\overline{1\frac{5}{6}}$$

   c. *Alternate method.* An alternate method is to change *all* whole numbers to fractions before subtracting and then reduce the answer to its lowest terms.

   Example: Subtract $2\frac{1}{2}$ from $4\frac{1}{4}$.

- *Step 1.* Find the LCD visually, or by the multiplication method, and you arrive at the LCD of 4.

- *Step 2.* Express all numbers (including the whole number portions) in terms of the LCD: $2\frac{1}{2} = \frac{10}{4}$ and $4\frac{1}{4} = \frac{17}{4}$.

- *Step 3.* Subtract:

$$\frac{17}{4}$$
$$-\frac{10}{4}$$
$$\overline{\frac{7}{4}}$$

- *Step 4.* Reduce to lowest terms: $\frac{7}{4} = 1\frac{3}{4}$, answer.

   19. **Multiplying fractions.** Going back to the three general rules, you know that multiplying the numerator or dividing the denominator by a given number, multiplies the value of the fraction by that number.

   a. *Multiplying fractions by multiplying the numerator.*

   Example: Applying the rule, multiply $\frac{3}{4}$ by 8.

- *Step 1.* Multiply the numerator: 3 x 8 = 24. Place the resulting number (24) over original denominator: $\frac{24}{4}$

- *Step 2.* Reduce to lowest terms: $\frac{24}{4} = \frac{6}{1} = 6$, answer.

   b. *Multiplying fractions by dividing the denominator.*

   Example: Applying the rule, multiply $\frac{3}{4}$ by 2.

- *Step 1.* Divide the denominator: 4 ÷ 2 = 2. Placing the original numerator (3) over the new denominator, you have $\frac{3}{2}$.

- *Step 2.* Reduce to lowest terms: $\frac{3}{2} = 1\frac{1}{2}$, answer.

c. *Multiplying fractions by fractions.* To multiply two or more fractions, multiply the numerators and denominators separately and reduce the obtained fraction to lowest terms.

Example: Multiply $\frac{7}{9}$ by $\frac{6}{14}$.

• *Step 1.* Multiply the numerators: 7 x 6 = 42, the new numerator.

• *Step 2.* Multiply the denominators: 9 x 14 = 126, the new denominator.

• *Step 3.* Make a fraction of the new numbers: $\frac{42}{126}$.

• *Step 4.* Reduce to lowest terms: $\frac{42}{126} = \frac{1}{3}$, answer.

d. *Multiplying fractions by fractions using cancellation.* Cancellation is a process of dividing both numerator and denominator of fractions by the same number. It is like reducing to lowest terms. When two or more fractions are to be multiplied (or divided), cancellation between the numerators and denominators not only works, but is time saving in most cases.

Example: Multiply the following: $\frac{7}{9} \times \frac{6}{14} \times \frac{1}{2}$.

• *Step 1.* Here you will divide seven into both numerator and denominator, making the 7 a 1 and the 14 a 2: $\frac{1}{9} \times \frac{6}{2} \times \frac{1}{2} =$

• *Step 2.* Here you will divide both the numerator and denominator by two, making the 6 a 3 and 2 a 1: $\frac{1}{9} \times \frac{3}{2} \times \frac{1}{1} =$

• *Step 3.* Here you will divide both numerator and denominator by three as before. No more such division is possible, so you multiply the numerators together and the denominators together, and if necessary, reduce to lowest terms: $\frac{1}{3} \times \frac{1}{2} \times \frac{1}{1} =$

• *Step 4.* Multiply the numerators and denominators: $\frac{1}{3} \times \frac{1}{2} \times \frac{1}{1} = \frac{1}{6}$, the answer.

In this example, you have made individual steps out of each of the division steps. In a real situation, you would do all of this in one step, as shown in the next two examples.

Example: Multiply $\frac{7}{9} \times \frac{6}{14} \times \frac{1}{2}$; $\frac{\cancel{7}}{\cancel{9}} \times \frac{\cancel{6}}{\cancel{14}} \times \frac{1}{2}$ $= \frac{1}{6}$, answer.

Example: Multiply $\frac{3}{10} \times \frac{9}{26} \times \frac{26}{54}$; $\frac{\cancel{3}}{10} \times \frac{\cancel{9}}{\cancel{26}} \times \frac{\cancel{26}}{\cancel{54}} = \frac{1}{20}$, answer.

e. *Multiplying two or more numbers, one or more of which is a mixed number.* To multiply mixed numbers, you must change them first to improper fractions, then proceed as with regular fractions.

Example: Multiply $\frac{1}{4} \times 1\frac{5}{8} \times 1\frac{1}{2} \times 5\frac{1}{3}$.

• *Step 1.* Change all mixed numbers to improper fractions: $\frac{1}{4} \times \frac{13}{8} \times \frac{3}{2} \times \frac{16}{3}$

• *Step 2.* Cancel and reduce to lowest terms:

$\frac{1}{4} \times \frac{13}{\cancel{8}} \times \frac{\cancel{3}}{\cancel{2}} \times \frac{\cancel{16}}{\cancel{3}} = \frac{13}{4} = 3\frac{1}{4}$.

20. **Dividing fractions**

a. Again going back to the three general rules, "If the numerator is divided or the denominator multiplied by a given number, the value of the fraction is divided by that number," you have the basis for division among fractions. In order to avoid error, it is best to put a 1 over the whole number, so that you do not inadvertently multiply the numerator instead of the denominator.

Example: Divide $\frac{3}{4}$ by 3. Multiply the denominator of the fraction by 3: $\frac{3}{4} \times \frac{1}{3} = \frac{3}{12} = \frac{1}{4}$.

  b. To divide a whole number or a fraction by a fraction, *invert* the divisor (the number by which you are dividing). This has the effect of placing a 1 over the fraction. Thus, inverting $\frac{2}{3}$ gives us $\frac{3}{2}$, or: $\frac{1}{\frac{2}{3}} = \frac{\frac{3}{3}}{\frac{2}{3}} = \frac{3}{2}$.

  (1) Example: Divide 4 by $\frac{1}{3}$. Invert the fraction by which you are dividing: $4 \times \frac{3}{1} = \frac{12}{1} = 12$.

  (2) Example: Divide $\frac{1}{4}$ by $\frac{1}{8}$. Invert the $\frac{1}{8}$; $\frac{1}{4} \times \frac{\cancel{8}^2}{1} = 2$.

  (3) Example: Divide $2\frac{1}{2}$ by $1\frac{1}{4}$. Here you must first change the mixed numbers to improper fractions, then proceed as before.

$2\frac{1}{2} = \frac{5}{2}$; $1\frac{1}{4} = \frac{5}{4}$.

$\frac{5}{2} \div \frac{5}{4} = \frac{\cancel{5}^1}{\cancel{2}_1} \times \frac{\cancel{4}^2}{\cancel{5}_1} = \frac{2}{1} = 2$.

21. Decimals

  a. Writing decimals. Fractions that have 10 or any power of 10 for denominators are called decimal fractions. *For example,* $\frac{1}{10}$, $\frac{3}{100}$, $\frac{126}{1000}$, and $\frac{1234}{10000}$ are decimal fractions. In writing decimals, the denominators can be omitted and a decimal point (.) placed in the numerator to show what the denominator is. There are as many digits *after* the decimal point as there were zeros in the denominator. Taking the examples above—

$\frac{1}{10} = 0.1$, $\frac{3}{100} = 0.03$, $\frac{126}{1000} = 0.126$, $\frac{1234}{10000} = 0.1234$.

Where there are less digits in the numerator than there are zeros in the denominator, zeros must be placed between the decimal point and the numerator as in $\frac{25}{10,000} = 0.0025$, and $\frac{21}{100,000} = 0.00021$. Be very careful to place the zeros to the right of the decimal and before (to the left of) the numerator.

  b. Movement of decimal point. Any error in the placement of the decimal is serious, for each movement of the decimal point to the right or left produces an error of tenfold. To illustrate what happens, consider the difference between $1.00, $10.00, $100.00, and $1,000.00. In each case, the decimal has been moved one place to the right and in each case, the amount of money represented has been multiplied ten times. Similarly, the dose of nitroglycerin is 0.4 mg.; to give a patient 4.0 mg. is a serious error. For this reason, be extremely cautious and exact when working with decimals.

22. Adding decimals

  a. When adding decimals, *always* make sure the decimal points are directly under each other. The actual addition is then the same as with whole numbers.

  b. The following three examples demonstrate the necessity of having the decimal points in line under each other. Compare examples (1) and (2) with example (3).

  (1) Example: Add $100.25, $50.69, and $18.10.

```
$100.25
  50.69
  18.10
$169.04
```

  (2) Example: Add 21.25, 36.17, 18.19, and 7.03.

```
21.25
36.17
18.19
 7.03
82.64
```

(3) Example: Add 1.324, 2347.1, 0.68235, and 11.0001. Remember to line up the decimal points!

```
   1.324
2347.1
   0.68235
  11.0001
─────────
2360.10645
```

23. Subtracting decimals

   a. Again the decimal points must be placed directly beneath each other, and again the procedure is the same as with whole numbers.

   b. The following two examples also demonstrate the necessity of having the decimal points in line. Study example (2) carefully. Here we must add zeros at the end of the shorter numbers so that we have something to subtract from. Adding zeros at the right of the number after the decimal point has no effect on the value of the number. Zeros cannot, however, be added before the number after a decimal point, or after a number before a decimal point.

   (1) Example: Subtract 11.59 from 102.21.

```
102.21
 11.59
──────
 90.62
```

   (2) Example: Subtract .675061 from 2.31.

```
2.310000
 .675061
────────
1.634939
```

Thus, 2.31 is the same as 2.310000. But 2.31 is NOT equal to 2.0031 or 20.31.

24. Multiplication of decimals. The basic principle in multiplication of decimals is that the number of places to the right of the decimal point in the product (answer) is the *sum* of the decimal points in the factors (numbers being multiplied).

Example: 43.789 (3 places to right of decimal)
         x .02 (2 places to right of decimal)
Product: .87578 (3 + 2 = 5 places to right of decimal)

25. Division of decimals

   a. How would you go about determining how much of a powder to pack into each of 12 capsules to evenly divide 64.8 grains of medication? You would divide 64.8 by 12. This division is shown below.

```
      5.4
12)64.8
   60
   ──
    4 8
    4 8
```

   b. Above you have divided and placed a decimal one place from the right because there was one place in the amount of powder. Division of a decimal by another decimal is basically the same except for one modification. We know that multiplying the numerator and the denominator each by the same number has no effect on the fraction. For this reason, we can eliminate the decimal from the divisor.

   (1) Example: Divide 225.6648 by 0.8.

● *Step 1.* Multiply both the numbers by 10 (simply moving the decimal one place to the right in each case): 08)2256.648.

● *Step 2.* Now the decimal will be correctly situated simply by placing it directly above the other decimal.

```
       282.081
08)2256.648
   16
   ──
    65
    64
    ──
     16
     16
     ──
      064
      064
      ───
       08
       08
```

   (2) Example: Divide 1.23456 by 0.02.

0.02)1.23456

● *Step 1.* Multiply both numbers by 100 (simply moving the decimal two places to the right in each case).

002)123.456

● *Step 2.* Now the decimal will be correctly situated simply by placing it directly above the other decimal.

$$\begin{array}{r} 61.728 \\ 002\overline{)123.456} \\ \underline{12} \\ 03 \\ \underline{02} \\ 14 \\ \underline{14} \\ 05 \\ \underline{04} \\ 16 \\ \underline{16} \end{array}$$

26. Roman numerals. Roman numerals are used in writing prescriptions. They are used to specify the amounts of ingredients when the apothecary system is being used, for example, "Codeine Sulfate gr. iii." They are used to specify the number of units (capsules, tablets, powders, or suppositories) to be dispensed, for example, "Disp. xxiv." And, lastly, they are used in the signa or directions to the patient, for example, "tabs. ii stat, then i q iv h." You should therefore be thoroughly familiar with the system of Roman numerals used in pharmacy. The basic symbols or numerals are—

ss or s̄s̄	1/2
i	1
v	5
x	10
L	50
C	100
D	500
M	1000

These basic numerals may be combined to represent *any* number and there are definite rules for the manner in which they are combined. The rules for Roman numerals are as follows:

a. Fractions. Except for "ss" meaning one-half (1/2), all other fractions are represented by the Arabic numeral, for example, 1/4, 3/8, 1/120.

b. Repeating numerals. Numerals may be repeated and when they are, the value of the number is repeated. Thus iii or III is 3, xxx is 30, and ccc is 300. Any numeral that would be the same as another when repeated is NOT repeated. *For example,* vv is NOT used for 10 (5 + 5) because x is 10. LL is NOT used for 100 (C = 100).

c. Smaller numerals before larger. A smaller numeral placed before a larger one is subtracted from that numeral. Only one number can be subtracted in this way. Thus iv (5 − 1) = 4, ix (10 − 1) = 9; XC (100 − 10) = 90; etc. But 3 is *never* written iiv.

d. Smaller numerals after larger. A smaller numeral placed after a larger one is added to it as viii = (5 + 3) = 8; xiii (10 + 3) = 13; CLX = (100 + 50 + 10) = 160.

e. Smaller numeral between two larger. A smaller numeral between two larger ones is ALWAYS subtracted from the larger numeral which follows it as CXL (100 + (50 − 10)) = 140; MCMLXV (1000 + (1000 − 100) + 50 + 10 + 5) = 1965.

f. Dotting the one. A dot over the numeral representing 1(i) is often used to distinguish it from a portion of the numeral v. When poorly written, \ / and v may be very similar. If the ones are dotted however, \ / can never be mistaken for 5. As a further precaution against error, the last i may be replaced by a j; 3 written in this manner would be written iij.

g. Table of Roman numerals. Table 2-1 shows Roman numerals and their equivalents. Memorize this chart. You must know these numerals as well as you do Arabic numerals.

Table 1. The Roman Numerals

ss	=	½	x	=	10	xx	=	20	li	=	51
i	=	1	xi	=	11	xxi	=	21	lix	=	59
ii	=	2	xii	=	12	xxix	=	29	lx	=	60
iii	=	3	xiii	=	13	xxx	=	30	lxx	=	70
iv	=	4	xiv	=	14	xxxi	=	31	lxxx	=	80
v	=	5	xv	=	15	xxxix	=	39	xc	=	90
vi	=	6	xvi	=	16	xl	=	40	c	=	100
vii	=	7	xvii	=	17	xli	=	41	ci	=	101
viii	=	8	xviii	=	18	xlix	=	49	cxxi	=	121
ix	=	9	xix	=	19	l	=	50	d	=	500
									m	=	1000

27. Weights and measures. Metrology is the study of measurement as applied to length, weight, and volume. During your study of pharmacy in your Army career, you will constantly be dealing with it, weighing, measuring, or transposing. To be effective, both while you are learning and while you are practicing pharmacy, you must have certain tables and equivalents *committed to memory.* The time you spend memorizing the tables of weights and measures now will be repaid with interest a hundredfold. Although there are other systems of weight and measure, there are three with which the pharmacist comes into daily contact; the metric system, apothecary system, and avoirdupois system.

28. *Metric system.* The metric system of weights and measures is the legal standard in the United States. All other systems are referred to it for official comparisons. It is used as the scientific system of measuring, the world over.

 a. Units of length, weight, and volume.
  (1) Meter. The standard unit of length, the meter, may be defined as a multiple (1,650,763.73) of the wave length of the light produced by a gas-discharge lamp filled with Krypton 86. This standard permits measurements to an error of 1 part in 10 million. This extreme accuracy degree is necessary in today's missile programs.
  (2) Liter. The unit of volume in the metric system, the liter, is the volume occupied by a kilogram of water at its greatest density (4° C.), and weighed in a vacuum.
  (3) Gram. The unit of weight, the gram, is the weight of one cubic centimeter of water at its greatest density (4° C.), and weighed in a vacuum.

NOTE

The internationally recognized symbol for a Gram is "g." This is also the symbol used by *The United States Pharmacopeia,* XVIII, and *The National Formulary,* XIII, which were published in 1970. Previously the official abbreviation for the Gram was "Gm." This was to distinguish the Gram from the grain (gr). Another commonly used abbreviation for the Gram is "gm." The change from the abbreviation "Gm" to "g." for Gram took place while this TM was being revised. The change came too late to convert all the "Gm" abbreviations in this text to "g." As a result, Gram is still abbreviated Gm. throughout even though the accepted abbreviation is "g."

 b. Advantages of the metric system. There are several definite advantages of the metric system over the other systems—
  (1) It has universal use.
  (2) Every weight and measure has a simple relation to the meter.
  (3) Every unit is multiplied or divided by 10 to reach the next higher or lower unit. As in our system of money, it is a system of decimal progression.

$$10 \text{ mills} = 1 \text{ cent}$$
$$10 \text{ cents} = 1 \text{ dime}$$
$$10 \text{ dimes} = 1 \text{ dollar}$$

  (4) It is the only system of weights and measures having a common standard where a unit of weight equals a unit of volume. The common standard is water. Therefore, under the standard conditions of temperature and pressure, 10 ml. of H_2O equals 10 Gm.: 100 ml. of H_2O weighs 100 Gm.

 c. Subdivisions and multiples. Each table of the metric system has a definite unit around which the subdivision and multiples are based; the meter for length, the liter for volume, and the gram for weight. Subdivisions and multiples of these principal units are indicated respectively by Latin and Greek prefixes.
  (1) Subdivisions (from Latin).

$$\frac{1}{1000} = \text{milli}$$

$$\frac{1}{100} = \text{centi}$$

$$\frac{1}{10} = \text{deci}$$

  (2) Multiples (from Greek).
   10 times = Deka
   100 times = Hecto
   1000 times = Kilo

 d. Learning the metric system. When you have learned the subdivisions and multiples above, the metric system will not be difficult for you to understand or to learn. Remember that it works just like our money system. Using tables 2-2, 2-3, and 2-4, those of lengths, weights, and liquid measure, memorize the metric system.

 e. Metric weights set. Figure 2-5 depicts the standard weight set you will be using in the pharmacy. It consists of weights from 10 milligrams to 100 grams. By combining these weights, it is possible to weight substances between 10 mg. and 201 Gm. *For example,* to weigh 20.750 Gm., you would select a 20 Gm. weight, a 500 mg. weight, a 200 mg. weight, and a 50 mg. weight. The combined total of these weights is 20.750 Gm.

Table 2. Metric Table of Lengths

Lengths			Abbreviations		
10 millimeters	=	1 centimeter	10 mm.	=	1 cm.
10 centimeters	=	1 decimeter	10 cm.	=	1 dm.
10 decimeters	=	1 meter	10 dm.	=	1 M.
10 Meters	=	1 Dekameter	10 M.	=	1 Dm.
10 Dekameters	=	1 Hectometer	10 Dm.	=	1 Hm.
10 Hectometers	=	1 Kilometer	10 Hm.	=	1 Km.

The metric table may also be written:

1 meter = 1000 millimeters
= 100 centimeters
= 10 decimeters
= 0.1 Dekameter
= 0.01 Hectometer
= 0.001 Kilometer

Table 3. Metric Table of Weights

Weights			Abbreviations		
10 milligrams	=	1 centigram	10 mg.	=	1 cg.
10 centigrams	=	1 decigram	10 cg.	=	1 dg.
10 decigrams	=	1 gram	10 dg.	=	1 Gm.
10 grams	=	1 Dekagram	10 Gm.	=	1 Dg.
10 Dekagrams	=	1 Hectogram	10 Dg.	=	1 Hg.
10 Hectograms	=	1 Kilogram	10 Hg.	=	1 Kg.

The metric table of weights may also be written:

1 gram = 1000 milligrams
= 100 centigrams
= 10 decigrams
= 0.1 Dekagram
= 0.01 Hectogram
= 0.001 Kilogram

Table 4. Metric Table of Liquid Measures

Liquid measures			Abbreviations		
10 milliliters	=	1 centiliter	10 ml.	=	1 cl.
10 centiliters	=	1 deciliter	10 cl.	=	1 dl.
10 deciliters	=	1 liter	10 dl.	=	1 L.
10 liters	=	1 Dekaliter	10 L.	=	1 Dl.
10 Dekaliters	=	1 Hectoliter	10 Dl.	=	1 Hl.
10 Hectoliters	=	1 Kiloliter	10 Hl.	=	1 Kl.

The metric table of liquid weights may also be written:

1 liter = 1000 milliliters
= 100 centiliters
= 10 deciliters
= 0.1 Dekaliter
= 0.01 Hectoliter
= 0.001 Kiloliter

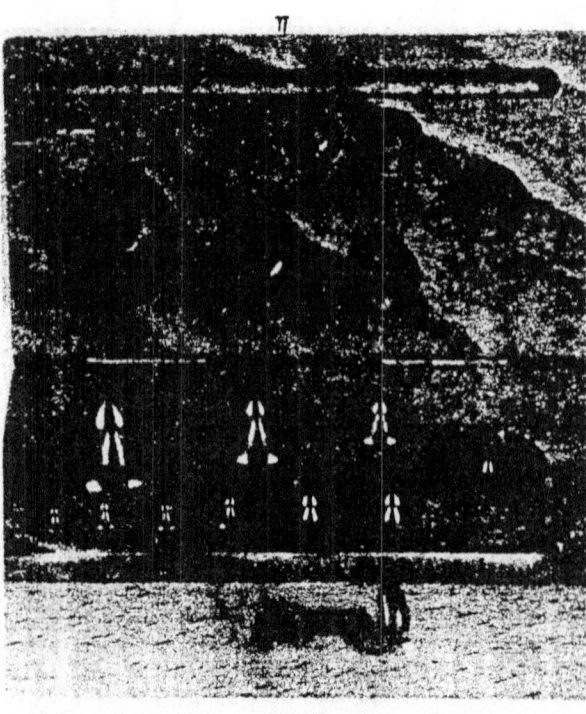

Figure 5. Metric weights.

f. Working with the weights and measures. Now that you have reviewed decimal fractions and have learned the metric system of weights and measures, apply the two as you will be using them in your job.

(1) Example: Addition and subtraction in the metric system. Suppose you dispensed the following amounts of a powder from your stock of 4000 Gm.—28 Gm., 500 mg., 14 cg., and 2 Kg. How much powder would you have remaining?

● *Step 1.* Since you are dealing with four different denominations of weight, you cannot add or subtract until you have a common unit to work with. Since you want the answer in grams (your shelf stock having been specified in grams), it will be simplest to convert all the quantities to grams as follows:

$$\begin{aligned}
28 \text{ Gm.} &= 28.0 \text{ Gm.} \\
500 \text{ mg.} &= .5 \text{ Gm.} \\
14 \text{ cg.} &= .14 \text{ Gm.} \\
2 \text{ Kg.} &= \underline{2000.0 \text{ Gm.}} \\
&= 2028.64 \text{ Gm. amount dispensed}
\end{aligned}$$

● *Step 2.* You started with 4000 Gm. and dispensed a total of 2028.64 Gm., so by subtracting you will determine the balance on hand. Therefore:

$$\begin{array}{r} 4000.00 \text{ Gm.} \\ -\underline{2028.64} \text{ Gm.} \\ 1971.36 \text{ Gm. remaining} \end{array}$$

NOTE

The same method is applied to liquid measure. How many ml. of alcohol would remain if you dispensed 240 from an original liter?

$$\begin{array}{r} 1 \text{ liter} = 1000 \text{ ml.} \\ -\underline{240} \text{ ml.} \\ 760 \text{ ml. remaining} \end{array}$$

(2) Example: Multiplication. How many grams of powder would be necessary to manufacture 20 capsules, each containing 300 mg.?

$$\begin{array}{r} 300 \text{ mg.} \\ \times \underline{20} \\ 6000 \text{ mg.} = 6.0 \text{ Gm.} \end{array}$$

(3) Example: Division. How many 30 ml. bottles of cough syrup can you dispense if you have 3 liters of the syrup on hand?

3 liters = 3000 ml.
3000 ÷ 30 = 100 bottles, answer

29. Apothecary system. Although the Army requires that all Army prescriptions be written in the metric system, the pharmacy technician must also be able to use the apothecary system. In civil practice the apothecary system is widely used and consequently many formulas are specified in terms of apothecary units. Many of the ready-made pharmaceuticals have strength and dosage listed in the apothecary system. Further, you will be filling prescriptions written by civilian prescribers who will use the apothecary system for quantity and dosage. In previous editions of the USP (Revision xiv and before), dosage of the official preparations was listed as an approximation of the apothecary system. The dosage is now completely in the metric system, the apothecary system being completely eliminated.

a. Units of weight and volume.

(1) Apothecary weight. The basic unit in the apothecary system of weight is the grain, which is approximately 64.8 mg. Divisions of the grain are expressed as fractions, for example, $\frac{1}{60}$ gr. Prescriptions will be written with a symbol for the weight denomination and a Roman numeral for the amount of that denomination. Study the table of apothecary weights and abbreviations (table 2-5). Thus, in prescriptions written in the apothecary system, you will see the following written:

Ɔiii　　　ʒii　　　gr iiiss　　　℥viii

Table 5. Apothecary Weights and Abbreviations

	Apothecary weights			Abbreviations	
20 grains	=	1 scruple		gr. xx	= Ɔi
3 scruples	=	1 drachm	= 60 grains	Ɔ iii	= ʒi
8 drachms	=	1 ounce	= 480 grains	ʒviii	= ℥i
12 ounces	=	1 pound	= 5760 grains	℥xii	= 1 lb.

(2) Apothecary liquid measure. The basic unit of the apothecary system of fluid measure is the minim (♏). Study the table of apothecary liquid measure below in table 2-6. Prescriptions are written with a symbol for the denomination to be used. Thus in prescriptions written in the apothecary system for liquids, you will see quantities such as the following:

f ℥ ss　　f ʒ ¼　　♏xii　　f ℥ viii

(3) Apothecary weights. Apothecary weights used in pharmacy are of two types—cylindrical weights and coin weights.

(a) Apothecary cylindrical weights. The apothecary cylindrical weights are

Table 6. Apothecary Fluid Measure and Abbreviations

	Apothecary fluid measure				Abbreviation	
60 minims	=	1 fluidrachm	=		♏lx	= f ʒi
8 fluidrachm	=	1 fluidounce	=	480 minims	f ʒviii	= f ℥i
16 fluidounce	=	1 pint	=	7,680 minims	f ℥vxi	= Ɵi
2 pints	=	1 quart	=	82 fluidounces	Ɵii	= qt i
4 quarts	=	1 gallon	=	128 fluidounces	qt iv	= Ci

similar to the metric weights depicted in figure 2-5. They usually range from one-half scruple to two drachms. The set contains grain weights in the form of wires; the number of sides indicates the number of grains (fig. 2-6).

   (b) *Apothecary coin weights.* Coin-type weights which have the weight embossed on their surfaces are particularly subject to error and should not be used.

  b. *Converting between denominations.* It is often convenient to express a weight or measure in its equivalent in a lower or higher denomination. This can be easily accomplished by either multiplying or dividing the weight by the number of units that equals either the higher or lower measure.

   (1) Example: Express 3/4 quart in its lowest terms in the apothecary system.

● *Step 1.* Since 2 pints = 1 quart; 2 x 3/4 = 1 1/2 pints which can be expressed—pt ii x qt 3/4 = pt iss.

● *Step 2.* Put aside and save the whole number, the one pint, and break the fraction to its next lowest terms.
   1 pint = 16 fluidounces
so, 16 fluidounces x 1/2 = 8 fluidounces
   or, f ℥ xvi x pt ss = f ℥ viii

● *Step 3.* Continue in this manner, changing each remaining fraction to the next lower denomination. In this case, however, you need go no further, 8 ounces is even. Now you have the whole pint saved from step 2, which equals 16 ounces plus the 8 ounces from step 3, or a total of 24 fluidounces for the answer.

   (2) Example: Express 2/5 gallon in its lowest apothecary terms.

● *Step 1.* 1 gallon = 8 pints.
    8 x 2/5 = 3 1/5 pt
    or, pt viii = gal i
   pt viii x gal 2/5 = pt iii 1/5

● *Step 2.* Continue in this manner, saving the whole and breaking the fraction to its next lowest terms:
   fl ℥ xvi x pt 1/5 = f ℥ iii 1/5
   fl ℨ xviii x fl ℥ 1/5 = fl ℥ i 3/5
   ♏ x x fl ℨ 3/5 = ♏ xxxvi

● *Step 3.* Putting the numbers previously saved together in sequence, you arrive at the answer: 2/5 gallons = 3 pints, 3 fluidounces, 1 fluidrachm, and 36 minims; or gallon 2/5 = ☉iii, fl ℥ iii, fl ℨ i, ♏ xxxvi.

   (3) Example: In order to proceed from a lower measure to highest terms, the procedure is just opposite. Divide the measure by the number of units of that measure that equals one unit of the next higher measure. Express 57,688 minims in its highest terms.

● *Step 1.* 60 minims = 1 fluidrachm, therefore
```
      961 ———→ 961 fl ℨ
60/57688
     540
     ‾‾‾
     368
     360
     ‾‾‾
      88
      60
      ‾‾
      28 ———→ 28 minims
```
Save the minims left over and break down the fluidrachms.

● *Step 2.* 8 fluidrachms = 1 fluidounce, therefore
```
     120 ———→ 120 fl ℥
 8/961
    8
    ‾
   16
   16
   ‾‾
   01
    0
    ‾
    1 ———→ 1 fluid ℨ
```
Save the fluidrachms and break down the fluidounces.

● *Step 3.* 16 fluidounces = 1 pint, therefore
```
      7 ———→ 7 pints
16/120
   112
   ‾‾‾
     8 ———→ 8 fluidounces
```
Save the fluidounces and change the pints to the next higher value (quarts).

● *Step 4.* 2 fluid pints = 1 fluid quart, therefore
```
     3 ———→ 3 quarts
  2/7
    6
    ‾
    1 ———→ 1 pint
```

● *Step 5.* Now, combine the various quantities you have saved in previous steps. Your answer is:

57,688 minims = 3 qts, 1 pt, 8 fʒ , 1 fʒ , 28 minims.

(4) *Checking your answers.* You can check your answers in both procedures by just reversing the procedure.

• In example (2), you converted 2/5 gallon to 3 pints, 3 fluidounces, 1 fluidrachm, and 36 minims. Going in reverse to check the accuracy:

60 minims = 1 fluidrachm

$\frac{36}{60}$ minims = 3/5 fluidrachm

3/5 + 1 = 1 3/5 fluidrachms
8 fluidrachms = 1 fluidounce
1 3/5 fluidrachms = 1/5 fluidounce
1/5 + 3 = 3 1/5 fluidounces
16 fluidounces = 1 pint
3 1/5 fluidounces = 1/5 pint
1/5 + 3 = 3 1/5 pints
8 pints = 1 gallon
3 1/5 pints = 2/5 gallon—the answer checks.

• In example (3), you converted 57,688 minims to 7 pints, 8 fluidounces, 1 fluidrachm, and 28 minims. To check this answer, you again proceed in reverse.

7 pt, 8 flʒ , 1 flʒ + 28 minims ⟶ 28 minims
7 pt, 8 flʒ , 1 flʒ
1 flʒ = 60 minims ⟶ 60 minims
7 pt, 8 flʒ
8 flʒ = 64 flʒ (8 × 8)
64 flʒ = ⟶ 3,840 minims
(64 × 60)
7 pt = 112 flʒ = 896 flʒ = ⟶ 53,760 minims
(112 × 8) (896 × 60)
adding the columns of minims ⟶ 57,688 minims
our answer checks.

c. *Addition and subtraction.* The arithmetic involved in the apothecary system is slightly more involved than that of the metric system. In the metric system, the units increase by multiples of ten. However, the apothecary system has no uniform scale of variation. You are again confronted with the problem that quantities of like denomination must be added or subtracted first, then converted to lowest terms. To illustrate this, look at the following addition problem.

(1) Example:
4 lb, 3 ʒ , 4 ʒ , 1 ᴑ , 18 gr.
+ 8 lb, 2 ʒ , 3 ʒ , 2 ᴑ , 19 gr.

• *Step 1.* By simple addition, adding pounds to pounds, ounces to ounces, you get—
4 lb, 3 ʒ , 4 ʒ , 1 ᴑ , 18 gr.
+ 8 lb, 2 ʒ , 3 ʒ , 2 ᴑ , 19 gr.
12 lb, 5 ʒ , 7 ʒ , 3 ᴑ , 37 gr.

• *Step 2.* This answer is not in its reduced terms, because 37 grains equals one scruple plus 17 grains, 3 scruples equal a drachm, and so on. To reduce this answer, begin at the right and work to the left, changing each quantity possible to the next higher denomination. Twenty grains equals one scruple, leaving 17 grains and adding 1 scruple to the 3 previously in the column. Likewise, since there are 3 scruples to the drachm, you must convert 3 of the 4 scruples you now have in this column to 1 drachm, leaving 1 ᴑ and increasing the drachms to 8. There being 8 drachms to the ounce, you have no drachms remaining, but increase the ounces to 6. The final reduced answer then beomes 12 lb, 6 ʒ , 1 ᴑ , 17 gr.

(2) Example: Subtract 4 lb, 6 ᴑ , 4 ʒ , 1 ᴑ , 19 gr. from 6 lb, 8 ʒ , 5 ʒ , 2 ᴑ , 15 gr.

• *Step 1.* Set up for subtraction.
6 lb, 8 ʒ , 5 ʒ , 2 ᴑ , 15 gr.
− 4 lb, 6 ʒ , 4 ʒ , 1 ᴑ , 19 gr.

Since you could not take 19 grains from 15 grains, it is necessary to convert one scruple to grains, reducing the number of scruples in the upper figure to 1 and increasing the grains to 35. You may never have a negative number in subtracting weights and measures.

• *Step 2.* Having converted the scruple to grains, your problem becomes:
6 lb, 8 ʒ , 5 ʒ , 1 ᴑ , 35 gr.
− 4 lb, 6 ʒ , 4 ʒ , 1 ᴑ , 19 gr.
2 lb, 2 ʒ , 1 ʒ , 0 ᴑ , 16 gr.

d. *Multiplication and division.*

(1) Example: Multiplication. Multiplication of compound numbers such as arise in the apothecary system may be accomplished in several ways, the easiest of which is to multiply each denomination individually, then reduce the answer. Multiply 2 gal, 3 qt, 1 pt, 9 fʒ , 7 fʒ , 18 min. by 6.

• *Step 1.*
2 gal, 3 qt, 1 pt, 9 fʒ , 7 fʒ , 81 min.
× 6

12 gal, 18 qt, 6 pt, 54 fʒ , 42 fʒ , 108 min.

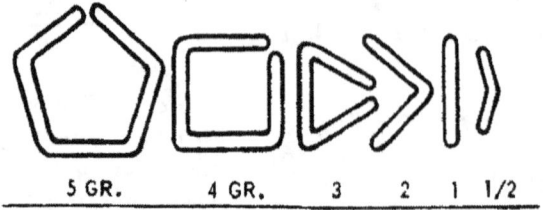

Figure 6. Apothecary grain weights.

Table 7. Approximate Equivalents

Weight

Metric	Approx apothecary	Metric	Approx apothecary	Metric	Approx apothecary
0.1 mg.	1/600 gr.	6 mg.	1/10 gr.	0.1 Gm.	1-1/2 gr.
0.2 mg.	1/300 gr.	8 mg.	1/8 gr.	0.12 Gm.	2 gr.
0.3 mg.	1/200 gr.	10 mg.	1/6 gr.	0.15 Gm.	2-1/2 gr.
0.4 mg.	1/150 gr.	12 mg.	1/5 gr.	0.2 Gm.	3 gr.
0.5 mg.	1/120 gr.	15 mg.	1/4 gr.	0.3 Gm.	5 gr.
0.6 mg.	1/100 gr.	20 mg.	1/3 gr.	0.5 Gm.	7-1/2 gr.
1 mg.	1/60 gr.	25 mg.	3/8 gr.	0.6 Gm.	10 gr.
1.2 mg.	1/50 gr.	30 mg.	1/2 gr.	1 Gm.	15 gr.
2 mg.	1/30 gr.	50 mg.	3/4 gr.	1.5 Gm.	22 gr.
3 mg.	1/20 gr.	60 mg.	1 gr.	2 Gm.	30 gr.
4 mg.	1/15 gr.	75 mg.	1-1/4 gr.	3 Gm.	45 gr.
5 mg.	1/12 gr.	90 mg.	1-1/2 gr.	4 Gm.	60 gr. (1 drachm)
				5 Gm.	75 gr.
				7.5 Gm.	2 drachms
				15 Gm.	4 drachms
				30 Gm.	1 ounce

Liquid Measure

Metric	Approx apothecary	Metric	Approx apothecary	Metric	Approx apothecary
0.03 ml.	1/2 minim	0.6 ml.	10 minims	15 ml.	4 f. drachms (1/2 oz)
0.05 ml.	3/4 minim	0.75 ml.	12 minims	30 ml.	1 f. ounce
0.06 ml.	1 minim	1 ml.	15 minims	60 ml.	2 f. ounces
0.1 ml.	1-1/2 minims	2 ml.	30 minims	120 ml.	4 f. ounces
0.2 ml.	3 minims	3 ml.	45 minims	250 ml.	8 f. ounces
0.25 ml.	4 minims	4 ml.	60 minims	500 ml.	16 f. ounces (1 pint)
0.3 ml.	5 minims	5 ml.	1 f. drachm	1000 ml.	1 quart
0.5 ml.	8 minims	10 ml.	2 f. drachms		

N.B. These are *approximate* equivalents. They may be used to compare prepared dosage forms such as tablets, capsules, and solutions. For converting *specific* quantities as are called for in formulas, use the exact equivalents provided in the U.S.P. For prescription compounding, use the exact equivalents rounded to 3 significant figures.

Step 2. Simply reduce the above answer to the lowest terms as previously explained.

17 gal, 2 qt, 1 pt, 11 f℥ , 3 fℨ , 48 min.

(2) Example: Division (usual method). Division of compound numbers is best done by dividing the highest measure first, keeping the whole number obtained and converting any remainder to the next smaller denomination and adding it to the given quantity. Then continue the division. Divide 8 gal, 2 qt, 1 pt by 3.

- *Step 1.*
  8 gal ÷ 3 = 2 gal (+ 2 gal remainder)
  2 gal = 8 qt + original 2 qt = 10 qt.

- *Step 2.*
  10 qt ÷ 3 = 3 qt (+ 1 qt remainder)
  1 qt = 2 pt + original 1 pt + 3 pt.

- *Step 3.*
  3 pt ÷ 3 = 1 pt.

- *Step 4.* Add the products from all steps (not the remainders!).
  2 gal, 3 qt, 1 pt, answer.

(3) Example: Division (alternate method). An alternate method is to convert the amounts to their lowest form; in this case, pints, then convert back to highest terms after dividing. Divide 8 gal, 2 qt, 1 pt by 3.

- *Step 1.*
  8 gal = 64 pt
  2 qt = 4 pt
  1 pt = 1 pt
  total = 69 pt

- *Step 2.* Divide.
  69 ÷ 3 = 23 pt

- *Step 3.* Convert back to highest terms.
  23 pt = 11 qt, 1 pt
  11 qt = 2 gal, 3 qt
  2 gal, 3 qt, 1 pt, answer.

30. Avoirdupois system. In the United States all items sold by weight are commercially bought and sold by avoirdupois weight. Exceptions to this rule include gems and precious metals. The weight which appears on a scale when you weigh yourself is avoirdupois weight. Unless expressly stated, all drugs and chemicals are bought and sold by avoirdupois weight. Therefore, it is *extremely* important to note that in receiving narcotics from the warehouse, an ounce bottle contains 437.5 grains (avoirdupois ounce), not 480 grains (apothecary ounce). As you can readily see, serious error could result in your narcotic records if you did not understand this principle. The grain is common to BOTH the avoirdupois and the apothecary system, *but* the ounces and pounds are different. Study the comparison below.

Apothecary ounce = 480.0 grains
Avoirdupois ounce = $\overline{437.5 \text{ grains}}$
42.5 grains *difference*

Apothecary pound = 12 oz × 480 grains = 5760 grains
Avoirdupois pound = 16 oz × 437.5 grains = $\overline{7000 \text{ grains}}$
1240 grains *difference*

31. Relationship and approximate equivalents. The metric system, apothecary system, and avoirdupois system are all used extensively by the pharmacy technician. Because you have and use three separate systems of weight and measure, it is necessary to understand their relationship and know how to convert from one to the other quickly and accurately.

a. Some relationships to remember.
- *Remember:* The pharmacist receives drugs and chemicals by avoirdupois weight at 437.5 grains per ounce, 16 ounces per pound.
- *Remember:* The pharmacist dispenses prescriptions in the metric or apothecary system. The apothecary system has 480 grains per ounce and only 12 ounces per pound.
- *Remember:* One apothecary fluidounce (H_2O) weighs 454.6 grains at 25° C. There are 480 minims in an apothecary fluidounce. It follows, then, that 1 minim of water at 25° C. weighs $\frac{454.6}{480} = 0.95$ grains.

b. Approximate equivalents. Table 2-7 should be thoroughly memorized. These equivalents will allow conversion between systems with a *relative degree of accuracy*. A facsimile of this table should be conspicuously placed near the work area in your pharmacy as a reference and check.

c. Exact conversion. Exact accuracy in conversion from one system to another as is needed for compounding prescriptions cannot be accomplished using approximate equivalents. Nearly exact conversion equivalents are given in a table in the USP.

32. Ratio and proportion

a. Ratio. Ratio is an expression of the relationship of one thing to another. For the purpose of arithmetic, ratio is the relation showing the amount by which one thing is different from another. Thus, if you have a solution of 9 grams of sodium chloride in 1000 grams of water, the ratio of NaCl to water is 9:1000 or $\frac{9}{1000}$, and is read "9 to 1000." The value of a ratio is the number obtained by dividing the first term (antecedent) by the second term (consequent); therefore, the value of 12:4 is 3.

(1) Ratios remain constant. Multiplying or dividing BOTH terms of a ratio does not change its value. Therefore, multiplying both terms of 10:5 by 5 gives us 50:25. In either case, the ratio is the same, 2:1. The terms of a ratio taken together are called a couplet.

(2) Equal units. Ratio can exist only between numbers of the same unit value—as ratio of percent to percent or weight to weight—but never weight to percent. (*Exception:* In pharmacy, we often make solutions which are expressed as weight to volume.) The comparing of numbers of the same unit volume follows as certainly as apples can be compared to apples and oranges to oranges, but never oranges to apples.

(3) Examples of ratio problems:
- What is the value of the ratio 10:100? Divide the first term by the second to get 1/10.
- Simplify 6:36. Divide both terms by 6 to get 1:6.
- What is the ratio between 18 percent and 9 grams? No ratio! Percent cannot be compared to grams.
- What do the following three ratios have in common? 1:5, 3:15, 5:25. When simplified, each is 1:5 or 1/5.

b. Proportion. 15:3 :: 10:2 is a proportion. It is read "15 is to 3 as 10 is to 2." Proportion is a means of showing equality between ratios. $15 \div 3 = 5$ and $10 \div 2 = 5$; they have the same value. The first and fourth terms of a proportion are called the *extremes* and the second and third terms are called the *means*. In the example cited above, 15 and 2 are the extremes; 3 and 10 are the means. The product of the extremes (15 x 2) equals the product of the means (3 x 10).

(1) Example: 50:10 :: 25:5
$50 \times 5 = 250$;
$10 \times 25 = 250$.

Thus, it is apparent that if one of the numbers were an unknown, it could easily be determined as follows:

(2) Example: If it takes 50 grains of powder to make 5 capsules, how many grains are necessary to make 3 capsules? This problem is nothing more than a proportion in which one of the terms is an unknown.

50:x :: 5:3
$5x = 150$ (arrived at by multiplying the means and extremes)
$x = 30$ grains, answer (to make 3 capsules)

It is customary to let x or y represent the unknown number in proportions. Thus you find that 30 grains would be necessary to make 3 capsules.

(3) Example: Rule of Words. Putting this example into a rule of words—"To find either extreme, multiply the means (2nd and 3rd numbers) and divide by the known extreme." Likewise, "To find either mean, multiply the extremes (1st and 4th numbers) and divide by the known mean." Notice how you progress from a statement of problem to a written proportion. If 500 Gm. of a salt solution contains 10 percent salt, to what weight must you evaporate the solution to make it 20 percent salt?

- *Step 1.* Write down the facts.
500 Gm. is 10%
? Gm. is 20%

- *Step 2.* Let x represent the unknown (?) quantity. Arbitrarily, let x take the fourth position.

- *Step 3.* Since we can compare only like articles, put the number with the same denomination as x in the third position.

- *Step 4.* Determine if the unknown is to be larger or smaller than the third number. In the preceding example, you are evaporating a solution and thus it will be smaller. Since the smaller follows the larger in the 3rd and 4th positions, the *same* must hold true of the 1st and 2d. Therefore, the larger number will be in first position, and the smaller in second position.

- *Step 5.* From the preceding 4 steps, you may conclude that—

    20:10 :: 500:x

- *Step 6.* Cross multiply (multiply the means and extremes).

    20 x = 5000

- *Step 7.* Solve for x.

    x = 5000 ÷ 20
    x = 250 Gm., the weight of the 20% solution, answer.

33. **Percentage preparations.** Many of the calculations you will be required to make in the pharmacy will be for the compounding and dispensing of percentage preparations (solutions or powders). The most important factor to keep in mind here is that *slight* errors in dilute preparations may be considered negligible, whereas even a slight error in a concentrated preparation may be serious. To firmly impress this in your mind, consider the difference between losing one quarter from your pocket containing ten quarters and losing ten quarters from another pocket containing 100 quarters. The loss in each case is 10 percent. In the first instance, 10 percent loss amounted to only 25 cents, while in the second instance the 10 percent loss amounted to $2.50. Thus, as the percentage of a solution or other preparation becomes greater, the error becomes more severe. The strength of a solution is the ratio of active ingredient to solvent and can be expressed as a percent or as a ratio.

   a. Percent solutions. The Latin "per centum" literally means "by hundreds." Ten percent, then, refers to 10 hundreds or 10 parts out of 100 parts. A 10-percent solution could be broken down as follows:

   Total volume of solution — 100% or 100 parts
   Solute (active ingredient) — 10% or 10 parts
   Solvent — 90% or 90 parts

   In solutions of solids or gases in a liquid, the solid or gas being dissolved is called the solute, and the liquid is the solvent. In solution of liquids in liquids, we arbitrarily say that the liquid present in greater quantity is the solvent and the liquid of lesser quantity is the solute. Thus we say that in mixing 25 percent water and 75 percent alcohol, we obtain a solution of water in alcohol. Reversing the situation, 25 percent alcohol and 75 percent water, we would term a solution of alcohol in water.

   (1) Variable meaning of percentage. Percentage in solutions can have different meanings under different circumstances. In solution, you are dealing with solids which are weighed, and liquids which can be weighed or measured; thus, it is necessary to define the expression of percentage concentration of solutions. There are three different percentage solutions:

   (a) Percent weight in weight (w/w)—expresses the number of grams of a constituent in 100 grams of solution.

   (b) Percent weight in volume (w/v)—expresses the number of grams of a constituent in 100 ml. of solution, and is used in prescription practice regardless of whether water or another liquid is used.

   (c) Percent volume in volume (v/v)—expresses the number of milliliters of a constituent in 100 ml. of solution.

(2) *Rules for percentage solutions.* Unless specifically stipulated otherwise, the following rules hold true for prescriptions of percentage solutions:
- Mixtures of solids are weight in weight.
- Solids in liquids are weight in volume.
- Liquids in liquids are volume in volume.
- Gases in liquids are weight in volume.

For example, to make a 10-percent solution, dissolve 10 Gm. of a solid or 10 ml. of a liquid in the amount of solvent necessary (qs) to make 100 ml. of finished solution. In the apothecary system, 45.6 grains of a solid or 48 minims of a liquid dissolved in enough solvent to make 1 fluidounce would yield a 10-percent solution. Slight changes in volume attributable to changes in room temperature are negligible and may be disregarded.

b. *Percent weight in volume solutions.* Weight in volume (w/v) percentage may be called the "key" to percentage and ratio solutions. You are dissolving a weight of solid in a volume of liquid (water, unless otherwise specified).

(1) *Metric system rule.* Multiply the specified percentage, expressed as a decimal fraction, times the required number of ml. The resulting number will represent the number of grams of solid in the solution, or percent (decimal) x ml. = grams solute.

(2) *Apothecary system rule.* Multiply the percent, expressed as a whole number times 4.5457 times fluidounces of solution required. The answer you obtain will be the number of grains of solute to be used. The weight of 1 fluidounce of water at 25° C. is 454.57 grains. Therefore, 4.5457 grains is the amount of solute necessary to prepare a 1-percent solution of 1 ounce. Expressed as a formula, this rule becomes percent (whole number) x 4.5457 x fl oz. required = grains of solute.

(3) *Example:* Prepare 300 ml. of 20-percent (w/v) solution of sodium thiosulfate. How many grams of solute are necessary? How much solvent is used?

- *Step 1.* Formula.
  % (decimal) x ml. = grams solute

- *Step 2.* Substitute.
  .20 x 300 = 60 grams of solute

- *Step 3.* Since the total solution is to be 300 ml., you add enough water to the 60 grams of solute to make the finished product measure 300 ml. If you assumed that 60 grams took up 60 ml. of volume, you could deduce that 240 ml. of liquid added to the 60 grams of solute would make 300 ml. This does not hold true. Many solids when dissolved do not take up a volume equal to their weight, so you must always add enough water to make the volume up to the required amount. This bringing up to the required volume is expressed in prescriptions as "qs ad" from the Latin, and means "add a sufficient quantity."

(4) *Example:* Work this similar problem in the apothecary system. Make ℥ iv (4 fluidounces) of a 20-percent solution of sodium thiosulfate.

- *Step 1.* Formula.
  % x 4.5457 x fl. oz. = grains of solute.

- *Step 2.* Substitute.
  20 x 4.5457 x 4 = 363.6 grains = (℥ vi gr iiiss)

The prescription could have been written:
  Rx Sod. Thiosulfate grs 363.6
  Pur. Water qs ad ℥ iv.

c. *Percent volume in volume solutions.* To calculate percentage of solutions of one liquid in another, multiply the desired percent, as a decimal fraction, of the active ingredient times the amount of total solution desired.

Example: How many ml. of an active ingredient must be used to produce 480 ml. of a 3-percent solution?
  480 x .03 = 34.4 ml., answer

d. *Percent weight in weight solution.* In some cases, a definite finished weight of solution is required. To find the percent of solid in the solution, multiply the total weight of the finished solution desired by the percent desired, expressed as a decimal. Written as a formula this would be—Gm. total solution x % (decimal) = Gm. of active solute. By subtracting this weight (the weight of the solute) from the weight of the total solution, the weight of the liquid required as solvent is found. This weight may be converted to volume by dividing the weight of liquid required by the specific gravity of the liquid. Specific gravity will be discussed below.

(1) *Example:* How many grams of acriflavine are required to manufacture 200 Gm. of a 10-percent (w/w) solution? How much glycerin will you use as the solvent? Express the amount of glycerin in both weight and volume (Sp. Gr. glycerin = 1.25).

200 x 0.10 = 20 Gm. acriflavine
200 − 20 = 180 Gm. glycerin
180 ÷ 1.25 = 144 ml. glycerin

(2) *Example:* Prepare 4 fluidounces of a 10-percent (w/w) solution of acriflavine in glycerin. This problem takes on more difficulty in the apothecary system. First reduce the total weight of solution to grains.

- *Step 1.* Reduce solution to grains.
  4 fl oz x 454.6 = 1818.4 grains (total solution)

- *Step 2.* 10 % of 1818.4 = 181.84 grains of acriflavine.

- *Step 3.* 1818.4 − 181.84 = 1636.56 grains of glycerin.

- *Step 4.* 1 fl oz of water weighs 454.6 grains; therefore, 1 fluidounce of glycerin weighs 454.6 x 1.25 = 568.25 gr.

- *Step 5.* Since you need 1636.56 grains of glycerin, by dividing this by the number of grains of glycerin in a fluidounce, you will obtain the volume of glycerin required in terms of fluidounces.
  1636.56 ÷ 568.25 = 2.88 fluidounces or
  f ℥ ii f ʒ vii ♏ii

34. Ratio preparations. Ratio is similar to percent, the entire solution is the total, the active ingredient is a certain part of the total, and the solvent or diluent is the remainder. Ratio solutions are expressed as so much in so much; for example, 1 in 10; 1 in 100; 1 in 1000. It means exactly what it says, 1 part in a total of 10 parts, or 1 part in a total of 100 parts; it does not mean 1 part plus 10 parts to give 11 parts. It is obvious that a 1 in 10 solution, therefore, is identical to a 10 percent solution. A ratio solution is expressed by parts—so many parts in a total of so many parts; 1 part in 10 parts = 1 in 10. The number of parts of active ingredient is taken as 1, and the total parts possible is variable as in 1 in 10, 1 in 20, 1 in 100. You remember in percentage, the total mixture was always 100 and the active part was variable, as 10 percent (10/100), 20 percent (20/100), or 50 percent (50/100).

a. Weight in volume solution by ratio. The following proportion is used in making ratio solutions of the weight in volume type.

weight of solute	:: *one part of solute*
wt of given volume of solution if it were water	No. of parts of completed solution containing 1 part of solute

(1) *Example:* What is the ratio strength (w/v) of a solution containing 25 Gm. of solute in 250 ml. of solution?
Substitute in the preceding formula.

$$\frac{25}{250} :: \frac{1}{x}$$

$$25x = 250$$

x = 10; ratio strength, then, is 1 in 10 (1/10)
Using this formula, any one of the four parts can be found, if the other three are known.

(2) *Example:* If the ratio strength (w/v) of a solution is 1:25, and it contains 50 Gm. of solute, what is the total volume of the solution?
Substitute:

$$\frac{50}{x} :: \frac{1}{25}$$

x = 1250 ml., the total volume of solution.

b. Volume in volume solution by ratio. Again, a simple proportion can be used to solve this type of problem.

vol. of ingredient	parts of ingredient
vol. of total solution	parts of whole

CAUTION
The two volumes concerned *must* be expressed in the same denomination; that is, if one is expressed in ml., the other must also be ml.

(1) *Example:* What amount of active ingredient must be used to produce 500 ml. of a solution (v/v) with a ratio strength of 1:20?
Substitute:

$$\frac{x}{500} :: \frac{1}{20}$$

$$20x = 500$$

x = 25 ml., answer

(2) *Example:* What is the ratio strength of a solution which contains 5 ml. of active ingredient in a total of 250 ml.? Substitute:

$$\frac{5}{250} :: \frac{1}{x}$$

$$5x = 250$$

$$x = 50$$

strength is 1 in 50 (1:50)

c. Weight to weight solution by ratio. For w/w solutions, two proportions may be expressed;

one shows the relationship between active ingredient and the total solution, the other between ingredient and diluent.

$$\frac{\text{wt ingredient}}{\text{wt mixture}} :: \frac{\text{parts of ingredient}}{\text{parts total mixture}}$$

or

$$\frac{\text{wt ingredient}}{\text{wt diluent}} :: \frac{\text{parts of ingredient}}{\text{parts of diluent}}$$

(1) Example: What is the weight in grams of a 1:10,000 (w/w) solution containing 150 mg. of active ingredient? Substituting in first formula:

$$\frac{150}{x} = \frac{1}{10,000}$$

$$x = 1,500,000 \text{ mg.}$$
$$x = 1500 \text{ Gm. (wt of solution)}$$

(2) Example: If 8 Gm. of a substance is dissolved in 128 ml. of water, what is the w/w ratio strength of the solution? Substituting in second formula:

$$\frac{8}{128} :: \frac{1}{x}$$
$$8x = 128$$
$$x = 16$$
$$1 \text{ in } 16 \ (1:16)$$

35. Specific gravity. Specific gravity, abbreviated Sp. Gr., is the relation between the weights of two substances, one of which is a standard. Determination of Sp. Gr. is accomplished under specific conditions, namely, 25° C. and normal barometric pressure. Distilled water is the standard for liquids and solids, and air for gases. Specific gravity is always expressed as a decimal; the standard substance has a Sp. Gr. of 1.000. Comparing equal volumes of glycerin and water, for example, we find that glycerin is 1-1/4 times as heavy. Since the Sp. Gr. of water is 1.000, the Sp. Gr. of glycerin is 1.250.

36. Specific gravity of liquids. There are several instruments used for determination of the specific gravity of liquids. We will discuss only two here, the pycnometer and the hydrometer.

a. Pycnometer. The pycnometer (fig. 2-7) is a specific gravity bottle. Pycnometer is derived from the Greek word pykno, meaning dense, and meter, meaning measure. It is, therefore, a device for measuring density. Any small, long-necked flask made of thin glass will serve as a pycnometer. It is preferable for simplicity of calculation that the pycnometer hold some simple unit volume of

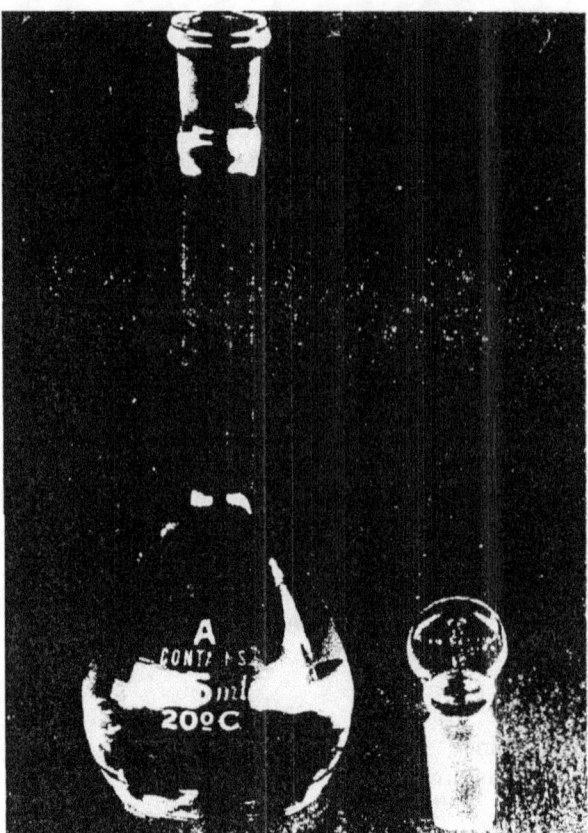

Figure 7. The pycnometer.

water, 25 Gm., 50 Gm., or 100 Gm. You will see the benefit of this in the following paragraphs. To find specific gravity using a pycnometer, proceed as follows:

(1) First, we must know the exact weight of the empty pycnometer. This is called the "tare" or "tare weight." Since dirt and moisture will affect this tare weight, it is important that the vessel be clean and dry. Make a note of the tare weight.

(2) Distilled water is then poured into the pycnometer until it reaches a convenient level in the neck. A line is marked on the pycnometer at the level of the lower edge of the meniscus (concave or convex surface of the liquid).

(3) Note the temperature of the water and record it. Now carefully weigh the pycnometer and its contents and record the combined weight.

(4) The weight of the water alone can be calculated by subtracting the tare weight of the pycnometer from the combined weight recorded in step *(3)* above. This is the weight of the water at the recorded temperature. The tare weight, temperature, and weight of the water may be permanently etched on the side of the flask for

future calculations. These figures will remain constant for all future specific gravity determinations.

(5) When the flask is again clean and dry, the specific gravity of any liquid may be taken by filling it to the same point with the liquid to be tested.

(6) Weigh the pycnometer, now containing a liquid to be tested, and subtract the tare weight of the vessel. The number resulting will be the weight of the liquid you are testing.

(7) Determine the specific gravity by substituting in this formula:

$$\text{Sp. Gr.} = \frac{\text{weight of known volume of substance}}{\text{weight of equal volume of distilled water}}$$

(8) *Example:* A pycnometer weighs 20.123 Gm. when clean and dry. When filled to a convenient level with water at 25° C., it weighs 44.678 Gm. The same bottle filled to the same level with glycerin at 25° C. weighs 50.816 Gm. What is the specific gravity of the glycerin?

- *Step 1.*

weight of glycerin + bottle = 50.816 Gm.
minus tare weight of bottle − 20.123 Gm.
the weight of glycerin 30.693 Gm.

- *Step 2.*

weight of water + bottle = 44.678 Gm.
minus tare weight of bottle − 20.123 Gm.
the weight of water 24.555 Gm.

- *Step 3.* Formula:

$$\text{Sp. Gr.} = \frac{\text{weight substance}}{\text{weight equal volume of water}}$$

- *Step 4.*

$$\text{Sp. Gr.} = \frac{30.693}{24.555} = 1.25 \text{ the Sp. Gr. of glycerin}$$

b. *Hydrometer.* The hydrometer is an instrument which gives us a quick but not as accurate a determination of specific gravity as the pycnometer. It can also be used to measure density of liquids and percent of solutions, such as the alcoholic content of liquids or the radiator of an automobile. The hydrometer consists of a closed glass tube, blown at one end and having a long stem at the other. The blown end is filled with a heavy weight (usually mercury or shot) to keep it erect when floated in a liquid. The long stem is internally calibrated with a graduated scale. For increased accuracy, there are hydrometers calibrated for use in light liquids and others for heavy liquids.

(1) *Theory of the hydrometer.* All floating bodies displace their own weight of a liquid in which they are immersed and sink to a depth proportionate to the volume of liquid displaced. Since this volume equals the weight of the immersed object, specific gravity can be determined by comparison of the volumes displaced. Thus a hydrometer is marked 1.000 at the level it sinks in distilled water at normal temperature. The scale is then carried above and below the 1.000 mark. When the instrument is placed in a different liquid, the specific gravity of that liquid can be read directly from the scale.

(2) *Testing the hydrometer.* Do not accept hydrometers as you receive them. Always test them first. By immersing your hydrometer in a number of liquids of known specific gravity, including water, you can observe its degree of accuracy. In the event a particular hydrometer shows consistent deviation of one or two points, you need not discard it as useless. Make a notation of the deviation on its box and merely add or subtract the error from the reading as you use it.

(3) *Hydrometer jar.* The hydrometer is generally floated in a hydrometer jar to take the reading (fig. 2-8). This device lessens the amount of liquid necessary for a reading because it is tall and narrow. It also facilitates cooling of the liquid to specified temperature, the jar being easily immersed in ice water.

(4) *Other applications of the hydrometer:*

(a) Urinometer—this hydrometer has a special scale for the determination of specific gravity of urine.

(b) Saccharometer—generally measures the percent of syrups rather than the specific gravity.

(c) Alcoholometer—determines alcoholic strength of hydroalcoholic solutions.

(d) Lovi's beads—also called specific gravity beads, are balloon-like, hollow globes of glass. They are of different sizes and weights and have a specific gravity number etched on their sides. When dropped into a liquid, those heavier than the liquid sink to the bottom; the ones lighter than the liquid float to the top; and the one which hovers in the liquid, neither floating nor sinking, represents the specific gravity. They must be used at a definite temperature for which they have been calibrated.

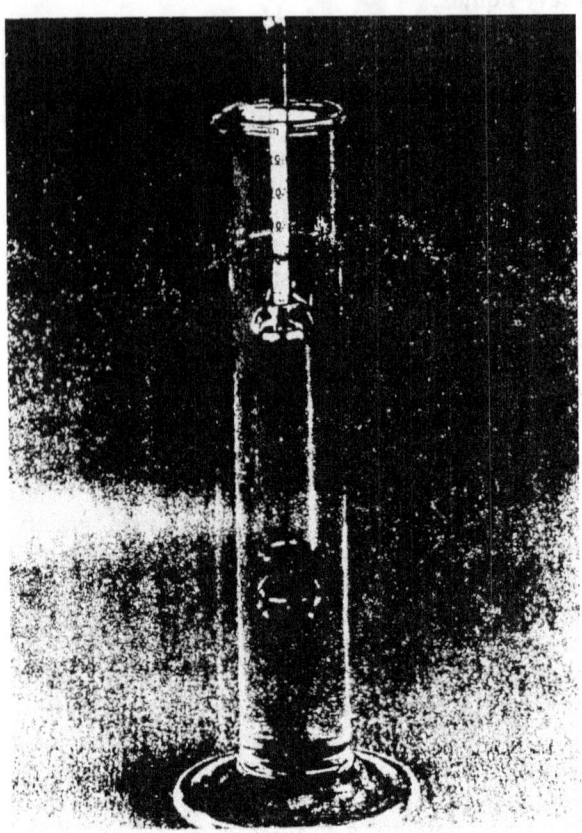

Figure 8. Hydrometer and jar.

37. **Specific gravity of solids.** Although various procedures must be used for determining the specific gravity of different solids, the formula used is always the same:

$$\text{Sp. Gr.} = \frac{\text{weight of solid in air}}{\text{weight of equal volume of water}}$$

Because of slight variations of technique necessary to establish the specific gravity of solids with different physical properties, we will break solids into groups according to their solubility and weight relative to water. Thus we have—
- Solids insoluble in and heavier than water.
- Solids soluble in and heavier than water.
- Solids insoluble in and lighter than water.
- Solids soluble in and lighter than water.

  a. Solids insoluble in and heavier than water.

  (1) When solid is a single piece. First, consider a solid in one piece, such as a block of metal or a strip of wire. The easiest method for determining specific gravity of a single piece of solid insoluble in and heavier than water is by using a balance.

● *Step 1.* Accurately weigh the sample to be tested on a good Rx or analytical balance and record this weight as the weight of the substance in air.

● *Step 2.* Attach a horsehair or fine, water-proofed, silk thread to the sample and to the beam of the scale. Immerse the sample in a beaker of water so that it is covered by the water, but not touching the bottom or sides of the beaker. The weight of the sample must be entirely supported by the beam of the balance. Make sure no air bubbles are attached to the sample which would provide buoyancy and make the weighing in water inaccurate. Record the weight of the sample in the water.

● *Step 3.* Apply the formula. *For example,* if a sample of copper weighs 10.52 Gm. in air and 9.34 Gm. when suspended in water, to find the specific gravity of the copper:

Weight in air   = 10.52 Gm.
Weight in water   9.34 Gm.
─────────────
1.18 = loss of weight in water

$$\text{Sp. Gr.} = \frac{\text{weight in air}}{\text{weight of equal volume of water}}$$

Since the loss of weight in water equals the weight of an equal volume of water, substitute in the formula:

$$\text{Sp. Gr.} = \frac{10.52}{1.18}$$

Sp. Gr. = 8.92 (copper)

  (2) When solid is fragmentary. Another method of determining the specific gravity of solids insoluble in and heavier than water is by the use of a pycnometer. This method is convenient when the solid is in fragments or smaller particles.

● *Step 1.* Weigh the sample in air and record the weight.

● *Step 2.* Drop the material into a tared pycnometer and fill with distilled water at 25° C. Weigh again, making sure that no water remains on the exterior of the vessel. This weight represents the weight of the pycnometer, the water, and the sample. Subtracting the tare weight, you have the weight of the sample plus the water in the bottle.

● *Step 3.* Apply the formula. *For example,* a sample weighing 10.5 Gm. is placed in a pyconometer which has been determined to hold

100 Gm. of water. You determine the weight of the sample plus the water plus the bottle to be 206.2 Gm. The tare weight of the bottle is 100 Gm.

206.2 Gm. weight of bottle, water, sample
− 100.0 Gm. weight of bottle
106.2 Gm. weight of water and sample
 10.5 Gm. weight of sample in air
100.0 Gm. weight of water held by bottle
110.5 Gm. weight of water plus sample
− 106.2 Gm. weight of water and immersed sample
   4.3 Gm. loss of weight in water

$$Sp. Gr. = \frac{10.5}{4.3} = 2.442, \text{ the specific gravity}$$

NOTE

The specific gravity of insoluble powders can also be determined by this method. Care should be taken to shake the powder with a quantity of water before filling the pycnometer to eliminate air bubbles and the error they can cause.

b. Solids insoluble in and lighter than water. The problem here is to make the solid sink into the water so that you can find out how much water it displaces. A weight or sinker, insoluble in water and heavy enough to cause the lighter sample to sink beneath the surface, can be attached. Since the loss of weight in water of the sample and sinker combined equals their total individual losses, it will be easy then to determine the loss of weight of the sample.

Example: A block of wax weighs 21.5 Gm. in the air. To this you attach a lead sinker which you have predetermined to lose 1.1 Gm. when immersed in water. Together they lose 25.8 grams when immersed in water. What is the specific gravity of the wax?

● *Step 1.*
Loss of weight of wax + sinker = 25.8 Gm.
Loss of weight of sinker   − 1.1 Gm.
Loss of weight of wax   = 24.7 Gm.
Weight of wax in air   = 21.5 Gm.

● *Step 2.* Apply the formula.

$$Sp. Gr. \frac{21.5}{24.7}$$

$$Sp. Gr. = 0.87$$

c. Solids soluble in and heavier than water. The problem here is solubility. By substituting a liquid in which the sample is not soluble for the water, you can then determine by proportion what the loss of weight in water would be. The following proportion will apply:

$$\frac{Sp. Gr. \text{ of oil}}{Sp. Gr. \text{ of water}} :: \frac{\text{loss of weight in oil}}{\text{loss of weight in water}}$$

Example: 20.311 Gm. of Copper Sulfate immersed in an oil having a specific gravity of 0.865 filling a 100 Gm. pycnometer weighs 98.859 Gm. Find the specific gravity of copper sulfate.

● *Step 1.*
Weight of $CuSO_4$ in air   = 20.311 Gm.
Weight of oil in pycnom.   = 86.5   (100 × 0.865)
Weight of $CuSO_4$ + oil   106.811 Gm.

Weight of oil +
 immersed $CuSO_4$ = 98.859 Gm.
Weight of oil displaced   7.952 Gm.

● *Step 2.* Substitute in proportion.

$$\frac{Sp. Gr. \text{ of oil}}{Sp. Gr. \text{ of water}} :: \frac{\text{loss of weight in oil}}{\text{loss of weight in water}}$$

$$\frac{0.865}{1} :: \frac{7.952}{x}$$

$$865x = 7952$$

x = 9.193, the loss of weight in water

● *Step 3.* Substitute in Sp. Gr. formula.

$$Sp. Gr. = \frac{20.311}{9.193}$$

$$Sp. Gr. = 2.209$$

NOTE

If the copper sulfate were in one solid lump, you could measure the loss of weight in oil directly by suspending it from a balance into the oil.

d. Solids soluble in and lighter than water. Here, the problem, and not a slight one, is to find a liquid lighter than the solid and one in which it is not soluble. When this is accomplished, the procedure is the same for solids soluble in and heavier than water (*c* above).

38. Application of specific gravity to pharmaceutical problems. Specific gravity, when known, is of great assistance to us as pharmacists in reducing metric and apothecary volumes to weight and, conversely, in reducing weights to volumes.

a. *Metric.*
- 1 ml. of water weighs 1 Gm.
- Sp. Gr. of water is 1.000.
- 1 ml. of any liquid with Sp. Gr. of 1.000 weighs 1 Gm.
- 1 ml. of a liquid with Sp. Gr. of 2.000 weighs (1 x 2.000) 2 Gm.
- 1 ml. of a liquid with Sp. Gr. of 1.5 weighs 1 x 1.5 or 1.5 Gm.

Therefore, the volume in ml. times specific gravity = weight in Gm.

(1) *Example:* What is the weight in grams of 1 liter of glycerin (Sp. Gr. 1.25)?

- *Step 1.* 1 liter = 1000 ml.

- *Step 2.* 1000 ml. x 1.25 = 1250 Gm., the weight of 1 liter of glycerin.

(2) *Example:* How many ml. of chloroform are there in 1480 Gm.? (Sp. Gr. of chloroform = 1.48).

x ml. x 1.48 = 1480 Gm.

$$x = \frac{1480}{1.48} = 1000 \text{ ml. or 1 liter of chloroform}$$

b. *Apothecary.* There is no convenient weight-to-volume comparison in the apothecary system. However, you may derive a working formula from the steps below.

- *Step 1.* In the metric system, 1 gram of water or any liquid with a specific gravity of 1.000, has a corresponding volume of 1 ml. In the apothecary system, a fluidounce of water or any fluid with a specific gravity of 1.000 does not weigh 1 ounce, nor does a fluidrachm weigh a drachm, nor a minim weigh a grain.

- *Step 2.* BUT, 1 fluidounce of water at 25° C. weighs 454.6 grains. Since there are 480 minims in 1 fluidounce, a minim of water weighs 454.6 ÷ 480 = 0.95 grain.

- *Step 3.* 1 fluidounce of any liquid having a specific gravity of 1.000 weighs 454.6 grain. 1 fluidounce of any liquid having a specific gravity of 2.000 weighs 454.6 x 2.

- *Step 4.* Conclusion. 1 fluidounce of any liquid weighs (in grains) 454.6 x specific gravity. Thus the following formula:
454.6 x Sp. Gr. x number of fluidounces = weight in grains.

(1) *Example:* How much does f℥ii, ℨiv of glycerin weigh? Sp. Gr. of glycerin is 1.25.

- *Step 1.* f℥ii, ℨiv = 2.5 fluidounces.

- *Step 2.* Substitute in formula:
454.6 x 1.25 x 2.5 = weight in grains

```
  454.6          568.25
x  1.25        x   2.5
-------        -------
 22730          284125
  9092          113650
  4546          -------
-------         1420.625, weight of glycerin
568.250
```

- *Step 3.* Convert to highest terms.
1420.625 rounded off (.625 → .63 grains)
20 gr./℈, so 1420 ÷ 20 = 71℈
3 ℈/ℨ, so 71 ÷ 3 = 23ℨ + 2℈ remainder
8 ℨ/℥, so 23 ÷ 8 = 2℥ + 7ℨ remainder

- *Step 4.* Collect the amounts.
℥ii ℨvii ℈ii gr ss(.63)

(2) *Example:* What is the volume of 250 grains of a liquid with a specific gravity of 0.942?

- *Step 1.* Formula.
454.6 x 0.942 x y (No. fluidounces) = weight in grains
454.6 x 0.942 x y = 250

```
   0.942
x  454.6
-------
   5652
   3768
   4710
   3768
-------
 428.2332
```

y(428.233) = 250

$$y = \frac{250}{428.233}$$

y = .583 fluidounce

- *Step 2.* Reduce to correct terms.
8 fℨ = 1f℥
therefore, .583 x 8 = 4.664 fluidrachms
60 minims = 1 fℨ
therefore, .664 x 60 = 40 minims

- *Step 3.* Combine the quantities:
fℨ iv ♏ x 1

39. Specific volume

a. Identification. Specific volume is much like specific gravity, except the comparison is between volumes rather than weights. Specific volume can be described as the ratio of the volume of one substance to the volume of an equal weight of a standard substance. As in specific gravity, the standard is water and the standard temperature is 25° C.

Since Sp. Gr. = $\dfrac{\text{weight of substance in air}}{\text{weight of equal volume of water}}$

Sp. Vol. = $\dfrac{\text{volume of substance}}{\text{volume of equal weight of water}}$

Then, Specific Gravity = $\dfrac{1}{\text{Sp. Vol.}}$ and

Sp. Vol. = $\dfrac{1}{\text{Sp. Gr.}}$; they are reciprocals

b. Sample problems.
(1) Problem: What is the specific volume of 750 Gm. of chloroform measuring 510.2 ml.?

● *Step 1.* Volume of chloroform = 510.2 ml.
Volume of equal weight water = 750.0 ml.

● *Step 2.* Substitute in formula

Sp. Vol. = $\dfrac{\text{volume of substance}}{\text{volume of equal weight water}}$

Sp. Vol. = $\dfrac{510.2}{750}$

Sp. Vol = 0.68

(2) Problem: Using the information in the previous problem, what is the specific gravity of chloroform?
Using the reciprocal formula:

Sp. Gr. = $\dfrac{1}{\text{Sp. Vol.}}$

Sp. Gr. = $\dfrac{1}{0.68}$

Sp. Gr. = 1.47, answer

```
        1.47
68/100.00
     68
     ───
     32 0
     27 2
     ────
      4 80
      4 76
```

40. Density

a. Identification. Density is the ratio between weight and volume of a substance; or, density = weight divided by volume, and is expressed not as a relative number, as specific gravity was, but with specific units as Gm./ml., lb/cu.ft., or gr./fl.oz.

From the formula:

$D = \dfrac{w}{v}$, we see that if we know density and volume we can determine weight; knowing density and weight, we can find volume; and knowing weight and volume, we can find density.

b. Sample problems.
(1) Problem: What is the density of alcohol if 250 ml. weigh 200 Gm.?

Density = $\dfrac{\text{weight}}{\text{volume}}$

$D = \dfrac{200}{250}$

D = 0.80 Gm./ml.

(2) Problem: How many ml. of mercury (density 13.6) would there be in a sample weighing 2000 Gm.?

$D = \dfrac{w}{v}$

$13.6 = \dfrac{2000}{v}$

$13.6\,v = 2000$

$v = \dfrac{2000}{13.6}$

v = 147.06 ml.

41. Temperature

a. Definition. What exactly is temperature? Temperature can be stated as being the degree of hotness or lack of hotness, or the *intensity of heat*. Relative temperatures can be sensed by touch in some cases, but the sense of touch can be very misleading. A piece of cloth and a piece of metal, although exactly the same temperature will feel differently to the touch. The cloth will not seem as warm or as cold as the metal. This is due to the rate at which the substance dissipates heat.

b. Measurement of temperature. Temperature, therefore, must be measured by a device which gives accurate degrees of heat. Such instruments are called thermometers. The thermometer is based on the principle of expansion and contraction of substances with change in temperature. The most common thermometers utilize alcohol or mercury. In order for readings obtained from expansion and contraction to be valid, the expansion and contraction must be uniform.

c. Liquid thermometer. The liquid thermometer consists of a fine capillary tube, hermetically sealed, with a bulb at one end. The tube is filled to a point on the capillary, the bulb serving as a reservoir. Upon elevating the temperature, the liquid expands and rises in the tube to a new level. Thus, calibrating the tube with known constant temperatures and dividing the space between with equal degrees, we have an instrument that will measure temperature. Figure 2-9 shows two liquid thermometers discussed below.

42. Temperature calculation. There are two different scales by which liquid thermometers can be calibrated—the Centigrade scale and the Fahrenheit scale.

a. Centigrade. The Centigrade thermometer is so calibrated that the melting point of ice is 0° C. and the boiling point of water is 100° C. By this scale, there is a difference of 100 degrees between the freezing and boiling points of water. The Centigrade scale has been adopted by the USP and NF as the official temperature standard. In fact, it is the standard temperature measuring device the world over.

b. Fahrenheit. The Fahrenheit thermometer is calibrated so that 32° F. is the melting point of ice and 212° F. is the boiling point of water. The difference between freezing and boiling on this scale is 180°. The Fahrenheit scale is used mainly for household purposes.

c. Importance of stating the scale. Because of the great difference between these two scales, you can see the importance of always stating which scale you are using when referring to a temperature. By itself, 40° means nothing; 40° Fahrenheit is approximately 4.4° Centigrade; 40° Centigrade is 104° Fahrenheit, a considerable difference.

d. Absolute temperature. We, as pharmacists, will not deal with the absolute temperature scale; however, you should be familiar with what it is. Remember only that *absolute* degree equals Centigrade degrees plus 273°. Expressed as a formula this becomes—

$$A° = C° + 273°.$$

43. Temperature conversion. Knowing that the range in degrees between the freezing and boiling points of water is 100° in the Centigrade scale and 180° in the Fahrenheit scale, it is obvious that one Centigrade degree is equal to 1.8 (9/5), the size of a Fahrenheit degree. Therefore, a 5-degree change in Centigrade temperature is a 9-degree change in the Fahrenheit scale. Since 0° C. equals 32° F., 1° C. must equal 32° plus 9/5° or 1.8°, or 33.8° F. Thus, we can derive several formulas. However, the basic formula is: 9C = 5F − 160, or 5F = 9C + 160.

a. Example: Convert −5° Centigrade to Fahrenheit.

- *Step 1.* Formula: 5F = 9C + 160

- *Step 2.* Substitute: 5F = 9 (−5) + 160
  5F = −45 + 160
  5F = 115
  F = 115 ÷ 5
  F = 23° F

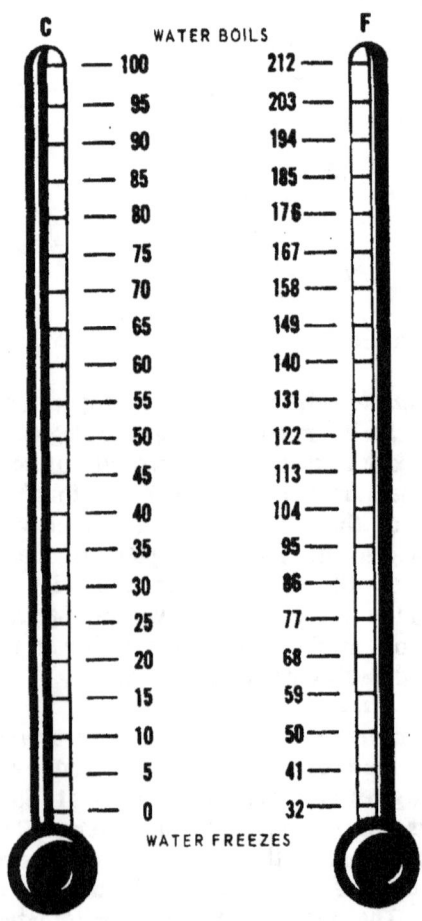

Figure 9. Thermometer comparison.

b. *Example:* Convert –40° Fahrenheit to Centigrade.

- *Step 1.* Formula: 9C = 5F – 160

- *Step 2.* Substitute: 9C = 5 (–40) – 160
  9C = –200 – 160
  9C = –360
  C = –360 ÷ 9
  C = –40° C

c. *Example:* Convert 80° Fahrenheit to Centigrade.

- *Step 1.* Formula: 9C = 5F – 160

- *Step 2.* Substitute: 9C = 5(80) – 160
  9C = 400 – 160
  9C = 240
  C = 240 ÷ 9
  C = 26.6° C

44. Dosage

a. Importance of dosage calculation to the pharmacist. When a prescription reaches the pharmacist from the desk of a prescriber, the ingredients are specified, the quantities listed (perhaps in specific amounts, perhaps as ratio, perhaps as percentages), and the instructions to the patient are written in Latin, in pharmaceutical or medical terminology. The pharmacist must (1) fill the prescription, (2) check the prescriber for possible error of amounts and dosage, and (3) write the directions upon the label in terms which can be easily understood by the patient. For these reasons, an accurate knowledge of dosage is mandatory for the pharmacist. Imagine the consequences of the following:

(1) Error in converting a percent ingredient to the specific amount.

(2) Prescriber's inadvertent error in amount of ingredient to be used in preparation of a medicinal (with the accompanying error of the pharmacist not observing the error).

(3) Prescriber's error in calculation of dosage (again combined with the pharmacist's missing the error). Although errors are the exception rather than the rule, the pharmacist must be forever on his guard against them. It is not his privilege to look for errors, but his *duty*. The pharmacist is held responsible equally with the erring physician. Overdose, even though it may originate at the prescriber, if not corrected by the pharmacy technician may constitute negligence.

b. Approximate household equivalents. The approximate household equivalents shown in table 2-8 are useful in making calculations for number of doses in a medication and for translating directions into terms understandable to the patient. These approximate equivalents are in obvious discrepancy due to approximating equivalency between three different measures. In table 2-8, one teasp, 1 f ʒ (approx 4 ml.) and 5 ml. are not equal at all. However, the directions to the patient cannot read "Take 1 drachm" or "4 ml." or "5 ml." They must be written in some language that all literate persons can understand—thus, "one teaspoonful."

c. Medicine glass. Because of inaccuracy in household equivalents and because household spoons, cups, and glasses vary considerably in size, the patient should be strongly advised to purchase a medicine glass (fig. 2-10) for accurate dosage.

d. Calculation of dosage. Some of the dosage calculations you will be making most frequently are listed below. The following proportion can be established which will aid in solving dosage problems:

$$\text{Total doses} = \frac{\text{total amount}}{\text{size of each dose}}$$

(1) Calculating the size of an individual dose. When given the total amount of medication and the number of doses to be made, the size of each can be calculated by dividing. *Example:* A

Table 8. Approximate Household Equivalents

Metric measure	Apothecary equivalent (approximate)	Household measure
2 ml	f ʒss	½ teaspoonful
5 ml	f ʒi	1 teaspoonful
8 ml	f ʒii	1 dessertspoonful
15 ml	f ʒiv	1 tablespoonful
30 ml	f ʒviii (f ʒi)	2 tablespoonfuls
60 m	f ʒii	1 wineglassful
120 ml	f ʒiv	1 teacupful
240 ml	f ʒviii	1 tumblerful

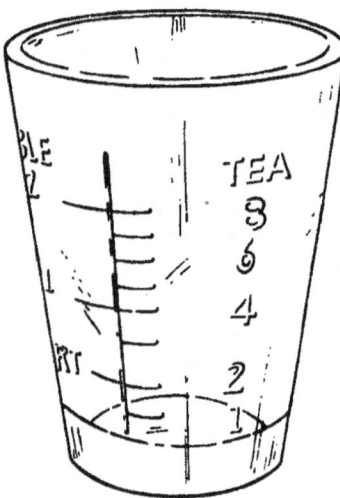

Figure 10. A medicine glass.

particular medication is to be taken 4 times daily for 1 week, and a total of 280 grains is being dispensed. What is the amount of this medication in a single dose?

- *Step 1.* What is the total number of doses?
4 doses daily x 7 days = 28 doses, total

- *Step 2.* Formula.

$$\text{Total doses} = \frac{\text{total amount}}{\text{size of each dose}}$$

- *Step 3.* Substitute—

$$28 = \frac{280 \text{ gr.}}{x}$$
$$28x = 280$$
$$x = 10 \text{ grains in each dose.}$$

NOTE

The answer will always be in the same denomination as the total amount, or if the total amount is the unknown, in the same denomination as the individual dose.

(2) *Calculating number of doses.* The number of doses in a specific amount can be calculated if you are given the total amount and the size of the dose.
(a) *Example:* How many doses of 5 grains each will result from a total of 75 grains of total medication?

- *Step 1.* Formula.

$$\text{Total doses} = \frac{\text{total amount}}{\text{size of each dose}}$$

- *Step 2.* Substitute.

$$x = \frac{75 \text{ gr.}}{5}$$
$$x = 15 \text{ doses}$$

(b) *Example:* If the dose of a medication is to be one-half fluidrachm, how many doses will a patient receive, given an 8-ounce bottle of medication?

- *Step 1.* Since there are 8 fluidrachms to the fluidounce, 8 fluidounces would contain 8 x 8 = 64 fluidrachms.

- *Step 2.* Formula.

$$\text{Total doses} = \frac{\text{total amount}}{\text{size of each dose}}$$

- *Step 3.* Substitute.

$$x = \frac{64 \text{ fluidrachms}}{.5}$$
$$x = 128 \text{ doses, answer}$$

(3) *Calculating total amount of medication.* If you know the size of the dose and the number of doses prescribed, you can determine the total medication to be dispensed.
Example: A patient is to receive 1 fluidounce of whisky morning, noon, and night for an indefinite period of time. What quantity would be dispensed for 1 week's medication?

- *Step 1.* 1 ounce dose x 3 doses per day x 7 days per week equals 21 ounces. The formula may also be used as shown in step 2 below.

- *Step 2.* Formula.

$$\text{Total doses} = \frac{\text{total amount}}{\text{size of each dose}}$$
$$21 = \frac{x}{1}$$
$$x = 21 \text{ ounces, answer}$$

(4) *Calculating amount of a single ingredient.* The amount of a single ingredient present in a dose of a mixture of several medicinal agents can be determined by dividing the amount of that ingredient by the total doses.

(a) *Example:* Calculate the amount of *each* ingredient in a single dose of the following prescription.

```
Rx Acetylsalicylic acid      ℥ii  ℈i  gr vii
   Acetophenetidin           ℥i   ℈ii gr v
   Caffeine                  gr xss
   M. Ft. M.
   Div in caps, no. xxi
   Sig: Cap i q 4 h, prn.
```

- *Step 1.* Reduce all ingredients to *grains*.

  Acetylsalicylic acid equals
2 × 60 grains (per drachm)	= 120	gr.
1 × 20 grains (per scruple)	= 20	gr.
7 grains	= 7	gr.
	147	gr.

  Acetophenetidin equals
1 × 60 grains (per drachm)	= 60	gr.
2 × 20 grains (per scruple)	= 40	gr.
5 grains	= 5	gr.
	105	gr.

  Caffeine equals
10 1/2 grains	= 10.5	gr.

- *Step 2.* You know that the total amount is for 21 capsules; therefore, the amount in a single capsule would be—

$$\text{Total doses} = \frac{\text{total amount}}{\text{size of each dose}}$$

$$21 = \frac{147}{x} = 7 \text{ grains acetylsalicylic acid per capsule}$$

$$21 = \frac{105}{x} = 5 \text{ grains acetophenetidin per capsule}$$

$$21 = \frac{10.5}{x} = 1/2 \text{ grain caffeine per capsule}$$

NOTE

To check this prescription for possible errors, consult the USP or Remington for the dose of each of the ingredients and compare the dose with the amounts you have calculated to be in each capsule.

(b) *Example:* A solution contains 4/5 grain of a potent drug in 4 ounces. What dose must be given to provide 1/120 grain of the drug?

- *Step 1.* Formula.

$$\text{Total doses} = \frac{\text{total amount}}{\text{size of each dose}}$$

- *Step 2.* Substitute.

$$x \text{ doses} = \frac{\frac{4}{15}}{\frac{1}{120}}$$

- *Step 3.* Remember that you can divide fractions by inverting the divisor and multiplying. Thus,

$$x \text{ doses} = \frac{4}{15} \times \frac{120}{1}$$

$$x = \frac{480}{15} = 32 \text{ doses}$$

- *Step 4.* Since you are to get 32 doses from 4 ounces, each dose must be one fluidrachm (8 fluidrachms = 1 ounce).

   e. Children's doses. Enough emphasis cannot be placed upon the calculation of dosage for children. Because of their size, weight, and incomplete development, they are not able to tolerate as much medication as adults. Although many factors besides weight and age play an important part in dosage, only these two will be discussed here. (Chapter 9 explains dosage factors in more detail.)

   (1) *Formulas for calculating children's doses.* Several formulas can be employed for calculating doses for children and infants; however, because of different degrees of response by children to different medications (e.g., children are extremely susceptible to morphine), it is best to become familiar with the correct doses through experience and to memorize doses as they present themselves. If at all in doubt about the size of a dose, ALWAYS check with the pharmacy officer or the prescriber. The most generally used formulas for calculation of doses for children are—

   (a) *Young's rule* (most widely used).

$$\frac{\text{child's age}}{\text{child's age} + 12} \times \text{adult dose} = \text{child's dose}$$

   (b) *Clark's rule.*

$$\frac{\text{weight of child (lb)}}{150} \times \text{adult dose} = \text{child's dose}$$

   (2) *Example problems.* Study the following examples carefully to see the application of the above rules.

   (a) *Example:* What would be the dose of elixir of phenobarbital for a child 3 years old? (Elixir phenobarbital contains 400 mg. of phenobarbital per 100 ml. Adult dose of phenobarbital is 30 mg., up to 4 times a day.) Use Young's rule.

- *Step 1.* Rule.

$$\frac{\text{child's age}}{\text{child's age} + 12} \times \text{adult dose} = \text{child's dose}$$

- *Step 2.* Substitute.

$$\frac{3}{3 + 12} \times 30 \text{ mg.} = \text{child's dose}$$

$$\frac{90}{15} = 6 \text{ mg., the child's dose}$$

- *Step 3.* Since 100 ml. of phenobarbital elixir contains 400 mg., 1 ml. would contain 4 mg. Therefore; 1:x :: 4:6.

$$4x = 6$$
$$x = 1.5 \text{ ml., the dose for 3-year-old child.}$$

(b) Example: What would be the dose of tetracycline hydrochloride for a 3-year-old girl weighing 30 pounds? Usual adult dose is 500 mg. Use Clark's rule.

- *Step 1.* Formula.

$$\frac{\text{weight of child (lb)}}{150} \times \text{adult dose} = \text{child's dose}$$

- *Step 2.* Substitute.

$$\frac{30}{150} \times 500 \text{ mg.} = \text{child's dose}$$

$$\frac{15,000}{150} = 100 \text{ mg., the child's dose}$$

45. Concentration and dilution. Many times in pharmacy it is necessary to dilute or concentrate a substance in order to dispense the right dosage; the dilution of nose drops is one of the most frequently seen examples. Phenylephrine hydrochloride solution is a standard nose drop preparation. Its strength as it comes to us is 1 percent. Most of the prescriptions for phenylephrine solution will call for 1/4 percent. You can see, then, that it will have to be diluted before dispensing.

a. Mechanics of dilution. If 1 ounce of a 1 percent-solution of phenylephrine hydrochloride solution was diluted to a new volume of 2 ounces, the percent of the new solution would be 1/2 of the original 1 percent, that is, 1/2 percent. Perhaps it will be more apparent if you consider that 1 ounce of a 1-percent solution contains approximately 4.5 grains of active ingredient. By diluting the solution to a volume of 2 ounces, you still have only 4.5 grains of active ingredient in a volume of 2 ounces. Thus, you have halved the percentage. If the active ingredient remains constant and the volume of the solution increases, the percentage decreases. And if the active ingredient remains constant and the volume of the solution decreases, the percentage increases. The percentage strength and the volume of a solution are inversely proportional to each other.

b. Concentration–dilution proportion. Since volume and percentage strength of solutions are inversely proportional, the following formula or proportion applies.

$$\frac{\text{\% concentration of original solution}}{\text{\% concentration of new solution}} :: \frac{\text{new volume}}{\text{original volume}}$$

This proportion can be used to solve any concentration or dilution problem arising in the pharmacy.

(1) Example: You have 30 ml. of a 10-percent solution and want to make a 1-percent solution. To what volume must you dilute the original solution? Substituting in the proportion you have—

$$\frac{10 \text{ (original \%)}}{1 \text{ (new \%)}} :: \frac{x \text{ (unknown new volume)}}{30 \text{ (original new volume)}}$$

$$x = 300 \text{ ml., the new volume}$$

In a practical situation, then, you would dilute the original 30 ml. of 10-percent solution to a total volume of 300 ml. to prepare the desired 1-percent solution.

(2) Example: Make a 4-percent solution from 60 ml. of a 2-percent solution by concentrating the volume. Again, substituting in the proportion, you have—

$$\frac{2\%}{4\%} :: \frac{x}{60}$$
$$4x = 120$$
$$x = 30 \text{ ml.}$$

You must concentrate the 60 ml. of 2-percent solution to a new volume of 30 ml. in order to obtain the 4-percent solution.

46. Alligation. Alligation is a process for finding the value of a combination containing known quantities of known strengths; *for example,* to determine the strength of a solution resulting from the mixture of 100 ml. of 20-percent alcohol and

20 ml. of 10-percent alcohol. Actually, alligation is two different processes, alligation medial and alligation alternate. Alligation medial is used for determining percentage strength and alligation alternate for proportional number of parts.

a. Alligation medial. Alligation medial is used in determining the percentage strength of a mixture of two or more ingredients of different strengths. Alligation medial can also be used to determine the resulting specific gravity of a mixture of two or more substances with different specific gravities.

(1) Example: What percentage of codeine sulfate is contained in a mixture of 60 grams of a 15-percent codeine powder and 15 grams of a 40-percent codeine powder?

- *Step 1.* Find the amount of codeine sulfate in the total mixture.

  60 x .15 = 9.0 Gm. of codeine sulfate
  15 x .40 = 6.0 Gm. of codeine sulfate
  15.0 Gm. total codeine in mixture

- *Step 2.* Find the weight of the total mixture.
  60 Gm. + 15 Gm. = 75 Gm. total weight of mixture

- *Step 3.* Divide the amount of codeine by the total weight to find the percent of codeine in the mixture.

  $\frac{15.0}{75.0} = .20$ or 20% codeine sulfate

(2) Example: You prepare a mixture of 3 ounces of liquid A and 13 ounces of liquid B. What is the cost per ounce of the resulting mixture if liquid A costs $4.00 per pint and liquid B costs $1.44 per pint?

- *Step 1.* Find the cost per ounce of each ingredient.
  A = $4.00/pint ÷ 16 = $ .25/ounce
  B = $1.44/pint ÷ 16 = $ .09/ounce

- *Step 2.* Find the number of ounces in the total mixture.
  3 ounces of A + 13 ounces of B = 16 ounces

- *Step 3.* Find the total cost of these two ingredients.
  3 ounces at $0.25 = $ .75
  13 ounces at $0.09 = $1.17
  $1.92 total cost of mixture

- *Step 4.* Find the cost per ounce of the mixture.
  $1.92 ÷ 16 = $0.12, cost per ounce

(3) Example: What is the specific gravity of a mixture of 250 ml. of Glycerin (Sp. Gr. 1.25) and 500 ml. of chloroform (Sp. Gr. 1.48)?

- *Step 1.* Find the number of grams in each of the volumes.
  250 ml. x 1.25 = 312.5 Gm. of glycerin
  500 ml. x 1.48 = 740.00 Gm. of chloroform

- *Step 2.* Find the total volume and total weight of the mixture.
  250 ml. + 500 ml. = 750 ml., total volume
  312.5 Gm. + 740 Gm. = 1052.5 Gm., total weight

- *Step 3.* Divide weight by volume to find Sp. Gr.
  $\frac{1052.5}{750} = 1.403$, the Sp. Gr. of mixture

b. Alligation alternate. Alligation alternate is a method of determining the proportionate number of parts of two or more ingredients of known strength when they are to be mixed to form a desired strength. The parts can then be changed to represent volume or weight. A substance of greater strength is mixed with one of lesser strength to form a mixture of a strength somewhere between that of the two ingredients. For example, 50-percent alcohol can be mixed with 25-percent alcohol to produce 30-percent alcohol. It is not possible to mix 50-percent alcohol with 25-percent alcohol to get less than 25-percent or more than 50-percent alcohol. The increase in percentage from the smaller ingredient to the percentage desired, equals the parts of the higher percent ingredient, and the decrease in percentage of the higher to the desired equals the parts of the lower percent ingredient.

(1) Example: What must be the proportion of 50-percent alcohol and 25-percent alcohol, mixed to obtain 30-percent alcohol?

- *Step 1.* Examine the situation. We desire a 30-percent alcohol solution from a 50-percent and a 25-percent solution. The 50-percent solution is 20 percent too strong and the 25-percent solution is 5 percent too weak. In other words, the 50-percent solution must decrease 20 percent and the 25-percent increase 5 percent.

- *Step 2.* Prepare a diagram and place the percentage you desire at completion in the center block. Place the highest percent ingredient (50 percent) on the left and the lowest percent ingredient (25 percent) on the right.

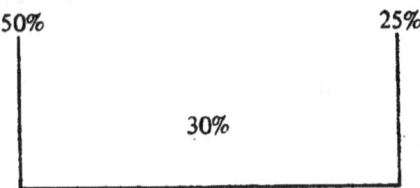

- *Step 3.* Subtract the percent you desire (center block) from the high percent and place your answer below the low percent. This answer represents the parts of the LOW percent you will need to make the desired strength solution.

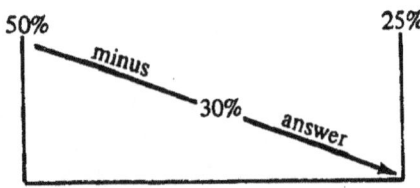

- *Step 4.* Subtract the low percent from the desired percent (center block) and place your answer below the high percent. This answer represents the parts of the HIGH percent you will need to make the desired strength solution.

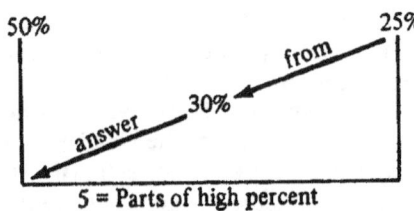

The paperwork from your completed problem, then, should look like this. It indicates that to make a 30-percent solution from 50-percent and 25-percent alcohol, you will need 5 parts of the 50 percent and 20 parts of the 25 percent.

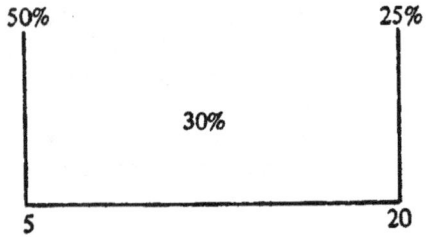

- *Step 5.* Express the number of parts in the denomination most suitable, such as ml., grains, grams, or ounces. Thus, 20 ml. of the 25 percent + 5 ml. of the 50 percent will make a 30-percent mixture; 20 ounces of the 25 percent + 5 ounces of the 50 percent will also make a 30-percent mixture.

(2) *Example:* In what proportion must you mix 95-percent, 10-percent, 50-percent, and 30-percent alcohol to make 40-percent alcohol?

- *Step 1.* Examine the situation. You desire a 40-percent solution by combining so many parts each of 95 percent, 50 percent, 30 percent, and 10 percent.

- *Step 2.* Although the setup looks a little different because there are 4 ingredients in this problem, use the same procedure, that is, to subtract the lesser percents from the desired to get the number of parts, and to subtract the desired percent from the higher percents to get the number of parts. This problem has been broken down into four diagrams to show each segment of subtraction. However, the problem should be worked from one diagram.

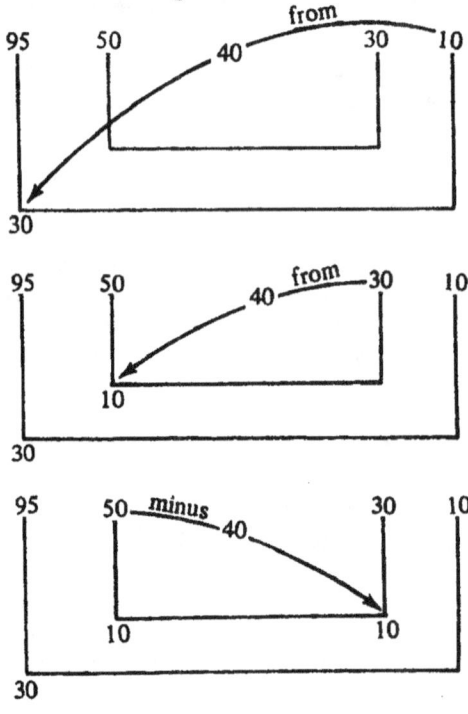

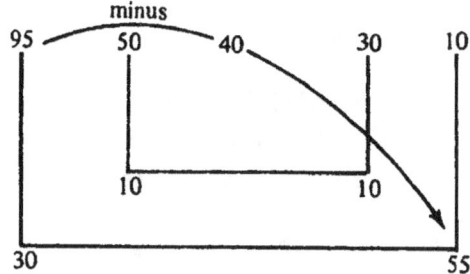

You therefore need—

30 parts of 95% alcohol
55 parts of 10% alcohol
10 parts of 50% alcohol
10 parts of 30% alcohol
105 parts of 40% alcohol

● *Step 3.* By expressing the parts as ounces, you mix 30 ounces of 95 percent, 55 ounces of 10 percent, 10 ounces of 50 percent, and 10 ounces of 30 percent to produce 105 ounces of 40-percent alcohol.

(3) Example: How many ml. of 10-percent, 20-percent, and 30-percent sodium hydroxide solution must be mixed to make a quart of 25-percent solution?

● *Step 1.* Examine the situation. You desire a 25-percent solution from the combination of 10-percent, 20-percent, and 30-percent solutions of sodium hydroxide.

● *Step 2.* Set up.

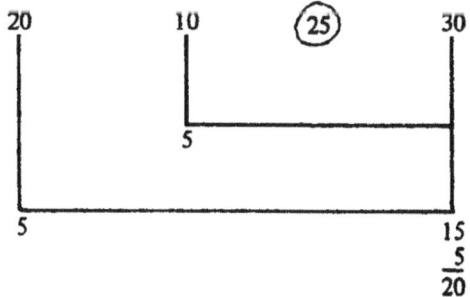

● *Step 3.* Thus you need—

5 parts of 20%
5 parts of 10%
20 parts of 30%
30 parts of 25% will result

● *Step 4.* Find what one part would equal. You know that there are 473 ml. in 1 pint, and therefore 946 ml. in 1 quart. The total number of ml. to be made is 946. You have a total of 30 parts of the solutions which are to equal 946 ml.; 1 part, then, would equal 946 ÷ 30 = 31.53 ml. per part.

● *Step 5.* Multiply the numbers of parts by the 31.53 ml. to find the number of ml. of each to be used.

31.53 × 5 = 157.65 ml. of 20%
31.53 × 5 = 157.65 ml. of 10%
31.53 × 20 = 630.60 ml. of 30%

(4) Example: How much water must be added to a pint of 95-percent ethyl alcohol to make 70-percent alcohol?

● *Step 1.* Examine the situation. You desire to make a 70-percent solution of alcohol from a 95-percent solution and a 0-percent solution (water).

● *Step 2.* Set up.

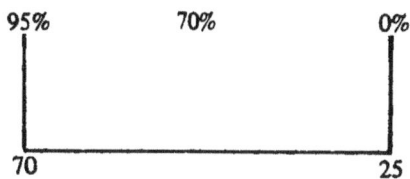

● *Step 3.* Thus you need—

70 parts of 95% alcohol
25 parts of 0% alcohol (water)
95 parts of 70% alcohol

● *Step 4.* Solve. One pint contains 473 ml.

70 : 473 :: 25 : x
70x = 473 × 25
70x = 11,825
x = 168.93 ml. of water required.

(5) Example: How many ml. of a 60-percent sulfuric acid by volume solution must be added to 344 ml. of 30-percent sulfuric acid and 172 ml. of 15-percent sulfuric acid to make 50-percent sulfuric acid?

● *Step 1.* Examine the situation. You desire to make a 50-percent solution of sulfuric acid by combining 344 ml. of 30-percent sulfuric acid, 172 ml. of 15-percent sulfuric acid, and x number of ml. of 60-percent sulfuric acid.

• *Step 2.* Find the percent strength of the mixture formed by combining the acids of known strength and volume.

$$344 \times 0.30 = 103.2 \text{ Gm.}$$
$$172 \times 0.15 = 25.8 \text{ Gm.}$$
$$516 \text{ ml.} \quad 129.0 \text{ Gm.}$$

$129.0 \div 516 = .25$, or 25%, the strength of the mixture of the two acids.

• *Step 3.* Set up for a mixture of the 25 percent and the 60 percent to be added.

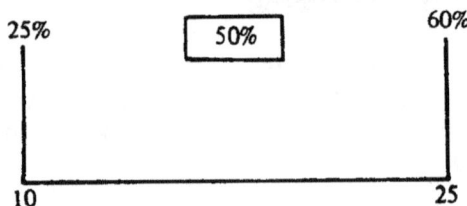

• *Step 4.* Thus you need—

$$\begin{array}{l} 25 \text{ parts of } 60\% \text{ sulfuric acid} \\ \underline{10} \text{ parts of } 25\% \text{ sulfuric acid} \\ 35 \text{ parts of } 50\% \text{ sulfuric acid} \end{array}$$

• *Step 5.* Since you have 516 ml. of the 25-percent strength solution, which represents 10 parts, find how many ml. will represent 25 parts.

$$10 : 25 :: 516 : x$$
$$10x = 516 \times 25$$
$$10x = 12,900$$
$$x = 1,290 \text{ ml. of the } 60\% \text{ sulfuric acid required.}$$

NOTES AND RESOURCES
CONTENTS

	Page
I- GLOSSARY OF DRUGS WITH NATIONAL NOMENCLATURES	
Anesthetics	1
Muscle Relaxants	1
Narcotics	2
Hypnotics	2
Antibiotics	2
Drugs Affecting Sympathetic Nervous System and Nerve Endings	3
Electrolytes	3
Plasma Expanders	4
Miscellaneous Drugs	4
Vaccines and Antitoxins	5
Antiseptics	5
II- USEFUL TABLES	
Table 1.- Atomic Weights, Valences, and Equivalent Weights of Certain Elements	6
Table 2.- Milliequivalent Per Gram of Certain Elements and Compounds	6
Table 3.- Normal Range of Concentration of Serum Constituents	6
Table 4.- Normal Range of Concentration of Whole Blood Gases and pH Values	6
Table 5.- Equivalent United States and Imperial Weights and Measures	7
Table 6.- Approximate Equivalent Metric and Imperial Doses	7
Table 7.- Equivalent Avoirdupois and Metric Weights	8
Table 8.- Equivalents of Centigrade and Fahrenheit Thermometric Scales	9

NOTES AND RESOURCES

I - Glossary of Drugs With National Nomenclatures
ANESTHETICS

United States	Germany	Netherlands	France
Chloroprocaine N.F	....	Chloroprocaine	
Cocaine hydrochloride U.S.P.	Cocainhydrochlorid DAB 7.................	Cocaine hydrochloride	Cocaine chlorhydrate.
Cyclopropane U.S.P	....	Cyclopentaan	Cyclopropane.
Droperidol	Dehydrobenzperidol	Droperidol	Haldol.
Ether U.S.P	Aether pro narcosi DAB 7 ..	Ether U.S.P............	Ether pur pour anesthesie.
Halothane U.S.P	Halothan	Halothaan	Halothane.
Lid.ocaine hydrochloride .... U.S.P.	Lidocainii hydrochloridum .... Ph. Int.	Lidocaine hydrochloride	Xylocaine.
Mepivacaine hydrochloride .... N.F.	Scandicain...............	Mepivacaine hydrochloride.	
Nitrous oxide U.S.P.	Distickstoffoxide, Lachgas	Lachgas, distikstofoxide.................	Protoxyde d"azote.
Prilocaine hydrochloride .... N.F.	....	Prilocaine hydrochloride................	
Procaine hydrochloride .... U.S.P.	Procainhydrochlorid DAB 7.	Procaine hydrochloride.	Lignocaine.
Proparacaine hydrochloride .... U.S.P.	....	Proparacaine hydrochloride, ... proxymetacaine.	
Tetracaine hydrochloride .... U.S.P:	Tetracainhydrochlorid DAB 7.	Tetracaine hydrochloride	Tetracaine.
Thiopental sodium U.S.P.	Trapanal	Thiopental-natrium..	Penthiobarbital injectable.

MUSCLE RELAXANTS

United States	Germany	Netherlands	France
Curare	....	Curare.	
Pancuronium bromide	....	Pancuronium bromide.	
Succinylcholine U.S.P	Suxamethonium chloridum .... Ph.Int.	Succinylcholine	Succinylcholine.
Tubocurarine chloride U.S.P.	D-Tubocurarini chloridum Ph.Int.	Tubocurarine chloride	Tubocurarine.

NARCOTICS

Codeine phosphate U.S.P	Codeinphosphate DAB 7...	Codeine fosfaat	Codeine.
Meperidine hydro- chloride U.S.P.	Pethidini hydrochloridum Ph.Int.	Pethidine hydrochloride.	Pethidine chlorhydrate.
Methadone hydrochloride U.S.P.	Methadoni hydrochloridum Ph.Int.	Methadon hydrochloride.	
Morphine sulfate U.S.P	Morphini sulfas Ph.Int.....	Morfine sulfaat..	Morphine.
Papaverine hydrochloride .... N.F.	Papaverinhydrochlorid DAB 7.	Papaverine hydrochloride	Papaverine.

HYPNOTICS

Amobarbital U.S.P...	Amobarbitalum Ph.Int.....	Amobarbital.........	Amobarbital.
Paraldehyde U.S.P..	Paraldehyd DAB 7	Paraldehyde	Paraldehyde.
Pentobarbital U.S.P.	Neodorm....................	Pentobarbital	Nembutal.
Phenobarbital U.S.P	Phenylaethylbarbitursaure DAB 7.	Fenobarbital	Phenobarbital.
Secobarbital U.S.P..	....	Secobarbital	Secobarbital.

ANTIBIOTICS

United States	Germany	Netherlands	France
Ampicillin U.S.P	Amblosin, Binotal.....	Ampicilline	Ampicilline. ....
Bacitracin U.S.P.	Bacitracin	Bacitracine	Bacitracine.
Carbenicillin.............	Anabactyl	Carbenicilline.	
Cephaloridine	....	Cefaloridine.............	Cephaloridine.
Cephalothin U.S.P ...	Cefalotin	Cefalotine	CepHalotine........
Chloramphenicol U.S.P	Chloramphenicol DAB 7....................	Chlooramfenicol	Chloramphenicol.
Colistin N.F.............	Colistin	Colistine	Colistine.
Erythromycin U.S.P .	Erythromycinum Ph. Int.	Erythromycine	Erythromycine.
Gentamicin sulfate U.S.P....................	Refobacin	Gentamicine sulfaat	Gentamycine.
Kanamycin U.S.P	Kanmytrex, Kanamycin, ... Resistomycin.	Kanamycine	Kanamycine.
Lincomycin U.S.P	Cillimycin	Lincomycine.	
Methicillin U.S.P	Cinopenil	Methicilline	Methicilline.
Neomycin sulfate U.S.P	Neomycin, Bykomycin	Neomycine sulfaat .	Neomycine.
Oxacillin U.S.P.........	Cryptocillin, Stapenor	Oxacilline	Oxacilline.
Polymyxin B sulfate U.S.P...	Polymyxini B-sulfas Ph.Int..	Polymyxine B sulfaat	Polymyxine B.

Potassium penicillin G, ... U.S.P.	Penicillin G-Kalium DAB 7.	Kalium penicilline B ...	Penicilline.
Potassium phenoxymethyl .... penicillin U.S.P.	Beromycin, Immunocillin, ... Isocillin, Aracil.	Kalium fenoxymethyl penicilline.	
Streptomycin sulfate U.S.P., ...	Streptomycinsulfat DAB 7..	Streptomycine sulfaat .	Streptomycine sulfate.
Tetracycline U.S.P ...	Tetracyclinum Ph.Int .	Tetracycline	Oxytetracycline.

DRUGS AFFECTING SYMPATHETIC NERVOUS SYSTEM AND NERVE ENDINGS

Atropine sulfate U.S.P	Atropinsulfat DAB 7	Atropine sulfaat	Atropine sulfate.
Cyclopentolate hydrochloride U.S.P.	....	Cyclopentolaat hydrochloride.	
Epinephrine U.S.P	Adrenalin DAB 7	Adrenaline	Adrenaline. .....
Homatropine hydrobromide U.S.P.	Homatropinhydrobromid .... DAB 7.	Homatropine hydrobromide.	Homatropine bromhydrate.
Isoproterenol U.S.P	Isoprenalini hydrochloridum Ph.Int.	Isoprenaline	Isuprel, isoprenaline.
Levarterenol bitartrate U.S.P.	Noradrenalinhydrogentartrat .... DAB 7.	Levarterenol bitartraat.	Noradrenaline.
Physostigmine salicylate U.S.P.	Physostigminsalicylat DAB 7	Fysostigmine salicyclaat..........	
Pralidoxime chloride U.S.P..	Pralidoximi methiodidum .... Ph.Int.	Pralidoxime chloride	Pralidoxime.
Scopolamine U.S.P	Scopolaminhydrobromid DAB 7.	Scopolamine U.S.P	Scopolamine.

ELECTROLYTES

Calcium gluconate injection .... U.S.P.	Calcium gluconicum 10%	Calcium gluconaat injectie.	Calcium levulinate.
Dextrose injection U.S.P	Traubenzuckerlösung 10%	Glucose injectie	Solution injectable de glucose, isotonique.
Lactated Ringer's injection .... U.S.P.	Ringer-Lactat-Lösung	Ringer lactaat injectie	Lactate de calcium.

Ringer's injection U.S.P.	Ringer-Lösung............	Ringer injectie.	Solution de Ringer.
Sodium chloride injection .... U.S.P.	Natriumchloridlösung, isotonisch, pyrogenfrei, steril (DAB 7).	Natrium chloride injectie.	Solution injectable de chlorure de sodium, isotonique.

PLASMA EXPANDERS

United States	Germany	Netherlands	France
Normal human serum albumin U.S.P.	Humanalbumin 20%	Normal humaan albumine uit serum.	Albumine humaine.
Plasma protein fraction U.S.P.	PPL, Humanalbumin 5%................	Protein fractie uit plasma..........	Gamma globuline.

MISCELLANEOUS DRUGS

Acetylsalicyclic acid U.S.P	Acetylsalicylsaure DAB 7	Acetylsalicyl zuur ..	Acetylsalicylique acide.
Amyl nitrite N.F		Amyl nitriet	Nitrite d'amyle.
Chlorpromazine U.S.P	Chlorpromazini hydrochloridum Ph.Int.	Chloor promazine	Chlorpromazine.
Digitalis U.S.P	Digitalisblatter DAB 7	Digitalis	Digitaline.
Digoxin U.S.P...........	Digoxinum Ph.Int	Digoxine.	
Ethacrynic acid U.S.P		Ethacryne zuur.	
Furosemide U.S.P...	Lasix	Furosemide	Furosemide-Lasilix.
Hydrocortisone sodium succinate injection U.S.P.	Hydrocortisonhemisuc cinat	Hydrocortison natrium .... succinaat injectie.	Hydrocortisone hemisuccinate.
Mafenide	Marfanil	Mafenide.	
Mannitol U.S.P	D-Mannit	Mannitol.	
Oxygen U.S.P	Sauerstoff	Zuurstof	Oxygene.
Petrolatum U.S.P.	Paraffinum solidum DAB 6, Paraffinum durum DAB 7.	Vaseline	Vaseline.
Probenecid U.S.P ...	Benemid	Probenecide.	
Silver nitrate U.S.P .	Silbernitrat DAB 7 ..	Zilvernitraat	Nitrate d'argent.
Sodium nitrite U.S.P	Natriumnitrit DAB 7.	Natrium nitriet	Nitrite de sodium.
Sodium polysterene sulfonate U.S.P.	Kationen-Austauscherharz	Natrium polystyreen sulfonaat.	
Sodium thiosulfate U.S.P.	Natriumthiosulfat DAB 7	Natrium thiosulfaat	Hyposulfite de sodium.

VACCINES AND ANTITOXINS

Gas gangrene antitoxin, pentavalent.	Gasoedem- Antitoxin, polyvalent.	Gas gangreen-antitoxine pentavalent.	Serum antigangreneux polyvalent. ....
Tetanus immune globulin (human) U.S.P.	Tetanus-Immunglobulin	Tetanus-immuno globuoline (menselijk).	
Tetanus toxoid U.S.P.	Tetatoxoid	Tetanus vaccin .	Vaccin antitetanique.

ANTISEPTICS

Alcohol U S P	Aethanol DAB 7	Alcohol	Alcool ethylique.
Hexachlorophene U.S.P	Hexachlorophen WHO	Hexachlorophene .	Exophene.

II - Useful Tables

TABLE 1.— *Atomic weights, valences, and equivalent weights of certain elements*

Element	Atomic weight	Valence	Equivalent weight
Sodium	23.0	1	23.0
Potassium	39.0	1	39.0
Magnesium	24.0	2	12.0
Calcium	40.0	2	20.0
Chlorine	35.5	1	35.5
Phosphorus	31.0	3	10.3
Sulfur	32.0	2	16.0

TABLE 2. *Milliequivalent per gram of certain elements and compounds*

Element or compound	Mini-equivalent	Element or compound	Mini-equivalent
Sodium	43.5	Potassium chloride:	
Potassium	26.0	Potassium	13.5
Magnesium	85.0	Chloride	13.5
Calcium	50.0	Sodium lactate:	
Chloride	29.0	Sodium	9.0
Sodium chloride:		Lactate	9.0
Sodium	17.0		
Chloride	17.0		

TABLE 3. *Normal range of concentration of serum constituents*

Constituent		Concentration per 100-milliliters	Milliequivalent per liter
Sodium	milligram	310-340	135-148
Potassium	do	13.6-20.7	3.5-5.3
Magnesium	do	1.8-3.0	1.5-2.5
Calcium	do	9.6-11.0	4.8-5.4
Chloride	do	348-383	98-108
Urea nitrogen	do	8-26	
Carbon dioxide		101-132	23-30 mM
Total protein	gram	6.0-8.2	
Albumin	do	3.8-5.0	
Globulin	do	2.3-3.5	

TABLE 4. *Normal range of concentration of whole blood gases and pH values*

Constituent	Concentration
pO_2 Arterial	90-100 torr[1]
Venous	30 torr
pCO_2 Arterial	35-16 torr
Venous	38-49 torr
pH	7.35-7.45

[1] One torr = 1 mm Hg at sea level.

TABLE 5. *Equivalent United States and imperial weights and measures*

Unit of measurement	Abbreviation	United States measure	Imperial measure
1 milligram	mg	0.015432 grain	0.015432 grain.
1 gram	g	15.432 grains	15.432 grains.
1 kilogram	kg	35.274 ounces (avoirdupois) 32.150 ounces (apothecary)	35.274 ounces (avoirdupois) 35.274 ounces (apothecary).
1 grain	gr	0.0648 gram 64.8 milligrams	0.0648 gram. 64.8 milligrams.
480 grains	gr	31.1035 grams	31.1035 grams.
1 ounce	oz	437.5 grains 28.350 grams	437.5 grains. 28.350 grams.
1 milliliter	ml	16.23 minims	16.894 minims.
1 liter	l	33.814 fluid ounces	35.196 fluid ounces.
1 minim	min	0.0616 milliliter	0.0592 milliliter.
1 fluid ounce	fl oz	29.573 milliliters	28.412 milliliters.
1 pint[1]	Pt	473.17 milliliters	568.25 milliliters.

[1] Sixteen fluid ounces, U.S. measure; 20 fluid ounces, imperial measure.

USEFUL TABLES

TABLE 6. *Approximate equivalent metric and imperial doses*

Milliliters	Minims	Grams	Grains	Milligrams	Grains
0.1	1½	0.1	1½	0.1	1/600
0.12	2	0.12	2	0.125	1/480
0.15	2½	0.15	2½	0.25	1/240
0.2	3	0.2	3	0.3	1/200
0.25	4	0.25	4	0.5	1/120
0.3	5	0.3	5	0.6	1/100
0.4	6	0.4	6	1	1/60
0.5	8	0.5	8	1.5	1/40
0.6	10	0.6	10	2	1/30
1	15	1	15	2.5	1/24
1.3	20	1.3	20	3	1/20
2	30	2	30	5	1/12
3	45	3	45	8	1/8
4	60	4	60	9	3/20
5	75	5	75	10	1/6
6	90	6	90	12	1/5
8	120	8	120	16	1/4
10	150	10	150	20	1/3
15	225	15	225	25	2/5
20	300	20	300	30	1/2
25	375	25	375	50	3/4
				60	1
				75	1 1/4

TABLE 7. *Equivalent avoirdupois and metric weights*

Pounds	Kilograms	Pounds	Kilograms
100	45.359	155	70.306
105	47.627	160	72.574
110	49.895	165	74.842
115	52.163	170	77.110
120	54.431	175	79.378
125	56.698	1 80	81.646
1 30	58.966	185	83.914
1 35	61.234	190	86.182
140	63.502	195	88.450
145	65.770	200	90.718
150	68.038		

TABLE 8. *Equivalents of centigrade and Fahrenheit thermometric scales*

Degrees C	Degrees F	Degrees C	Degrees F	Degrees C	Degrees F
-10	14.0	31	87.8	72	161.6
-9	15.8	32	89.6	73	163.4
-8	17.6	33	91.4	74	165.2
-7	19.4	34	93.2	75	167.0
-6	21.2	35	95.0	76	168.8
-5	23.0	36	96.8	77	170.6
-4	24.8	37	98.6	78	172.4
-2	26.6	38	100.4	79	174.2
-2	28.4	39	102.2	80	176.0
-1	30.2	40	104.0	81	177.8
0	32.0	41	105.8	82	179.6
1	33.8	42	107.6	83	181.4
2	35.6	43	109.4	84	183.2
3	37.4	44	111.2	85	185.0
4	39.2	45	113.0	86	186.8
5	41.0	46	114.8	87	188.6
6	42.8	47	116.6	88	190.4
7	44.6	48	118.4	89	192.2
8	46.4	49	120.2	90	194.0
9	48.2	50	122.0	91	195.8
10	50.0	51	123.8	92	197.6
11	51.8	52	125.6	93	199.4
12	53.6	53	127.4	94	201.2
13	55.4	54	129.2	95	203.0
14	57.2	55	131.0	96	204.8
15	59.0	56	132.8	97	206.6
16	60.8	57	134.6	98	208.4
17	62.6	58	136.4	99	210.2
18	64.4	59	138.2	100	212.0
19	66.2	60	140.0	101	213.8
20	68.0	61	141.8	102	215.6
21	69.8	62	143.6	103	217.4
22	71.6	63	145.4	104	219.2
23	73.4	64	147.2	105	221.0
24	75.2	65	149.0	106	222.8
25	77.0	66	150.8	107	224.6
26	78.8	67	152.6	108	226.4
27	80.6	68	154.4	109	228.2
28	82.4	69	156.2	110	230.0
29	84.2	70	158.0		
30	86.0	71	159.8